She

Was

Horrid

Morgan Waites

Attention schools and businesses: for discounted copies on large orders,
please contact the publisher directly.

For information contact:
Unsolicited Press
Portland, Oregon
www.unsolicitedpress.com
orders@unsolicitedpress.com
619-354-8005

Cover Design: Kathryn Gerhardt
Editor: Jay Kristensen Jr.; Kristen Marckmann
ISBN: 978-1-956692-31-0

Chapter One

It's the same old shit, always the same.

But then one day it's not, when I get home to my apartment and discover that there's been a sprinkler malfunction. The carpet in the hallway is soaked and squishes beneath my feet as I walk to my unit at the end of the hallway, making an awful noise only someone who watches those ASMR videos would like. The sprinklers are still releasing a feeble stream of fluid that reminds me of water trickling out of a gutter or off a sloped roof when there's been a heavy rain, except it's inside. Some of the water drips on my head. It all feels very strikingly wrong, like I'm in a Murakami novel and I've entered another dimension. If only.

When life feels surreal like that, it's not magical, it's just disconcerting.

"What a hot mess this is," I declare resignedly and also loudly, because I am speaking to the fireman striding down the hallway towards me just then, and because of the incessant, obnoxious beeping of the fire alarm that's been going off for God-knows-how-long. I am hoping for some form of consolation from the fireman in that solemn outcry. He is supposed to be the pillar of society, the civil servant come to rescue us all, clean the mess up, and assure us of our safety, thus restoring the delicate balance of civilization. It's strange, how fragile our security has become in this modern era. How a simple sprinkler malfunction or power outage can reduce us to helpless, fretful little infants. People are crowded in the lobby and the hallway whispering frantically to one another. One girl is crying. Another is screaming into the phone at the property management company.

"Yep, sure is," he agrees, really not giving a shit. He doesn't live here. He'll be leaving the wet carpet and sodden furniture and endlessly beeping fire alarm as soon as he's sure he's done the bare minimum the job requires. He isn't paid enough, I'm sure, so I can't really blame him. But still, I want him to summarize exactly the cause, when it occurred, how they'll be resolving the issue, and when it will all be finished, and last of all, I want him to assure me that everything's going to be all right. But apparently, he isn't in the business of doing that. He works for the fire department after all; I'm sure a sprinkler malfunction is just a minor inconvenience to them.

When I get to my unit with the anxiety of what I will discover wringing at my pounding heart, I am able to summon some shred of relief at the fact that the sprinkler in my studio unit happens to be located right in front of the door, which means stepping into a puddle of water as soon as I walk in that puts me in an immediate state of doom, but then there is the lack of furniture in the very front meaning none of my stuff has been ruined. Everything else is safe and unsodden. Just a puddle. Not so bad. Though the sprinkler is still going. I'm grateful and I breathe a silent thank you to the universe.

There are other things to be grateful for. For instance, I'm lucky I haven't brought a man home today, which I am wont to do more-than-occasionally. It would've been awkward and so many of the tenants would've seen him and they've already seen several of the men I've brought home before, but not all the tenants at once, though I suspect they've had plenty conversations about me behind my back, about the girl in B10 with all the different men she regularly brings home. I sometimes worry with nagging paranoia the inaudible whispering outside my apartment is in fact about me.

I was spotted once with an Indian man whose balding head barely reached my chest, and once with a sixty-something-year-old, and with a handsome Brooklyn boy and a short, transgendered man with impeccable manners and a Chad who worked out every day and was addicted to protein bars and a blond bespectacled hipster with a propensity for crying when he came, and so many nameless others I've lost count of. When I was younger it was fun and like a game—racking up an inordinate number of conquests—now it's just sad. Now, it's just a vocation, and when I sometimes remember I don't know the number of people I've slept with anymore, I feel nausea turning in the pit of my stomach. There are so many people I couldn't possibly recount or pull from my foggy memory—I've willfully repressed much of it. I used to know the number so definitively, so proudly. Now that unknown number is just a brutal reminder of how horrid I've become. It's shrouded in shame rather than pride.

And I know with equal shame that my neighbors on the first floor can hear the sex noises reverberating from within the thin walls of my tiny studio apartment. I can hear theirs, of course, but the ones escaping mine are far more frequent, perhaps annoyingly so. Sometimes I take multiple clients a day, up to ten a week, though lately business has been slowing down a bit. No more than five a week.

And then after having sex with the many men I lure into my apartment, there's always the walk of shame to the laundry room or through the lobby as I go to leave or wash the tainted bedsheets. I get a creeping sickly sensation whenever I walk outside freshly fucked, the sin a slimy intangible layer upon my skin that I'm so sure they can see. And I wonder if they wonder about me as I glance into their curious watchful eyes, then flicker mine away evasively. I wonder if they think I'm a whore, or easy, or unhinged, or if they suspect the awful truth. That I'm a prostitute. I see it in their politely downturned eyes, flickering sideways glances, and friendly but cautiously tendered hellos.

But yes, I'm very grateful today I didn't happen to be ushering a client into my apartment when the sprinklers malfunctioned. But I'm even more grateful that I didn't decide to binge today.

If they had seen me lugging an excessive quantity of takeout and grocery bags laden with junk food, I would've been mortified, and also outraged, because this would've gotten in the way of my binging. Which is always infuriating when the switch has gone off. The switch of self-control, I mean. I behave like an automaton when I inevitably lose control.

I've been good lately in terms of my eating disorder. I have not been eating in a disordered way, like restricting then breaking down and binging then purging, and then surrendering hopelessly to that seductive cycle. But my thoughts are still as disordered as ever. Actions rarely portray the inner turmoil of the fucked up human brain. Regardless, I haven't binged or purged in nine days, my longest streak in a while.

And today, I haven't come home as I have so many other days in the past, with my reusable grocery bag glutted with junk food or deep-fried, sauce-smothered takeout and a pressing, impatient sense of urgency to get home with it so I could hole myself up in my 220-square-foot-sanctuary and engulf the food mindlessly while watching YouTube videos or scrolling with equal mindlessness through Instagram or Facebook with an earnest belief that this is what I've been denying myself for X amount of days of good behavior and now I am finally rewarding myself, and this is what I truly want more than anything. Then, I'd eventually become so full, my belly so uncomfortably distended, I'd struggle to breathe, and then I'd throw it all up with tears squeezing out of my eyes and heart pounding like it's gonna explode. And afterwards, my teary eyes would be pink with a fine gauze of broken blood vessels, and my head aching from the force of vomiting.

And I'd feel ragged at the edges and seeing stars and dirty to my core, still reeking of grease and pungent spices. And I wouldn't feel rewarded any longer. Only gross, stupid, weak, and worthless.

But I can feel rewarded for my good behavior today. Relieved and rewarded, for there is also no evidence of a recent binge in my apartment when I walk in and step in that puddle. There are no wrappers, no old takeout boxes, no acrid stench of vomit wafting from the bathroom. No vestige, not a single swollen lymph node or broken capillary, evident on my skin, which is clear but for the small pimple I wear like an honorary badge. So if a person with building management were to knock upon my door, I wouldn't feel self-conscious or intensely guilty like someone just caught in the act of stealing. Not that I don't do illegal things. But that's probably obvious by now.

So with relief I take in the scene, then realize that it's my fire alarm leaking water, not the sprinkler. I hadn't known fire alarms could spout water out of them until today.

I put an old coffee cup—stained brown inside and with a congealed layer of old coffee at the bottom—on the floor directly below it to catch the continuous dripping water.

The problem temporarily mitigated, I decide to change into some comfy clothes. I'll light some candles and put on a face mask and try not to be self-destructive, for once. But then there is a knock on the door.

"Evelyn?" I can tell by their whiny, quivering voice that it's the building manager, Mary. I've always disliked her because she's nosey and strict and notices every single time someone puts their garbage in the wrong bin or leaves a sock in the laundry and I know it's inevitable she'll find out about me and my deviant, less-than-savory activities, whether it be the occasional bulimia or the more-than-occasional solicitation.

"Yes?" I call out, my voice taut with worry. I can't help but assume I'm being either chastised or evicted. But then, I always assume the worst. That has kept me safe, in a way, ever since my father died, mentally preparing myself for the worst possible outcome.

"It's Mary, can you let this man—what was your name?" she pauses for a moment and there is another, fainter and lower voice that replies. I can't decipher their words though or who they are, just that they're male. They say women can't hear low noises that well because our hearing is evolutionarily primed for the high-pitched cries of infants. So we can't hear men as well as babies, but they aren't much different, as it turns out. "Joseph. Can you let Joseph in to check your sprinkler?"

Joseph. A nice name. A biblical name. I know because my mom is very religious and made me read the Bible and learn the books and names and whom begot whom and recite verses and all that. It's both sad and ironic that she chose my name, Eve—supposedly the mother of all humanity, but also the perpetrator of original sin.

I let them in—my annoying building manager and the mysterious stranger with the biblical name.

I had been hopeful he'd be a fireman, and that we'd have some erotic, porn-worthy tryst in the near-future, and I'd finally have good sex for the first time in forever, because despite having had countless sexual partners in the past, truly mind-blowing transcendental sex has eluded me. But instead of a burly fireman, it is a wiry plain-looking guy near my age, dressed in a t-shirt and jeans that look like they were bought from Goodwill. They just have that threadbare and thrifted look about them. I know it well from growing up poor. The clothes make him look like a college student, but I notice some light creases on his otherwise youthful face.

"Hi, I'm the new maintenance guy," he says. He has a nice voice, not especially deep or masculine, but it reminds me of a voice you'd hear on the radio in the fifties, and when I meet his earnest, unfaltering gaze and am able to do a quick study of his features, I realize he is actually quite good-looking, and older than I initially thought, probably in his very early thirties. His face isn't actually plain either, just classically handsome, and kind. He's has kind, green eyes that pierce right through the guarded wall I constantly erect around myself, especially around strangers. And I'm so shaken by their innocent delving I have to avert my gaze, because I fear they'll see the ugly truth that lies beyond that protective veneer.

But I can't help but look again, peering up at him with the same innocent curiosity. Because hiding beneath that scruffy beard of short and soft, golden curls, I think I see the outline of a surprisingly masculine jawline. The way he holds himself though is almost effeminate. And his scrawny frame makes him look even less masculine. But then I notice there is strength in his lean arms as he reaches up to fiddle with the alarm. I stare quite rudely at the bulging bicep and branching veins, finding I cannot look away because I am so surprised by them. His jaw is square and features perfectly symmetrical. Everything is just as it should be, like out of a movie, and I find it unsettling, how utterly flawless yet guileless and earnest his face is in that quick study of mine.

"You'll have your work cut out for you, it seems," I remark. I avert my gaze but want to look at him again, to verify his appearance as it is still not quite impressed upon my memory. Sometimes, upon first glance, your brain vastly misconstrues the pattern of a stranger's features, in order to rush to a conclusion of familiarity. But he is wholly unfamiliar—I've never seen anyone like him—so I need a second, a third, perhaps even a fourth look, to truly gauge his attractiveness.

There is something cherubic about his short golden-brown curls cropped close to his head, and his slender yet sinewy neck, and the humble working clothes he's garbed in, and the modest compactness of his long, lean body. Sometimes I look at a guy passing by and I think he's handsome, but then on the second or third glance, I realize he's not, or there's nothing special about him, or there's a feature or form of asymmetry throwing everything off. But this guy is decidedly attractive.

"I hope this doesn't happen every day," he mutters.

"Well, it is always something, around here," I say in a voice ripe with resentment, and I glance pointedly at Mary, the property manager.

"I'd hardly say that, Evelyn," Mary states with her usual staid dryness. She's staring at me critically, her eyes narrowed and wreathed by a fine ray of creases, and I remember all of the "community" emails she's fired off, and tremble with misplaced guilt and fear. Even though I didn't leave the stove on that time or leave the garbage outside the designated trash area or play loud music after quiet hours, I always get the sense that those caustic emails are somehow in fact directed at me and that she knows about my less than savory activities and she's secretly admonishing and threatening me.

But really, all those caustic emails that make tiny, routine, perfectly understandable mistakes seem like catastrophic events are likely just indications that she hasn't been laid in a long, long while. I contemplate, for a moment, whether she's a lesbian, and if she fantasizes about me sitting on her face. I contemplate, too, whether or not I'd like that, and deduce I might in some twisted way, as a mere power play. I'm not a lesbian, but my sexuality isn't exactly rigid either, especially when my ego's in the equation.

The idea doesn't quite turn me on though, as precious little does. I'm mostly just getting antsy for them to leave. I don't want Mary to find something wrong with my apartment to reprimand me for. It's no pigsty, but I've never been the meticulous cleaner either. I glance around at the mess and see with plummeting dread a torn, empty condom wrapper on the floor. There's also a dirty pair of underwear with its crotch area exposed, crusted with yellowy discharge long-since-dried. I'm mortified that Joseph should get this first impression of me and forever remember me as the ratchet girl with the messy apartment and dirty underwear and condom wrapper on the floor. But neither of them seems to notice. God, I hope they don't.

They are wrapping things up now. I edge slowly backwards and kick the underwear, at least, beneath my bed.

"Thanks Evelyn; that's all we needed," Mary says in a curt manner, and giving me a final look over, her stiff brow wrinkled by contempt, concludes, "I figured I'd give Joseph the tour." Yeah, she definitely wants to sit on my face. But she's as old as my mother and I don't have an Oedipus complex. My mother and I get along just fine—as well as we can, anyway, despite her living on the opposite corner of the country, or being a devout Christian, or being a Trump-voting conservative, or being a pious and self-righteous proselytizer, or being absolutely impossible to argue with. And, of course, she knows nothing about my vocational activities.

"Thanks!" I say, banishing my mother temporarily from my head.

"Nice meeting you, Evelyn. I guess I'll see you around," Joseph says, and I'm very anxious to get them out of my messy apartment, away from the crime scene of my past sins, especially when Joseph looks at me with that earnest, fixed, penetrative stare, which pierces right through my walls again, reducing them to rubble. I've been so diligent to keep them up. To hide my innermost secrets.

"Yes. I guess you will. I mean. I live here. So…so I'll be around. B-bye. Good luck," I say, my voice wrung taut with despair at my own stuttering ineptitude. He looks at me and smiles with his eyebrows cocked up all bemused-like and it makes my stomach churn and face flush with warmth from the mortification of it all. Why do I care what this maintenance guy thinks?

Chapter Two

I lead them out, holding the door open, then shut it and wait to hear the sound of their footsteps squishing on the wet carpet outside, then lock the deadbolt. It locks with a satisfying click and I exhale with relief. So much pent-up anxiety. So much regret which lingers long after they've left. The air is frenetic from my frazzled nerves, and the main light in my apartment is flickering erratically, probably about to go out. Another inconvenient malfunction. I guess I can always call the new resident handyman.

Why is it when I'm around older, ugly men like my clients, I can be the most charming human on Earth, but when I'm around someone even vaguely attractive, I can't flirt to save my life? In moments like these, I am struck by the humbling reminder that I'm not as captivating as I think I am. Or perhaps I'm just not as cold and frigid and impenetrable as I like to think I am either.

When I get out of the shower, slick and wet and cleansed by the scalding water, I feel like both my degrading sins and embarrassing blunders have been temporarily wiped away. But I'm in a low mood now. The hot water beating down on me didn't help with that. Perhaps it made it worse. I remember reading an article about how frequent and long showers are an indication of being depressed.

Then, when I check my phone for the millionth time that day, in spite of my recent resolution to cease checking it so frequently, I see I have a new email, and my heart lifts. It's from the site I use for escorting—perhaps the most ubiquitous one out there, used by aspiring sugar babies and sex workers. The message is from someone whose username I don't immediately recognize. Fresh meat.

"Care to meet me for a drink tonight and explore a potential arrangement?" he asks.

Their profile picture is the all-too-familiar anonymous silhouette that never ceases to evoke an unnerving, eerie feeling in my gut. No matter how many faceless, nameless strangers I meet, the feeling never changes. The fear and anxiety never go away. But there is a certain excitement to it as well. The thrill of a potentially lucrative match.

"I'd love to," I reply, and reel him in with, "Meet me at the Ramshead Pub on 23rd at 8?" Making solid plans as soon as possible is always best.

As I get ready, the promise of income peps me up with more efficiency than a quad shot of espresso. It's the promise of money for such a finite amount of time that is so thrilling, to be handed a wad of cash for simply using one's wiles and body, by exploiting a rich man you despise. Not by climbing the ladder, but fucking it instead. It's way more validating than getting a match on Tinder. Years ago, that might've been exciting for me. But now, free sex seems futile, and I don't need the attention what with my other multitude of avenues for receiving it.

Not that I'm getting off with clients when they fuck me, but I wasn't getting off with Tinder hookups either. A part of me does get off on getting the money though, to be exploiting some rich bastard for such a short amount of time and effort on my part. I lie supine (usually) and simulate moans and look good, and that's all. And I get paid an obscene amount for it.

He doesn't reply for another thirty minutes, and I'm starting to get antsy as I try on five different outfits and attempt to hide a pimple that's got a head just begging to be popped, while also being dry and flaky from the tea tree oil I tried to annihilate it with to no avail. The best thing to do is gingerly apply a thin layer of ointment, wait, then cover with makeup in hopes of disguising the redness, at least.

The first few times, I'm unhappy with the result, as my concealer only seems to draw attention to the raised pustule with its white center, lightening the surrounding area without covering the actual pimple.

I think I've gone through the process of washing off the makeup then reapplying it about seven times before I finally give up and decide to check my phone again, and I wonder if this is just my OCD coming out as a coping mechanism in times of stress or anxiety, just like the binging and purging. Something to fixate on besides the deep inner turmoil and unhappiness dwelling in my heart. But I'm not nervous, I reassure myself in the mirror.

This time, he's actually replied.

"Sure, that works," his message reads, and I sigh with relief.

So often, on the site in this sort of vocation, a guy tells you he's interested, asks to meet, then you offer a time, and he's unfortunately not available, or fails to reply after the time's elapsed, and you go back and forth like that until you've wasted way too much effort for zero return on investment, and have to resign yourself to the fact that for whatever reason, this man wants to toy with the idea of meeting you but likely never will, and you don't want to be made a fool of or keep having your time wasted. So you block him and delete the conversation, making it as though it never happened at all. Or, worse case, you agree to meet, and he flakes, making you look like a total fool. Or, yet worse still, he actually meets you but turns out to be a creep or a dud who's actually broke but desperate for any form of female attention he can get.

Then there is the rare rejection, which never fails to make me feel like shit, and what could've been a very lucrative arrangement turns into just a waste of time.

When I put on my eye makeup, I feel reassured, because I no longer recognize the girl looking back at me. I've erected a mask I can hide behind. In my day-to-day life outside of the escorting, I don't bother with makeup, not even foundation, so the barest amounts of mascara and lipstick totally transform me.

"See you there," he texts again, illuminating my phone.

I reply with a smiley face, thus ending the conversation for now, while solidifying our plans, and keeping things fun, most importantly. It's all about making the client feel comfortable, while still not giving too much of yourself away in the process. Save the flirting for in-person. Save the intimacy for the bedroom. Never send nudes when he hasn't paid you a dime. Et cetera.

I check my messages again for his name, but realize he never told me. I also check to make sure we've been discreet and haven't discussed money yet, in case he's a cop. I've never actually met a cop while escorting, but I've heard plenty about entrapment and their erratic stings on dating sites—and it's possible I've been messaged by them before and just don't know it. The ones that try to name a price right off the bat, or ask to come over without meeting in public, or offer to send money without even speaking to me, I block and delete automatically. In my trade, one has to be cautious.

I've asked him to meet me at a bar that is low-lit and unpretentious. So unpretentious, it's part of a regional chain with over sixty locations and known for its tater tots. As I walk down the trendy Northwest 23rd Avenue. I become conscious of my appearance. There are people watching me as I walk by, in my thin, red slip dress and heeled leather boots that practically scream sex. Sometimes I do wonder if strangers perceive me that way; if they look at me and contemplate the possibility of my being a hooker. I am one, essentially. Sex work has become grayer and grayer since the internet came around, since men stopped automatically taking care of women, and women had to get smarter. Because now we are free and liberated, and so we must work hard for our money. Not that the old paradigm involving pregnancy and child-rearing wasn't difficult; it's just a different sort of struggle. If given the option of this or giving birth and raising a child, even if the latter promised a comfortable life, and never having to worry about money or my future financial stability again, I'm not sure I'd choose it.

But mistresses and brothels have been around since long before supposed female liberation.

I'm four blocks away now. I catch a glimpse of my reflection passing by a darkened storefront window, and I reassure myself of my attractiveness. Then the jitters come. I shove my way past people crowded outside Salt & Straw with their ice cream cones, and I feel their eyes on me, creeping over me, undressing and dissecting me. Sometimes I wish I was invisible. Surprising, perhaps, for someone so vain, whose sole source of income depends upon being highly visible, and beautiful, and tangible enough to be fucked and fondled. But I secretly dread the perception of others, and I oftentimes wish I could simply melt away.

He's outside waiting on me, on time for once. People in Portland are unbelievably flakey and perpetually late. It catches me off guard, his unabashed presence there.

"Eve," he says, eyes lighting up at how real and tangible I truly am. I always get this reaction—the men are always fretful that I'm going to turn out to be a catfish or a cop or no one at all, just a remote entity in Pakistan or Romania, trying to scam and humiliate them.

"That's me, in the flesh," I reply once I have crossed the street, and feeling like I've just blessed his life with my existence.

He has a pitiful look in his big brown eyes. I feel something akin to sympathy suddenly, as I take in his dark skin and short stature. Indian men actually make up about half my clients. Many of them are in arranged marriages or don't know how to navigate the dating scene here. And they are all considerably well-off because Intel or some other tech conglomerate hired them. These types aren't *rich* rich, but they make enough for me to not feel guilty about robbing their retirement for all that long. Especially knowing that they're married. I note the silver band on his ring finger he hasn't bothered to remove.

I am at least three inches taller than he is, and I regret wearing the heeled boots, since it makes me feel like a giantess next to him.

My lips curl into a droll smile as my previous insecurities and fears, which had been consuming me only seconds ago, melt away in an instant. It's like muscle memory, as I unfurl like the tender new frond of a fern, all dewy in the morning light. And then I begin the act of employing all the esoteric powers of my sex that even I don't comprehend. The deft, sequential captivation of luring a man into my apartment and making him pay me an arbitrary but not insignificant sum of money is strikingly similar to a hunter luring its prey.

I put my arm around his shoulder, and he trembles slightly from the contact. I wonder when he was last touched by a woman. He is wearing a clean yellow polo and pair of trousers, freshly starched. At least he's clean. That isn't the case for many of my clients. Occupational hazard.

"What do you do for work?" he asks. Among other questions. I loathe these questions, but I suffer them, nonetheless. They go as follows:

"What do you like to do for fun?"

 "How long have you been on the site?"

"Have you been in an arrangement before?"

"Would you be open to pay-per-meet? Until we build trust, of course."

"So, your place—you said it was close to here?"

"I bet you get a ton of messages."

"What turns you on?"

"Do you like sex? I bet you're a freak in bed."

"Do you have Venmo?"

"Are you ready to head out?"

Always the same idle questions, prying inquiries, mildly annoying and lascivious remarks, the presumptive statements, all the same, tedious bullshit, every time without fail. It's a script I know by heart, though I always pretend to have never heard it before. I laugh at all the right times, I smile and maintain eye contact, and caress their leg with my hand and flip my hair and lick my lips and pick at my food daintily, administering the same restraint and poise I handle my prospective client with, while making sure the dialogue stays on track. Sometimes I find myself growing impatient or even irritable, like when they mention the birth control, and all the dormant frustration that's been brewing inside of me threatens to bubble over.

"Are you on birth control?" he asks.

"I don't think that's any of your business," I answer succinctly. "Or relevant." The words might seem curt, but they are doled out with a flirtatious smile. Yet behind that smile, I'm beginning to grow angry.

"Relevant—" he chuckles, looking incredulous, and on the verge of being offended. "I don't want to get anyone pregnant."

"And you won't. Why would you? I use condoms every time, and I've never gotten pregnant. How could you even assume we wouldn't be using them?" I berate him, my blood pressure rising and face growing hot. This happens far too frequently.

But you'd think that after having gone through this hundreds of times with men—clients and one-night stands and Tinder hookups alike—that I would have learned by now. You'd think I would have learned how to be unfazed by their total lack of respect and flagrant disregard for their own health, or would've grown adept at assuring them in my pretty feminine way that everything would be fine, and the condom wouldn't somehow divest them of their masculinity, or make them incompetent or bite their tiny dicks off as they seem to fear. Otherwise, why would they avoid them so vehemently?

"Well, it's just," he mumbles ineffectually, almost whining as his voice quivers then falters. "I don't like the way condoms feel," he states matter-of-factly, but still in that pathetic, whiny tone like a child who is telling his mother he doesn't like broccoli and thus refuses to eat it, even though it's good for him and the very act of refusal—of making a fuss about it at all—is a juvenile one that warrants derision.

But this is far worse than refusing to eat one's vegetables. This is another human's bodily autonomy and safety we're talking about. But the vast majority of men these days don't seem to care.

But I'm not allowed to actually say these things to him. I can't actually deride and admonish him. That's the quickest way to sour the mood and kill a man's capricious libido.

So I have to conjure up some reply to assuage his insecurities and simultaneously bolster that frangible sense of dominance.

"Don't worry, I'll still make you cum," I whisper through the veil of my lashes. "I've never had a man complain. And I know how to use my mouth."

"I bet you do," he says, shifting in his seat excitedly. Now I've gotten his attention. "You don't use condoms when you—"

"When I suck you cock? No. I won't. If we can come to an arrangement that is. Per hangout is fine, for now," I tell him, pretending we'll see each other again when I know that probably won't happen. "We could even call it a gift. I prefer cash though. I'll show you to the ATM by my house."

I walk with him to the bodega a couple blocks away, where they have a reliable ATM in the back. I've been through this routine too many times to count.

Perusing the aisles of processed junk, I'm tempted to ask him for some powdered doughnuts and a bag of chips, but I decide against it. I'm ravenous, having neglected to eat both lunch and dinner. I should've ordered something at the pub—some fries or a pizza. But eating greasy finger food is another sure-fire way to turn a guy off. I know the tricks of the trade too well by now. Never eat too much. Eat daintily. Don't eat garlic. Don't eat with your hands. Don't eat onions. Don't eat at all. Order only one drink. Don't finish it. Wear tight clothing. Don't wear too much makeup. Wear some makeup. Don't shower beforehand— that's a waste. But don't stink either. But don't use too much perfume. Wear heels, but not too high—you're not trying to be a stripper, and in his eyes, you're not a hooker either. He needs you to match the lie he tells himself, to make it seem like he's not paying you to have sex with him. But you still have to look like sex on legs with a dash of supermodel while still espousing that approachable and humble girl-next-door vibe.

The owner of the bodega—who also happens to work the cash register—keeps eyeing me suspiciously as I loiter around the individual packages of Pop-Tarts on display that look ever-enticing with their crisp blue wrappers, like I'm about to steal one. I'm not even carrying a handbag though. When we go to leave, he looks at the both of us suspiciously, and I have the nagging paranoia that I often have that he's assuming the worst, which happens to also be the truth. And in moments like these, I also have this latent worry that they'll call the cops on me, or report me to someone. The ever-pervasive guilt and paranoia plaguing me to my grave.

I lead him back to my apartment. There's a tenant hanging outside, smoking a joint. I tense when I see him, like there's a rod in my back that goes utterly stiff. I'm all-too-familiar with this guy. Even if I can't seem to remember his name for the life of me, I know his voice by heart. It's high-pitched and whiny and downright obnoxious how loud it is. There is a presumptive officiousness to the way he projects his voice and enunciates his words, as if everyone on the whole floor ought to hear him. But everyone, even the busy-bodied building manager Mary who is probably dying for friends, avoids him like the plague. And he's oblivious.

I can see him in my periphery as we walk up, taking me in, recognizing me. My heart sinks with morbid dread. I know he will speak to us. He will speak to anyone and everyone in his desperate, groping way when given the opportunity.

"Hey, Elizabeth, isn't it?" he asks, like he doesn't know my name. Actually, maybe he doesn't. He's not that bright, so maybe his memory is not that good either. And he talks to so many people, even if only fleetingly, I can imagine the names getting easily scrambled in his tiny pea for a brain.

"No. Evelyn," I tell him.

"Oh, sorry. Evelyn. Of course. We were going to get coffee, weren't we? Sorry I spaced on that—and your name—I'm terrible with—"

"It's okay. I don't remember your name, either," I interrupt abrasively, unable to suffer his babbling, then I laugh—a laugh that is both innocent and icy, and causes an injured look to replace his dopey smile. "And honestly, I don't have time for coffee with you anyway. So busy." I pull a pained expression that is not remotely sincere. Then I chime, "Have a nice night." My drawl comes out in the most condescending way possible. I wince, because I sound like my mother, but then I smirk to myself, because, based upon his dumbfounded, wounded expression, I've achieved precisely the reaction I wanted. Maybe I should be thanking her. If only she could see me now. I wince again.

I lead my client in and slam the door behind us before that guy can form a response. And yet I still worry at what he must think of me, seeing me with this older man. Even though I dread that guy's inevitable presence—as he lurks perpetually outside the complex smoking his joints, or in the communal kitchen harassing the property manager with

23

his inane questions, or flirting with the cute petite girl down the hall, or trapping some unlucky fool into conversation as they wait anxiously for their pizza to finish cooking or their laundry to finish drying—I also dread his judgment and worry at what thoughts are possibly going through his head as he takes in the much older man I'm with, as he tries to work out why I'm with him, because he's so very old and ugly and lecherous-looking. But then, he didn't see the money. He didn't overhear our date. But he must come to that simple conclusion as I fear so many people do. He must be able to piece together this plain and universal puzzle. Just like the man at the bodega, or the couples that passed us on the street, or the bartender that asked for our IDs and no doubt mentally calculated the age difference.

I strut down the hallway towards the end where my apartment is, unlock the door, then let him in. The dormant but ever-present fear of being raped awakens in these moments, then I willfully quell it. It resurfaces innumerable times during my meetings, but I've gotten proficient at discounting it.

He pauses to take in the sparse furniture, the sleeves dripping out of the drawers, the plush comforter lazily draped over my bed, the plants in mismatched pots and books stacked along the wall, the window with its gauzy curtain and the sad, half-dead succulents perched upon the sill with crumbling white glaze, the unwashed dishes in my kitchenette. Every little mess and imperfection is visible in my micro studio apartment. I've justified to myself that it gives the place character—a certain bohemian *je ne sais quoi*—but then through the lens of a wealthy unbiased newcomer, it simply looks squalid and untidy. But he doesn't seem to care, as he doesn't waste much time before pressing me against the wall.

"Wait," I whisper in a flustered breath. "What about my present?" I ask as if I am a child on Christmas morning, my hands planted on his chest and pushing him away.

Sometimes, I'm nice enough to wait until after sex to request payment, but not with this one. After his annoying series of questions at dinner, my patience is worn thin.

He obliges, only mildly exasperated that I've ruined the illusion, and momentarily deprived him of his authentic experience.

Then it's the usual merry-go-round, and I'm sticky with sin again.

Chapter Three

The post-meeting ritual.

Once he's left, I can breathe a sigh of relief and fart in peace. Then I race to strip the bed, which involves me hurriedly lunging at all four corners of my queen-size mattress to ply off the sheet befouled by his vile sweat and cum. And then I disgorge the pillows from their cases and pluck the damp towel he used off the floor. His masculine odor has imbued itself into the towel's fibers. I almost gag as the stench wafts into my nostrils, and I toss it into the hamper. I have a few clothes—specifically underwear—that needed washing anyway. As if I need a source of consolation for the $3.50 I'll spend feeding the coin-operated laundry machines. I've just made one hundred times that in about two hours and that's not even the most I've made before. The trick is to never feel too entitled; it's a dangerous tendency to begin thinking you deserve a certain amount just because you've received it before. Some rich old bastards are willing to shell out five hundred for one night while richer and older ones won't part with over two hundred. It's better to settle sometimes though, when there's no other option, otherwise I'd just be screwing myself over by waiting around and trying to reel in a higher-paying client. And meanwhile, I'm not making a dime and rent day is ever approaching. I fucking hate rent day.

I emerge from my apartment in a silky oriental duster I only wear when lounging around, with a lacy bralette and shorts beneath it, because I frankly don't give a damn, and sometimes I like looking the part of the mistress because it suits me aesthetically. I had always dreamt of being the girl that slinked around in a silky bathrobe smoking a cigarette on the balcony of an apartment in some exotic, romantic European city like Paris, looking tragically sad and tragically thin. Now

I'm all those things, if you can call Portland exotic. It's certainly like a foreign country compared to the small Southern town I grew up in, where the Appalachian foothills were strewn with creeks and black bears and trailers or dilapidated shacks.

As soon as I turn the corner, I realize there's someone else in the laundry room and let out a yelp of surprise. It's the maintenance guy, Joseph, sitting there eating a sandwich as if it's the most normal and commonsense thing to do. He's reading a small dog-eared paperback too.

When I yelp, he looks up from his sandwich, not seeming at all miffed. I blush as I recall the dirty underwear and the condom wrapper and the act I've just done, and wonder whether or not he can see any evidence of it on me, like cum on my face or on the sheets balled up in the hamper I've got clutched closely to my chest as a means of protection.

"Oh, hi," I peep innocently, though I'm not quite the image of innocence, am I? I watch as his green eyes rake over my body involuntarily. There is nothing lewd about that curious gaze that quickly takes me in, this strange, sexy-looking girl who's interrupted his sandwich-eating. "Lunch break?" I ask in a high-pitched, awkward voice. "It's nine o'clock," I inform him, because who the hell eats a sandwich this late at night?

"Yeah, well, these sprinklers won't fix themselves. And the carpets need drying. Now I'm waiting up on the cleaners to arrive, then I'm off the hook. And boy, am I glad. This is the first chance I've had for a break since I got here at twelve. So it's egg salad sandwich and Hemingway for me."

I'm not sure why he just volunteered all that information I'm not particularly keen on knowing, until I consent that yes actually, perhaps I was a little curious and still am about him, even though I don't know why.

I catch a whiff of his sandwich, which smells like rotten eggs, and a scoffing laugh escapes my throat. I go around where he's seated so that I can get to the laundry machines. I open up the washer and toss my clothes inside. I try to do this as quickly and neatly as possible out of fear that he'll see the dirty underwear again, or God forbid, the cum stain.

"What?" he asks, chuckling, more befuddled than defensive, which is odd, coming from a man. Men usually don't like being laughed at by a woman and that's why I laugh at them, and often.

"Egg salad? Who in their right mind would choose to eat that? It's almost as off-putting as Hemingway."

"Well first of all, you really shouldn't make fun of another person's food preferences. It's rude. And secondly, Hemingway's a genius."

"I guess being a genius and an asshole aren't mutually exclusive, unfortunately," I remark, feeling a swell of genius in myself. But I ought to calm down. I'm such a narcissist, not just about my looks, but my intelligence too, despite being a high school dropout. "But the fact is, I've never been able to get through one of his books. And it's not because I'm illiterate, or don't understand the misogynist drivel, mind you," I add defensively before he even has a chance to reply.

"I would never have suggested that," he finally says in a voice that's feather-soft, once I finally let him get a word in edgewise. His grass-green eyes are twinkling with a devious spark that isn't quite malicious, but I don't trust it either. I can't put my finger on what it means, or what he's thinking, as he looks at me studiously with that steadfast, unfaltering gaze and serene, unnerving smile that penetrates my protective walls again.

"Say, you know that scene in the movie *Silver Linings Playbook*," I ask, folding my arms and trying to hide how disconcerted I am. I recall the scene with vivid clarity. "When Bradley Cooper's character throws the book out the window in frustration, breaking the glass?"

"Yeah. It was *A Farewell to Arms*," he answers after only a very short pause of deliberation and sounding slightly exasperated that I've brought it up.

"You actually seen that movie?" I ask in a tone of genuine disbelief as my Southern accent comes out involuntarily. I purse my lips as soon as I hear that discordant twang leaving my mouth, and that backwards hillbilly tendency to drop the auxiliary verb.

I watch the quizzical quirk of his brow and a look of bemusement ripple across the quiescent planes of his annoyingly perfect face.

"I love films," he states matter-of-factly.

"Me too," I retort, as if it's a challenge. And praying he won't bring up the accent.

"Maybe we could go watch one sometime," he coolly suggests.

"Not if you smell like egg salad," I retort without the vaguest hint of flirtation teasing my staid monotone. But secretly, my stomach is wildly fluttering. He's asking me out. Then as he attempts to read my poker face through narrowed eyes, a slow and infectious grin breaks out across his handsome face. "Or read Hemingway," I add, hoping that I sound cruel.

"Listen, I don't agree with all the things Hemingway said or did. I'm a feminist, I'll have you know," he says defensively.

"Oh, you're a feminist? Of course you are," I say with a pie-eating grin.

"Sure, I like women," he says, as if it's the simplest thing in the whole wide world. "I like you."

Something hot and irresistible swells inside of me at that statement. A swift and sure unfurling. The tendrils of it clasp my heart, like an insidious plague, like a warm hug.

He likes me. I knew it. Part of me is disappointed by how predictable this is. And part of me is flattered and that dumb fluttering is exacerbated by his big beautiful smile. When a client gives me money, it's thrilling, but this is a different sort of thrill, one that's both pure and pernicious. Because I have no control. There is nothing more vulnerable than being in love or in lust. And the feeling, this queasy queer fluttering and faint tremor of the heart, triggers a deep-seated pain I've repressed for many years.

And then in response to that trigger, I get this frantic, anxious feeling, a tautness in my chest, as if I'm about to be in some sort of predicament I cannot escape. I flee at the first signs of a romantic entanglement.

Several years ago, after my first tortuous brush with heartbreak—which was really no more than a high school crush that ended with rejection—I built walls around myself very carefully, to ward off any potential intimacy and make myself unapproachable, unavailable, and therefore inviolable. No one could break my heart. Because I'd never let anyone in. I became the ice queen. And prostitution was the perfect way to monetize my frigidity. I realized that if I was indifferent towards men and sex, I could control them and exploit them.

"Well, I promise not to eat egg salad just for you, then."

This poor handyman with awful taste in food probably isn't worth the risk in ruining all my hard work.

"Look, I was only kidding. You can eat all the egg salad you want. I can't go to the movies anyway," I explain vaguely, my face hot and voice flustered. I can't let this flirtation go any further. But I also know what's going to happen. I'm weak, after all. I've never had much self-restraint when my feelings got in the way.

"It's not because you have a boyfriend?" he inquires in a lower voice, the same deep resonant tone I'd heard behind my apartment door before first meeting him. I feel a tingling up my spine. His voice had been high and ebullient before, so what's this? I feel myself unraveling, right at the pith he's so impertinently bitten into.

"Why would you think that?" I snap, now even more flustered. I tighten my crossed arms that shield my chest. As if they offer any sort of protection, or will prevent him from getting beneath the cage of my slender frame and to my heart.

"Well, someone mentioned they saw you bring a guy home. That they see you with guys," he remarks with a shrug while gazing out the window behind me. His gaze had been so penetrating, I'm relieved he's shifted it at least momentarily.

"Who was it that told you that?" I demand, suddenly angry, defensive, and no longer all fluttery inside. "The chatty guy who stands outside smoking joints?"

"The Jewish guy, Peter?" he says.

"Yeah," I answer, though I'm honestly not sure—I certainly didn't know the annoying chatterbox was Jewish, and I don't know how he does either. "Did you actually talk to him? You better watch out, he might think you're his friend now."

"Why's that a bad thing?" he chuckles, clearly amused. "Are you afraid of making friends, Evelyn?"

I say nothing. It feels strange, hearing him say my name. It unsettles me like the calm, penetrative way his green eyes gaze at me now, zeroing in on me again. But I don't exactly hate it, either.

"Hey! I—you've totally changed the subject. Did this Peter guy," I ask, saying the name with disdain, "tell you that he'd seen my boyfriend or something?"

"He said he saw you with a man—a few in fact," he mentions nonchalantly.

"Is this the fucking Salem whore trial or something?"

"Geez, no," he hisses defensively, throwing his hands up in an act of both surrender and exasperation. He can't handle a woman's emotions, like most men. At least his reaction is deferential versus hostile. "I'm all for female sexual liberation."

"I'm sure you are," I say, crossing my arms again and staring at him judgmentally.

"It's just that people talk. There might've been more than one tenant that mentioned something. But like I said, it's your business, not mine. Just stating facts." He's pulling an awkward expression as he says this, no longer quite so aloof.

"The people here must be bored out of their minds. Poor, lonely cunts," I mutter under my breath, not angry necessarily—they're too pathetic to deserve such a strong, self-immolating emotion—but genuinely feeling sorry for them in the most deprecating way possible.

"God," he exclaims, as if my words have injured the innocence of his very person, or made him physically ill. "Do you always have such a dirty mouth?"

"This conversation is growing tedious. I have to go," I huff, picking up my hamper and walking off so that my duster floats behind me theatrically, like a cape. I live for these moments.

Then he says, "I'm sure you do," in a surly voice that gives me pause. In fact, I halt outside my door for some time groping with the unsettled feeling pervading my conscious, bristling it into discontent, and wondering at what my reply should've been. I hate how witless I become when faced by an unpredictable riposte or uncomfortable social interaction. Or worse, someone I'm attracted to. It happens so rarely.

Inside my apartment, my inner turmoil turns to hunger, as I realize I haven't eaten in twelve hours. And the hunger goes beyond physical appetite. I want to forget the embarrassment gnawing at me as I recount the cringe-worthy conversation and my needless cuntiness. I want to eat and forget. Food has always been my comfort and my escape, maybe because I was raised poor and rarely had it. Or maybe because it's a damn cheap form of therapy.

I walk up to Papa Haydn, which I'd been side-eyeing earlier, and order a big slice of German chocolate cake to-go. Then I go to the specialty coffee shop closer to my apartment that is mysteriously, magically open until nine, unlike the majority of the coffee shops that close by six, and order a latte. I've successfully stopped myself from getting takeout or more than one slice of cake or going to the grocery store and buying a bag full of junk food, thus staving off the inevitable binge and purge.

I don't see the maintenance guy or his dog-eared Hemingway novel for several days, and I go about my business as if I'd never met him, though I don't forget about him completely. The anticipation of seeing him in the lobby or down the hall, and having to relive that dreadful embarrassment, is temporarily lifted whenever I pass by the empty lobby of my apartment, or hear the sound of Peter and the chatty girl down the hall from me in apartment B15, or even Mary, and speed past them as discreetly as possible. But when that anticipation subsides, and I feel preserved again from those dangerous emotions Joseph alone seems to mysteriously provoke inside of me, it is not relief I feel, but a sentiment more akin to disappointment.

Chapter Four

The languid days during which I don't have any meetings with potential or regular clients scheduled feel like long, drawn-out vacations that are more nerve-wracking than relaxing. When I used to work my waitressing or department store job, and I'd take the rare, well-earned week-long vacation—which is now hilarious to think about—I'd grow so anxious about the work that would need to be caught up on, or how jarring and difficult it would be to get back in the swing of things. And the longer my vacation was, the more acutely I felt this agonizing anxiety, until I grew paranoid that the vacation would never come to an end and I'd inevitably lose my fragile hold on financial stability and my place in society as I knew it. And so, I could never properly, thoroughly enjoy that hard-earned vacation because of the eternal rat race, and the fear of becoming homeless or in debt so deeply ingrained in my conscious. It is different in some ways now. I have more money than I did then. But the days still go by agonizingly slowly, while the weeks melt away, and the months change in the blink of an eye, and the passing years give me whiplash, and I'm still here. Unemployed. Untethered and restless. Whoring around and hanging around in sterile coffee shops with the aroma of roasted beans imbued into the laminated walls with endless cups of coffee, the endless vacant hours of lazing and waiting around, or filling the day with meaningless activities. But all the while frantic, fretting over when I'll get my next client, and whether or not I'll make enough for the bills, or if the tiny creases below my eyes are deepening, or if my breasts are beginning to sag as they inevitably will.

I'll have to re-enter society and the miserable traditional working class again at some point, I reckon. I've eluded it for an inordinately long time as it is.

But there are thousands of other people in the Portland area who've eluded working the typical nine-to-five job or escaped the rat race completely. Trust fund babies, musicians, college students living off loans or grants or their parents, artists and yoga instructors living in communal houses and growing their own food. Or people who aren't the breadwinners and are fortunate enough to have partners that actually enjoy their work and make a lot doing it, enough to support their partner.

My friend Stephanie is one of those parasitic partners. But she's not exactly parasitic, because Stephen doesn't mind supporting her, supposedly.

She hits me up at eight in the morning on a day when I'm not otherwise occupied and tells me to come over in her needy, presumptuous way, as if I've nothing better to do—I haven't—and will unquestioningly obey her command. And I do. I'm thankful for the diversion. I had been tempted numerous times the past couple days to hit her up myself, but it's not my style. I don't want her to think I need her, or something. I'm always so cavalier about how I don't need anyone and have sworn off traditional dating as well as the idea of a soulmate. I think of Joseph suddenly, at the idea of a soulmate—but that's ludicrous—and willfully banish him from my thoughts.

I gather my things, stuffing them into the pockets of my light fall jacket, and head out, and Joseph, goddamn him, is standing in the hallway a few feet from my door tampering with the electrical box.

"Hi," he says as soon as he sees me, as if he was waiting for me. Or maybe he's just got quick reflexes. His shirt has a hole under the armpit, and I can see the outline of a couple of his ribs beneath his sun-kissed flesh sticking out, and I wonder at how he's so tan given that he's a

Pacific-Northwest-boy, and the sun has become scarce these days. The whole world is cloudy and gray and wet outside and he's as radiant as a July day as he smiles at me, his smile like summertime. And what does he expect from me? He doesn't ask anything of me. Really, he's like every other pussyfooted Portlander.

"Hey," I sigh, and shrug past him.

Then there's some hope as he runs up to the door as I go to walk out. I'm holding a bag in one hand and my phone in the other, so perhaps he thinks I need a hand, but I don't. But this rare display of chivalry is admittedly extremely attractive. He holds the door open, still smiling that infectious stupid smile.

"Sorry I made you mad the other day. I didn't mean to rile you up," he says, sounding sincerely apologetic as he stands there holding the door open and gazing at me with his gorgeous face. I notice that his beard has been freshly trimmed and cropped closer to reveal his square, sharp jawline, and my ovaries threaten to explode.

"I don't know what you're talking about. I wasn't riled up."

"You sure seemed like you were, Eve."

"Stop saying my name."

"But that's your name, isn't it?" When my only reply is a silent frown, he says, "Look, do you not like me or something?"

"No. I do," I mutter reluctantly, sounding perfectly abysmal about it, and hoping he won't misconstrue it as something more than platonic.

"Then why do you sound so miserable about it?" he asks, as if reading my mind.

I roll my eyes at him, silently wishing he'd either just ask me to suck his cock already or leave me the fuck alone, and end this sudden misery that's taken up residence in my heart. "I gotta go," I huff in exasperation, and hurry off.

I wonder what his cock looks like.

36

Chapter Five

Stephanie's apartment is located only ten blocks from my own, making it almost too easy to hang out with her whenever boredom strikes. But I know from past experiences that I grow tired of people when I hang out with them too frequently. I begin to feel claustrophobic, that same sort of feeling I felt when the stupid maintenance guy named Joseph with the gorgeous face and probably gorgeous cock suggested we go to the movies together, or just now when he cornered me in the hallway, and yet I had wanted something else, too. And that's what really disconcerted me, that sure and steady crumbling of my protective walls, and the desire aching beneath them.

"What've you been up to?" Stephanie asks me when I get there. I automatically go to the kitchen, and help myself to some of the herbal tea she has brewing constantly throughout the day, in one of her chunky ceramic mugs with shiny multicolored glaze that she's amassed quite the collection of. The steam that rises from the cup, heating my face, smells of chicory and licorice and unidentifiable roots and herbs. Outside, the rain drips, dribbles, and splatters intermittently on her windowpane and the dark waxy leaves of a magnolia tree.

"Nothing much. Running, brunching, reading, hanging out in coffee shops."

"I don't know how you don't go crazy."

"Why? What do you do all day except sleep?" I ask with a teasing smile, and she frowns at me.

"I run a business, I'll have you know," she informs me coolly.

The business she refers to is a service she advertises on Instagram as "therapeutic divination," which encompasses tarot card readings, horoscopes, astrology, healing crystals, aromatherapy, and more recently, cuddling sessions. She claims they're for treating PTSD. Cuddling for money is all the rage these days. A sign, I guess, of how lonely our generation has become.

"All right, and how many clients did you have last week?"

"One," she pipes up, a little self-consciously, then adds defensively, "It was a slow week. And I had to drive my mom to the hospital. And I've been reconceptualizing my space."

"Reconceptualizing" is just a fancy way of saying she's moved a chair to the other side of the living room, then burned some sage to cleanse the apartment of bad energy or whatever. It would hardly qualify as redecorating.

"And Mercury's in retrograde," I conclude in a droll voice. She knows I'm only teasing. "Still, you have a lot of downtime."

"I don't have the energy to do all the things you do. I need at least ten hours of sleep a day. Speaking of sleep, let's go back to the bed."

"Ugh. I've been lying around all day. Let's go do something."

"We can smoke and watch Netflix," she suggests, glancing at her bong on her bedside table.

I don't smoke weed usually. Even though it's totally legal here. My vice is that I like too much control, not that I like losing it, or my grasp on reality.

"I don't think I'll smoke, thanks."

"I figured. So lame," she moans, pulling herself into her bed and lifting the cover for me to get in beside her. "Always such a stick in the mud," she pouts, "refusing to let your guard down. You're such a Capricorn." She takes the bong from her bedside table and lights it with a flickering flame. The water bubbles like a witch's cauldron, and her dangling crystal earrings knock against the bowl, tingling like a chandelier. And the smoky perfume of weed fills the room, making me cough because I've still never gotten used to it. I've only smoked a handful times, myself.

I end up relenting, feeling more reckless than usual. I do one hit, to her shock and excitement, and sink into that deep, heavy abyss, by which my melancholia only intensifies, even as I giggle at the dumbest things, and my thoughts evaporate, and we watch *The Office* reruns and burrow beneath her blanket, and I contemplate my existence, my purpose, and my life way more than I like to when given the choice. And Michael Scott is blathering away. I'm convinced he's the most annoying, selfish, and idiotic little cretin I've ever laid eyes on, but I can't stop laughing at his dumb face when it appears on the screen.

Something about his face reminds me of that guy Joseph, even though they don't actually look alike. But there's still something there— an openness, an earnestness, a sense of faultless childlike purity—about that dopey, innocent, readily wounded countenance.

"I met someone," I tell Stephanie in an idle voice as I stare at the screen in a fixed daze.

"A guy?" she blurts in astonishment. "You mean, like, one who's not paying you?"

"He's the maintenance guy at my apartment," I say, ignoring the last comment. She likes to pretend she's never used her body for money, even though Stephen's practically her sugar daddy and she's cuddled an untold number of men in her so-called business venture.

"A handyman?"

"A poor one, I take it. He hasn't paid me a dime."

She looks dubious. "And you fucked him?"

"Well, no. It hasn't gotten that far. It probably won't. I don't even know if I like him. He's kind of annoying," I say, turning suddenly evasive and vague, though I don't know why. I just know it's a struggle to convey my thoughts—to even know my own thoughts—but maybe that's just the weed.

"Then why did you bring him up?"

"I don't know. I guess because he caught my eye, at least. It's so rare for that to even happen, you know?"

"Yeah," she agrees. "You never talk about anybody. There must be something about him. What's his sign?"

"I don't know," I reply with a scoffing laugh.

"What do you mean, you don't know?"

"Believe it or not, that's not the first thing people usually discuss when they meet. Usually, there's the name, and the interests and whatnot. Or, I don't know, whether or not they have a girlfriend."

"Does he?"

"I don't know," I answer meekly, ashamed that I don't know even that vital detail with utter certainty, despite the fact that I brought it up. And now I'm also wondering about his stupid astrological sign. "But he sort of asked me out, so I don't think so."

"And?" she asks with a smile. She's always rooting for romance. She's a shameless romantic. It comes with the horoscopes, I think.

"I kind of blew him off. You know I'm shit at flirting when it actually matters. Besides, it's impossible; I can't date people. If he really found out who I am—what I do—he wouldn't want anything to do with me."

"Well, it's so rare you get excited about anyone, you don't generally have to worry about this sort of thing, right?" she asks sympathetically, looking at me with her puppy-dog eyes.

"Yeah," I say vacantly, finding it difficult to switch gears and string my thoughts into words. Weed seriously affects my cognitive abilities, and I hate that about it too. I regret the single hit. "I'll ask him what his sign is, okay?" Not that it matters. Nothing can come of it and I'm deluded if I think otherwise.

Stephanie's partner, Stephen, walks in shortly after we stop talking. His name being so similar to Stephanie's has always disturbed me. A lot of things they do—their couplisms, like Frenching in public or baby-talking to each other or their pet names for one another—disturb me. It's a natural reaction, to feel discomfort at witnessing another couple's intimacy, what society would deem an inappropriate display of affection. But I ought to be better than all that petty bullshit, living the lifestyle I do that is not only looked down upon, but more or less illegal.

Still, deep down I know my disgust originates from a pernicious breed of resentment and jealousy, at having been deprived of the same universally-desired experience. But at the same time, I've deprived myself, so I'm at an impasse. It's easier to just look at the couple and be disgusted, and view them as derisive and pathetic for being so codependent, rather than admit to my own jealousy.

"Hey baby!" Stephanie calls out to him, as he walks through the hallway and into the bedroom. He takes in the scene of us lying in bed together with an amused smile.

"Hey ladies; you two sure look comfortable," he remarks judgmentally. His lanky, six-foot-four frame towers above us, as slender and stoical as an ancient spruce tree.

"What's that supposed to mean?" she barks, and I tense warily at that prickly tone of hers.

"Well, some of us have to work eight hours a day."

"Excuse me? Are you shaming me? You were the one that encouraged me to start my divination business. And now you're giving me this shit?!" she exclaims, becoming unhinged as she is wont to do. For being so spiritually enlightened, her mood is very volatile.

"I'm sorry. I wasn't trying to."

"You don't like helping support me?" she asks, her lips pouting like a petulant child's.

"Of course, I do. I love it," he grovels like a whipped dog, his head bent down and back hunched over in capitulation. He might be tall and intelligent and hardworking, but he is also the most passive and weak-willed man I've ever met.

He goes over to Stephanie's side of the bed and leans down to kiss her, a tactic to shut her up and end whatever small tiffs they frequently have. Her moods are mercurial but short-lived, and while defensive and entitled, she craves affection more than anything. She moans softly, unnecessarily, and I shift awkwardly beneath the covers. There is an almost incestuous wrongness to lying in my best friend's bed while she kisses her boyfriend.

Thankfully, their kiss is not a prolonged one and doesn't turn into something else. They don't have much regard for my being there, generally. In addition to being overly-affectionate, they are also in an open relationship, like so many other couples in Portland, and have asked me to be their unicorn—the plus-one in their hopeful threesome—on multiple occasions.

I decide I best leave before they have the chance to try that on me again.

"I'll just be going now," I chime, throwing off the heavy layer of blankets and jumping out of her immense bed. The much heavier blanket of that weed-induced mental fog lifts miraculously as well, allowing me to get out of there lightning-fast before Stephanie even has a chance to beg me to stay a while longer, or worse.

Chapter Six

When I get back to my apartment, I am afflicted by an acute pain at the emptiness of it, at the perpetuity of my solitude, and the prospect of another long evening stretching out before me.

I go to switch on the main light, which has gone dim since the day the sprinklers went off. But this time, it doesn't even turn on, or flicker erratically. It's gone out once and for all, making my sparsely furnished space all the gloomier. The lights in the bathroom and kitchenette provide enough light for me to get by without it, and my clients rarely want all the lights on anyway. This makes it easy to justify not worrying about it, given that I don't even know how to change a lightbulb. And I'm certainly not calling the new resident handyman. I'm tempted, but I really shouldn't.

Besides, I don't want anyone bothering me tonight, even if I feel lonely.

I've gotten used to being alone. I've intentionally and methodically partitioned my private life from others, which means hiding my sex work shenanigans. Stephanie and Stephen and my other friend, Gertrude, are the only ones that know about it, and I can therefore confide in them about my misadventures. My mother and the rest of my family back home don't have a clue, and it's quite convenient I don't have any family or childhood friends in Portland, and that I just happened to choose to live in a place on the opposite corner of the country, some three thousand miles away, where I can lead precisely the life I want to lead without anyone's nose in my business. My mother's anxiety-wrought, shyly inquiring tone does sometimes tempt me to open up to her. But there are some things, many things, in fact, that shouldn't be shared with one's mother.

I think about being in her womb, of being submerged within her as a still-forming embryonic thing, and about how she birthed me, and cleaned me, and fed me, and cradled me, and loved me unconditionally, and I feel hot tears rising to my eyes, because I feel suddenly so alone and foreign to even myself, and I wonder at what I've become. She would never want to know the things I've done. How debased I am from whatever idyllic image she might've once envisioned when she cradled me as an infant in her warm maternal arms.

And then, the next moment, I'm beneath a man named Peter, if that's even his real name. Married, obese, obscenely wealthy, and otherwise completely strange to me. I like to keep it that way. It's easier to repress any memory of them that way. I don't want to later dwell on the memory of him humping me right now, or his heaving breath the smell of decay, or the guttural grunts or sweaty, hirsute back.

Once he finishes, then gives me the money, I slip on a dress that already needs washing then open the door for him to leave. His moistness has rubbed off on my skin, as well as his smell, and I can't wait to jump into the shower.

As I open the door, the last person I want to see is walking down the hall. He is deep in thought and looking down, and the furrowed ridge of his brow makes him look more serious than usual, and perhaps even more attractive, and my heart catches for a fraught second. Then he looks up and our eyes connect and the world stops. But then my client leaves, shouldering past me through the open door and shattering that frozen moment in time and only leading to my humiliation. Because Joseph's eyes shift from mine as he takes in this stranger, this old and hirsute man leaving my apartment. I wonder if he heard the bestial grunts, my affected moans, or the stranger's voice as he told me I was beautiful and worth every penny and really know how to suck dick. My insides turn to liquid. Then his brow furrows again as he pieces together what's happened. There is only one conclusion. What else could it be? It's fatally simple, and the fatality of it is evident on his surprised but resigned expression. I wouldn't have sex with a man like that willingly; surely, he must know that. I almost want him to know that I'm a prostitute, to shout it out to him, because the only other explanation—that I would willingly fuck a dude this old and ugly for free—is even more mortifying.

I would tell him that now that the man is gone—that I only fucked him because he paid me five hundred dollars—but he looks so innocent with that handsome earnest expression, that I'm not sure such an explanation would be preferable to whatever assumption he's formed about me. Maybe he thinks that I'm easy, which isn't necessarily unacceptable in this day and age. But to actually be confronted by my myriad of sexual partners, that's another matter entirely. Either way, I feel dirty and debased.

He continues walking down the hall, apparently not as eager as usual to engage me in conversation, and I can see why. I quickly shut the door and lock the deadbolt.

I take a scalding hot shower to cleanse myself of the previous client, as well as the humiliation I've just experienced. I wonder at what I could've done differently. If there was something I could've said, or a lie I could've told. I can be good at lying, at least when it concerns my vocation.

I get out of the shower, my skin scalding red, then I ensconce myself in a bathrobe. I go about my standard routine of stripping the sheets and putting them in my hamper and gathering my things. Always the same routine. Always the same low feeling, until I am clean and confidently rid of them, and I can count out the loose bills with that thrilling feeling usurping the sadness and self-disgust, for a while, at least.

After putting the money in the small safe beneath my bed, I pause with the hamper in my arms, frozen by fear, at the prospect of having to see Joseph again and suffer the judgment of his vernal gaze. I'm not usually like this. I'm usually confident and unapologetic, pompous, even. Yet here I am, cowering behind my door because of a stupid broke hipster handyman—a boy. Barely a man.

"This is stupid," I mutter to myself, unclosing it brusquely and going out into the world. Of course he is in the laundry room in the front, this time with a cup of herbal tea instead of a sandwich, and he's traded Hemingway for a large textbook. When he looks up from it and sees me, I halt in the entryway and release a shaky breath.

His eyes return to the book.

"Hi, how are you?" he asks me, though his eyes are still glued to the tiny, inscrutable text. His tone is perfectly cordial but leeched of any feeling. I can tell he's only feigning this guise of friendly nonchalance, but in reality, he's disappointed and perhaps even angry with me.

"I'm well, thanks. And what about you?"

"Oh, you know, I'm right as rain," he says, looking lackadaisical with his legs sprawled out in front of him as he leans back, not nearly as tense as he was when I first entered the room. I'm still unconvinced, though. I'm all too aware of the affectations people don.

Without thinking, my eyes fall involuntarily to the space between those long lanky legs, where his pants sag around his crotch, teasing me. His pants are bit too baggy and too short at the same time, so that his knobby ankles are exposed. I bet he got his pants from a thrift store too.

My usual reaction towards men like him would be apathy, if not disdain, not because I feel superior to them, but because my brain's been wired to perceive men as mere tools to be extorted, and those without wealth, without anything to offer me, I automatically categorize as useless. But he somehow eludes this stereotype. Because I'm not stupid and I know perfectly well that our consumerist society is driven by money and greed and is actually very corrupt and evil and I, like most intelligent but jaded working class people, yearn to escape the shackles of it. But only in the same way I yearn to escape the rigid confines of civilization—I don't actually, because if I were to live in a tent in the woods, I'd quickly grow bored and want a latte and the internet, and long to return to the enthralling excitement of modern city life, shackles and all.

But I get the feeling from his threadbare clothes, homemade sandwiches, and thrifted books that Joseph is different. He could probably go days without spending a dime on lattes or frivolous trinkets and be quite content eating his stupid egg salad sandwiches in the woods alone. And that's why, rather than being deterred, I'm in awe of him.

Outside, the rain is falling. And suddenly, all is right in the world.

The world is insular and contained when the rain falls lightly like this for copious hours with its penetrative dampness. I feel healed by it. It washes away thoughts of all the men I've been with. It bathes me in all its glorious gloom.

I chuckle idly as I turn away from him because I can't come up with any other natural transition, and go about loading the washer, trying to be at ease with the silence that falls over us. It's difficult to bear, even though I loathe small-talk with strangers. But he isn't quite a stranger, or an annoying tenant, or a creepy homeless man at the bus shelter, or another chatty woman in the checkout line. I want him to bring up the man. I want him to be more irked, rather than appear unperturbed as he coolly reads his textbook in silence.

I'm in a good mood suddenly. Perhaps it's the rain, or being paid recently, or the tension of him being there which has created a sort of drama I find deliciously exciting. It's broken the monotony, at least, and then there's still the fresh thrill of having received five hundred dollars. The novelty of that thrill never quite fades, though the intensity of it, the elation it once incited, isn't nearly as strong. And it's so short-lived now. And there's the inexorable shame that taints it. By evening time, I'll be worrying about getting another client, and fretting over the possibility that my beauty will wane before then, or that men's tastes will change. Women look so different now anyway and I can't keep up with the everchanging fashion trends and the contouring and lip fillers.

But for right now, I'm still on Cloud Nine, and wondering what I'll eat—and he's here, and for some reason, I want to ask him to dinner, even though I know he can't afford it, and we'll likely go Dutch, given his modern "feminist" sensibilities.

"Say, are you hungry? Would you like to get something to eat?" I ask suddenly, no longer so bothered by his failing to ask me out first. But maybe that's because I feel like I owe him one after being so prickly and hostile towards him, and his having to see that other man coming out of my apartment.

"Sharing a meal, now there's a foreign concept," he says, looking up from his book. "I'm on the clock though. Just taking a quick break." He's totally aloof. Why does it make me want him more?

"Well, when do you get off?" I ask, then my face colors at the obvious association there. Getting off. *Masturbating.* I wonder what his cock looks like again. I'm horrid.

He seems too pure and unconcerned to catch the possible implication though, and perhaps he's too pure for masturbation at all, and I'm beginning to fear he's asexual—because his flirtations in the past might not be flirtations at all, given his already open and friendly demeanor—when he looks up at me with that earnest expression and annoyingly perfect jawline and says, "Five o'clock. I'd be down to get a meal with you. But don't you have a boyfriend?"

"That question again?" I whine. "I told you I didn't."

"You never actually got around to telling me. Or explaining all the men."

"Hmm, that's interesting," I murmur idly while I die inside.

"You're evasive. You're uncomfortable talking about yourself, aren't you?" he asks, his face darkening as he psychoanalyzes me. Then his lips twists with cruel amusement. "You're hiding something, aren't you, Eve?"

"Yes. You're triggering me. Stop it," I plead. I hadn't anticipated being confronted like this.

"Wooooow," he exclaims in a long-drawn out voice. Effeminate. Whiny in a way that is not obnoxious but rather part of his accent. Like so many other Portland men. Of course, he grew up here, I think with an internal groan. That explains the unidentifiable boyishness and breezy nonchalance about him.

"You're a tricky one," he adds. Then he leaves it at that. He gives up so easily. It seems to be part of his disposition.

"I can talk about myself. It's just not exactly my idea of fun, and certainly not laundry room repartee," I quickly explain. "So...five?"

"Sure thang," he chimes with a smirk, and I think he's mocking me. I usually disguise my Southern accent pretty well. But something about Joseph puts me in a state of discomposure. Then it comes out involuntarily.

I change into a crop top and high-waisted jeans and oversized knit cardigan with some clogs, and do my hair up in a messy bun and put on a new pair of dangly earrings, then gingerly dab on a tiny bit of concealer to hide the fresh blemish that has suddenly, unexpectedly emerged from the mysterious network of glands beneath my epidermis. I blame it on my client rubbing his oily, sweaty face on mine.

Luckily there's makeup, a modern invention that women in my position, who constantly have to look good, must unfortunately depend upon.

But I'm putting it on now, and fretting over my looks, even though I don't have to, even though I'm not meeting a client who expects me to look perfect. I'm going on a date, and with a poor guy, at that. And as I stare fixedly into the mirror, I pause to wonder why I'm fretting so damn much. I'm not even getting paid for this. My brain's been wired at this point to associate sex with money, so that I can't even properly enjoy it, so this date will probably be futile, and I should've never engaged with this man to begin with. I know this because I've tried one-night stands with hot men in bars before. It doesn't matter if I'm sexually attracted to them, the sex always falls flat. They cum and then they leave me without paying a dime and never text me again or perhaps hit me up a week later when they're horny again expecting me to eagerly open my legs for them again, but then I ghost or outright reject them and then they resent me for it and perhaps even send me a hateful text as if they're entitled to my body, my attention, and my affection.

And yet, I chase after that ephemeral orgasm anyway. And not the ones I get on my own. Those don't count. They're hardly fulfilling. They only leave me feeling emptier and more pathetic. And I'm not talking about the machine-like kind that I'm sometimes able to produce with clients, either. Or the ones I simulate, complete with spasms, purely to inflate their fragile egos and finish them off sooner so they'll pay me then get the hell out of my apartment.

And still, the prospect of sex with Joseph makes me both excited and anxious. I don't care what my clients think—what the guys at the bar think—what the Tinder and Bumble and Hinge hookups think— but I care what he thinks. And I have the smallest shred of hope that it'll be different with him. And I suspend all rationale for that silly shred of hope. When I leave my apartment, for a moment, I'm no longer a sex worker, and only a woman—timid, naïve, and almost virginal in my excitement.

Chapter Seven

When he sees me coming into the lobby, he stiffens and jolts a little, as if I've startled him. I look very different in this outfit and with my hair done up. It's five o'clock sharp.

"What, never seen a girl before?" I tease, and as I walk up to him, I am reminded of his height. The t-shirt he's changed into flatters his tall, lithe frame and sinewy arms. It reads "Virgo" in big, faded letters. I immediately think of Stephanie. For once, I'd like to employ her knowledge of astrology. I wonder what she'd say about him.

We go to a Thai restaurant on the trendy Northwest 23rd Avenue, where tourists and locals stroll along the shop-lined streets with ice cream cones in hand, and the trees are strung up with glowing Christmas tree lights. It's only a bit past five and already sundown, which would usually be depressing, but I'm too excited right now for that. We walk beside each other with a small but suggestive gap between us, and I pretend to be chill, though my heart is pounding in my chest.

"So, you're a Virgo?" I ask him once we're safely inside the dimly-lit Thai restaurant. I've assured him that while it doesn't look like much, it's one of the best Thai places in town, which says a lot considering the sheer quantity of Thai restaurants in Portland.

"Yeah. Don't try and do a reading or whatever on me though."

"What makes you think I'm into that?" I ask defensively.

"You have a witchy vibe. Actually, I'm fairly convinced you're a witch."

I pretend to be offended by that remark, though it secretly amuses me.

"I actually don't know much about that stuff. That's my best friend's forte." All I can remember from Stephanie's unsolicited rants is that Virgos are an Earth sign and that my mother's a Virgo, but that's it. I don't know what their strengths or weaknesses are, or what drives them, or if they're even-keeled or impulsive, introverted or gregarious. And I certainly don't know if they're sexually or romantically compatible with me. And I usually wouldn't care, but suddenly I do. Very much. I think of my phone in my handbag and contemplate googling it in the bathroom.

I've truly reached a new low.

"Oh, so you're saying she'd be more proficient at picking me apart?"

"I'm sure she'd love that," I answer, then pause at the squeamish thought. She'd likely try to seduce him during her divination. She likes to think she's some kind of sex goddess. Even though I have no claim to him, the idea alone of someone else having him, and especially my friend, bothers me. But what bothers me more is that I'm already so jealous. "Especially since I'm interested in you," I add emphatically, emboldened by that jealousy. Seconds after, I regret that boldness. But my heart is stuttering excitedly in my chest. And I remind myself he's already said he liked me.

"You are?" he asks, his face brightening and that same radiant sparkle coming into those grass-green eyes. I realize there're tiny flecks of gold in them too.

"Sure. You're attractive," I say coolly. I look up at him, though it requires some courage. But he averts his gaze, tipping his head up to the ceiling just to frustrate me, it seems, with his sharp jawline and prominent Adam's apple and insufferably cute grin. It's hard for me to fathom that he's just as nervous as I am, given his otherwise-flippant act.

"Oh, gee, thanks. So you just want me for my body," he replies once he finally condescends to meet my anxious gaze. "That's very superficial of you, Miss Evelyn."

"Ugh. Call me Eve. Evelyn sounds like an old lady's name."

"Well, Joseph isn't the most popular for our generation either."

"I like it. There's something soft about it."

"Thanks," he groans in that whiny accent I'm beginning to find adorable. I smirk at him. We connect eyes from across the table. His eyes look oddly severe beneath the brooding ridge of his eyebrows in this dim restaurant lighting, and then they dart away. "So, Eeeeeve," he practically sings, "you're interested in me?"

"Even though you're abysmally simple, yes," I say, and it sounds far more incisive than I intended. He looks utterly nonplussed, his gentle, open expression inexorably wounded, so that I feel compelled to amend it. "I'm kidding, of course. I find you frustratingly good-looking in addition to being incredibly intriguing. Reading Hemingway *and* being a self-proclaimed feminist?"

"Yes, I'm an unsolvable puzzle. There's unchartered depths in this one," he remarks sarcastically. "But personally, I think you're the intriguing one." He looks at me with the same quiet but penetrative curiosity as the first time we met, but this time it is also slightly sad, as if he's discovered something about me even I haven't, which is disconcerting. He doesn't know, does he? Has he guessed? It's not that difficult.

"I am, probably. But not necessarily in a good way," I say, arrogant and all at once self-deprecating. I contemplate telling him the truth then as the fact of my occupation hovers unspoken in the air. But I decide against it because I am anxious and impatient to have sex with him. It feels imminent, now that it's been established we both like one another, yet it is still not wholly certain, and he could slip through my fingers at any moment, at the smallest blunder. So I decide to put off telling him, and the waiter conveniently arrives with our food.

"So, you're a handyman. You fix things for a living," I say as we shuffle our silverware around.

"Yeah, but I can't seem to fix myself," he laughs, but there's some truth to his deprecating tone.

"You don't seem the troubled, angsty type."

"Well, looks can be deceiving," he says, totally earnest now. "But we all have our shit, don't we?" Still, there is a lighthearted twinkle in his eye. He never lets things get too sad or heavy, I can see.

"I suppose."

Then we start eating. The curries are still steaming.

"This is incredible," he mutters under his breath as he slurps the second spoonful of his curry. It's electric yellow from the turmeric, and aromatic steam is coming up from both of our large soup bowls, smelling of fresh basil, kaffir lime leaves, and star anise.

"I thought it would be good on a cold, rainy night. It really warms you up."

He makes an affirmative hum and continues eating, so I do as well, then I don't have to worry about saying the wrong thing if we eat in silence.

I'm thinking to myself as I slurp away that he's not being very forthcoming, when he sets down his spoon and says, "I used to be a waiter here in Portland, before I got into maintenance. And before that, I was a delivery driver in LA, and before that, a tour guide in Africa, and before that, an English teacher in Spain."

"How old are you?" I ask. He doesn't seem that much older than I am, despite having lived multiple lives already.

"Thirty-one."

"That's young considering everything you've done—all the places you've been."

He shrugs apathetically and goes back to eating his curry.

"I've never been abroad," I remark sadly. The life of a vagabond sounds enviable.

"Never?" he asks, more surprised that I haven't managed to go anywhere than I was about his having travelled around the world. Maybe I could sense the cultured air about him, and it's what lured me to him, even if it was simultaneously intimidating.

"Nope. Not many states either. I'm from Tennessee originally, so I guess I've been there. But that's about it."

"I thought I detected a Southern accent," he remarks with a smile, the sort of flirtatious smile men often give me when they discover my sultry origins. Perhaps they romanticize the South because it seems exotic and old-fashioned. If only they knew about the giant cockroaches and mosquitos, or the flea-infested trailer I lived in as a child.

"It's faded a lot. I moved away seven years ago."

"You're practically a local."

"I'm still just white trash." He quirks a confused brow at me. "But you're a local," I say to him, before he can try and refute my self-deprecating statement.

"I am," he agrees with a serene smile.

"Portland boy. That's why you've moved around so much. You were spoiled, growing up in a city."

"I guess. Why did you move to Portland, of all places?"

"Why not? It's beautiful. It's fun. It's got great food. People aren't as judgmental."

"I guess. There are more interesting places though. Like Budapest, or Berlin, or New York or Chiang Mai."

"You just say that because you grew up here. This place is an oasis compared to where I'm from. Besides, traveling costs a lot of money. I'd be poor if I traveled as much as you have."

"But you're poorer for not having experienced it. Travel enriches a person in a different way. I don't feel poor. And in reality, I'm far better off when it comes to quality of life than the vast majority of people in the world. If you traveled a bit, you'd realize that."

"And what constitutes richer?" I ask, my curiosity getting the better of me. For some reason, I want to know precisely how rich or poor he is. "Do you make more than, say, the global median household income of nine or ten thousand dollars?"

He rolls his eyes and balks at me. "That's money talk. I don't like to confine myself to such a consumerist, capitalistic mindset," he says almost condescendingly, or maybe it's just that Portland accent that comes off as so condescending.

"Oh, you're so enlightened," I balk right back. "You don't care deeply about anything, do you?" I say with an edge of resentment, and I'm not sure why. Perhaps because of those dark depths of melancholia I often fall into despite my strident efforts to elude it, by exercising and making lots of money and buying pretty clothes and hanging out with friends and taking my vitamins and getting enough sunshine and calling my mother and filling my day with these mindless activities to distract myself from the truth of my deep, internal sadness. "You don't have a serious thought in your head."

"Quite the opposite actually. I have too many. I'm very serious," he assures me, grinning all the while because it sounds so ridiculous to say as he says again, "I'm a very serious person," as if he's trying to convince himself as much as me.

"See, you don't even sound serious when you say that!"

"I can't help it! This particular environment isn't very conducive to existential angst."

"Does it have to do with me?"

"Yeah, you. You've got that witchy way about you," he laughs, bringing up the fucking witchy thing again like I'm trying to bespell him, and perhaps I am, though I'd rather it have been of his own volition. "I'm enraptured by you, Eve."

Why would he be enraptured by me? I'm not special. I blush and look away.

Then the check comes out. After his enlightened little speech, I figure him conforming to tradition and picking up the check is out of the question, so I go to reach for my purse.

"No, Eve. Don't worry your pretty head about it. I'm going to get it," he assures me, his condescending tone re-emerging as he reaches into his back pocket for his billfold and takes out two twenties, tossing them on the table as if even touching the evil tainted currency sickens him.

And then there's the inevitable walking back to the apartment building. And there are other couples strolling down 23rd Avenue, clasping each other's hands and looking utterly besotted with one another, and I think to myself how nice it would be if Joseph and I were like that and surrendering to all those atrocious romantic clichés that suddenly seem incredibly appealing. And I also realize how much I want them to think we're a couple as we walk side by side, and I long for him to hold my hand or wrap his arm around me protectively, possessively. I've never felt this way before. I certainly don't feel that way about my clients when I'm forced to walk down the street with them, and fear being seen by potential friends or acquaintances, or even strangers. But with Joseph, I would be so proud. And only because I like the way he looks so much and find him so irresistibly charming, and it's a vile disease taking over me, this superficial lust. I of all people ought to know better.

Then we get to the door at long last, and my stomach is churning nervously with what feels like butterflies or indigestion, and he turns to me with that resigned and regrettable look someone gives you when they must part with you at long last.

"Well, dinner was lovely, Miss Eve," he says, really laying it on thick with the polite niceties. But he's looking like he's about to go and leave me.

No. I want to cry out to him. *Don't leave it like this.* I want him to kiss me so badly. His soft green gaze shifts from my eyes to my lips. But he doesn't kiss me, he just stands there looking at me, and it's infuriating. It must mean he doesn't like me like that, like I thought he did. Something didn't go quite right during our short date and he's decided he won't kiss me.

"Do you want to go back to my place?" I hear myself ask, buckling so quickly, because I don't want to miss my chance, and I'm willing to shame myself—to become so vulnerable. Why must I be the one to ask? Why must I crumble so easily?

"We could," he sighs reluctantly, and in that sigh, all my confidence is decimated. It's not exactly the response I expected or hoped for. "Are you sure you want to? Maybe we shouldn't." Then I realize he's reluctant because it's a conflict of interest. Because it could be misconstrued as inappropriate and perhaps put his job at risk. Because he's afraid of someone seeing us and reporting him to building management for fucking a tenant. Valid fear, I suppose.

"Oh," I murmur helplessly, and not sure what we're supposed to do now. Why did he have to talk to me in the first place, and be so goddamn charming, and agree to go to dinner, if he knew dating a tenant was inappropriate? "Now I feel dumb."

"Hey, Joseph. You're still here?" a female voice is coming from behind me, and Joseph smiles suddenly, no longer looking nervous or regretful.

"Hey, Katy. Yeah. Worked late," he explains, subtly furthering the gap between us. I feel my heart sink, then burn with jealousy. Has he been having the same friendly and flirtatious repartee with her? Have they fucked already? They seem to know each other, at least. But then again, Joseph is effortlessly charming and I can see him making fast friends with everybody.

"I'm having an issue with the fridge in my apartment. I don't think it's getting cold enough; could you take a look at it?" she says sweetly, batting her stupid long eyelashes. She opens the front door and holds it open so that he has no choice but to step through the threshold and abandon me. His altruistic niceness behooves him to help her.

"He's actually off the clock," I state in an incisive tone, and step inside as well, my possessiveness emboldening me.

Her mouth forms a grim line as she glances at me then looks away. She seems annoyed by my presence, which is really rich considering she's the one who just intruded into our moment and stole Joseph away.

Even more upsetting is the fact that she's not ugly and a lot more petite than I am. I usually don't mind my tall, statuesque frame, and even embrace it by wearing heels and clothes that flatter my long legs, but there's nothing like a tiny, curvy girl standing at five-foot-two to make me feel self-conscious.

"I don't mind," Joseph says congenially, and much to my irritation. He's far too obliging, but maybe it's because she's cute and he knows her name, so perhaps they're good friends, or he's excited he'll have the opportunity to fuck her, because he actually likes her more than me, and the idea is infuriating. But instead of boiling with rage, I'm wilting with despair.

"Well, I'll see you around, then?" he says to me, not coldly, but certainly not in a way that suggests he's sorry to part with me. Something snaps inside me—a chord that was affixed to my heart—and I reel from the jarring blow.

"Yeah, yeah. Of course," I murmur lowly, and stumble to the side so that he can follow her down the hall, feeling feeble and dejected. I watch as they go to her apartment, which is on the same floor as mine. Despair resounds in my chest at having been abandoned so unexpectedly. I trudge back to my own apartment. The light's still out so it's impossibly dim. I realize I should've asked him for help with this just like Katy did, but then I feel silly, trying to fight for this poor unimportant handyman's affections.

I hear voices outside as people walk by in conversation, which reminds me of how impossibly thin the walls are here and how I better put some headphones on quickly, and watch some YouTube videos or listen to music or something, lest I should hear them having sex, the possibility of which fills me with dread, even though it's none of my fucking business and ridiculous I should care when I've had three men inside me this past week alone. So why should I feel so possessive of Joseph, whom I barely know? But I've put him on some sort of pedestal. And with the other men, it's different. I don't have sex with them out of love or lust, so they don't count. Katy would count. He'd actually be getting off with her. And I am so perturbed that even the possibility antagonizes me to the point that I must drown out any and all noise for the next three hours.

I listen to some music and mindless YouTube videos about nothing in particular, but still can't stop thinking about them. I wonder if they've slept together. And if he hasn't slept with her, I wonder if he wants to. He did leave me for her, after all, and gladly abandon all hope of sleeping with me so that he could help her with her stupid fridge, supposedly. And now the jealousy and insecurity I once fancied I was immune to is infecting me like a virus.

I am more incensed by my caring at all than the fact that he went off with her in the first place. I'm not supposed to care about men or whom they sleep with. In the case of my clients, it's preferable if they sleep with other people. Because the clients who see me exclusively—except, perhaps, their wife whom they aren't sleeping with anyway—

usually end up catching feelings and becoming the worst sort of client, the sentimental possessive stalker type that forget what I am and the bounds of our arrangement.

I drift off, but wake up some unknown amount of time later to the sound of someone softly knocking on my door. It stops, I get up, my heart pounding with fear. I look through the peek hole and it's a distorted view of Joseph.

He's come back for me. But I'm groggy and disoriented. "Joseph," I croak.

"Shit, sorry. I didn't mean to wake you. I thought you were still up. Sorry," he apologizes in a breathy whisper. It all feels like a dream, and I wonder if I am dreaming and never woke up at all.

"You came back. What about Katy?" I ask.

"I was just fixing her fridge. But then there was something I forgot to do."

"What?" I ask confusedly. I don't fully believe that he was just fixing her fridge, but I want to.

And then he mumbles softly, "I have to head out soon. I have to get up early." But then he bends down and kisses me. I probably taste like death since I drifted off without brushing my teeth, but apparently he doesn't care, because he kisses me long and hard, and I unravel in his arms even though my reflexes are slow and sleep-drunk. He smells like the forest and tea tree oil and home. Then, next thing I know, he's walking off, abandoning me again, and this time I'm worse off than before. Why didn't he ask to come in? Then I remember he said it was late. But he had time for Katy. And maybe he did fuck her. Then he kissed me right after, the bastard.

I float back to my bed. Sleep returns to me, and I dream there's someone knocking on my door again, but I'm stuck in dreamworld this time and can't answer it. Then I wake up and it's morning. Was that kiss even real? Or was it just a dream? Even if it was, even in my dreams, he didn't want to come in. But would I have let him? I still don't know if he fucked that girl Katy. One thing's decided, though: I'm a fool for caring at all.

Chapter Eight

And my limbs are heavy and ache when I try to get up. I hate mornings. Rather than being excited about what transpired last night, I am wracked by conflict. It's all bad news. It doesn't mean anything. Nothing can come of it. Just like the gray damp weather outside.

I relent to lying back down and submerging myself further under the covers. I often get this heavy feeling that settles over me as soon as I wake up. A deep, abysmal depression I readily surrender to. It's difficult not to when you live alone and haven't got anywhere to go to in the mornings. No job. No obligations. No exciting plans. The only plans I ever have happen strictly in the evening, so the only things really to inspire me to get up are coffee and food, when the hunger pangs and the throbbing caffeine headaches inevitably come.

I ought to sign up for a yoga class, or a volunteer job, or move in with Stephanie. She has a spare room she currently uses for her divination business, but she has nagged me about moving into it. But then, if I moved in, she'd also harass me about the threesome thing more. I shiver in my bed, repulsed by the thought.

I get up finally when I realize more sleep isn't in the cards for me, though I only got five hours, and go about my usual routine, which involves brushing my long hair with painstaking slowness and body-checking myself about a dozen times, and switching outfits before deciding on some stretchy striped flares and a cropped shirt and jean jacket with frayed accents. Then I walk to the coffee shop a few blocks from my apartment, which just so happens to have my favorite coffee in town. I like looking like I'm straight out of an Instagram picture, but when people stare, it makes me uncomfortable. I want attention, yet I can't bear it when I actually receive it. I make no sense.

"Give me your finest cup of battery acid," I mutter without even saying hello to the barista. She doesn't look amused, and I wonder who pissed in her cereal this morning, then I remember I'm the grumpy one. Still, I can't decide if she hates me or just has resting bitch face. It's not uncommon for other females to dislike me.

"Sorry, I just really need my caffeine." I'm wondering where Ricky—my usual barista—is, when he suddenly appears.

"We're just a nice-looking clinic shelling out your next fix," he says, waving off the other barista so that he can take over. "The succulents and fancy house-made syrups are just a ruse."

"What's her problem?"

"She probably just hates you 'cause you're pretty. That's a girl thing, right?"

Ricky and I hit it off the moment I started frequenting this coffee shop. He's from Tennessee too, and he detected my Appalachian twang right off the bat.

Once I get my coffee, I find a table and get to work, researching volunteer opportunities near me. But all I find are those centered around children and homeless people, neither of which are my cup of tea. I keep scrolling. There are programs for volunteering with handicapped people and pets and at a nursing home. I click the link for the nursing home and see that it's only a ten-minute walk from my apartment, so I'd never have much of an excuse for not showing up twice a week. I think about my grandmother, whom I was close to before she died when I was only twelve, and I fill out the application.

Then I go about the usual checking of emails and replying to messages from potential clients, which rarely materialize into something profitable as they are mostly flakes or merely flirting with the idea of paying someone for sex or entering an arrangement and obtaining a mistress and cheating on their wife. Or they are hopeful scammers, or cops on a sting, both of which I have a way of screening out, but there's always the initial introductory messaging with tedious greetings and inane questions one has to get through. It's like making cold calls. It's a numbers game. Today, there are two I find somewhat promising, and make plans with one to meet this afternoon for coffee.

People start steadily crowding into the coffee shop as I sit there for the next hour, until I can't hear my own thoughts and feel claustrophobic as a lady's baby-stroller blocks the door and the aisleway, making it impossible for me to leave if I wanted.

Ricky is bringing over lattes, threatening to spill over their ceramic cups with painstaking slowness.

"What's with all the people? It's crazy in here."

"It's Saturday. It's always like this, unfortunately," he says apologetically.

"Shit, it's the weekend already?" I remember I'm meant to meet Stephanie for lunch today at our favorite smoothie bowl place in thirty minutes, and it will take me just about that to get there, so I rush to gather my things and make my way through the labyrinth of huge strollers, purebred dogs, and trophy wives standing around in their activewear. I can't help but judge them for being jobless, vacuous, superficial, and rich, even though I fit half of those categories myself and am actually insanely jealous. They've truly made it.

When I get to the smoothie bowl place, the first thing Stephanie notices are the new flares I'm wearing.

"I love those pants, oh my god. How much were they? They look expensive."

"They were ninety-eight dollars," I state with a shrug. "Free People."

"Wow. One day you'll be like one of them," she remarks in a clandestine whisper, and her long-lashed eyes flicker to the women sitting near the front. They're clad in designer clothes and spotless, chunky designer sneakers that are as ugly as they are distinctive.

Growing up in Portland and coming from a family that was better-off than mine, Stephanie has been acquainted with the bourgeoisie since a young age, unlike me, who was wholly shook when I was confronted by it after having spent my life in a rural town on the outskirts of Chattanooga with a median household income just under $18,000.

"I despise them."

"Why? I mean I get it, but—"

"They're just so…rich." Admitting this sentiment so frankly for the first time while wearing my expensive britches makes me realize I'm the biggest hypocrite on the planet. "I should stop buying so many things all the time. It's addicting."

"I know." She sighs, bemoaning her own spending habit. She lifts up her smoothie bowl, and I give her a surly look.

"I didn't mean food." God forbid I should stop eating out for every meal and buying my six-dollar oat milk lattes. "Don't be crazy; we can't stop going out to eat. That'd be torture. Besides, you've got plenty of money."

"Whatever. I've got debt, you know."

She likes to use this elusive debt as leverage whenever I tease her for being so bougie.

"True. College, the biggest scam of the twenty-first century. That's why I didn't go." I fail to add the fact that I couldn't even get in if I wanted to, considering my lack of a diploma or GED.

"If I didn't have debt, maybe I wouldn't feel trapped with Stephen," she mutters abysmally, so that I know she's being plagued by some tragedy. She looks at me with her sad doe eyes, practically begging that I inquire about it and bathe her in sympathy and affection—she really gets off on that. But we all have our love languages. Mine just happens to be receiving gifts and money and being told I'm gorgeous, while hers is any form of attention or pity.

"Where's this coming from?" I ask, indulging her. "Since when do you feel trapped? You love him so much it's nauseating. Y'all're like, THE perfect couple," I lie.

"Well, we've got problems," she says defensively. "He's been withholding intimacy again. He says he's tired. But it's been almost two weeks since we last made love."

I try to hide the reflexive disgust I feel when she uses that icky phrase.

"That's perfectly normal for a relationship that's long-term like y'all's," I say, putting my hand on her arm consolingly. "Besides, you're in an open relationship, can't you just fuck someone else?"

She tenses slightly at my bluntness.

"Well, sometimes I'd like to just fuck my boyfriend. Is that too much to ask?" her voice raises as she says this, so that the entire restaurant can hear her, and the bougie group of women from before seem visibly perturbed as they glare at us through their veil of fake lashes. I am not usually embarrassed by these sorts of things, but because it's Stephanie, I feel a second-hand sort of shame that I'm with her and therefore party to her unnecessarily theatrical antics.

"Don't worry, the one guy I want to fuck isn't even remotely interested in me," I whisper under my breath, hoping my obvious change in volume will implicitly tell her to do the same.

"Wait, what? Who?" she demands.

"That stupid maintenance guy at my apartment complex."

"Maybe he's interested, and you just don't know it."

"If a man's interested, you'll know." I don't bother mentioning him leaving me to fix another girl's refrigerator when I invited him into my apartment. Or the kissing. That might've all been a dream, after all.

"So Stephen isn't interested anymore then, is that what you're suggesting?" she asks defensively. That wasn't my implication, but I'm just relieved she's changed the subject.

"Maybe if you weren't so clingy, worrying about it all the time, maybe if you got out of the house more, he'd be more interested."

"I am out of the house. I'm right here with you," she exclaims. "Besides, why are you attacking me right now?"

"I'd hardly call well-intended advice an attack. I'm your best friend."

"Then why are you taking his side?"

"I'm not," I say, tempted to tell her how I really feel. It's not that I hate Stephen, I just don't trust him entirely, like I don't trust any man. But I know saying so will be counter-productive.

"Well maybe, I don't want your rational advice, maybe I just want you to listen to me vent."

She pouts out her bottom lip like a child as she says this in the most pitiful voice. Then she lays her head on the table until I consent to running my hands through her glossy natural curls. Her occultic powers are lost on me besides the witchy way she incites my sympathy.

My hand freezes suddenly when I see someone familiar-looking passing by outside through the window of the restaurant. And my heart skips a beat.

Stephanie jerks her head and says, "Excuse me," offended that I've stopped rubbing her head.

It's him. He's walking down the sidewalk beside the restaurant with long, confident strides, looking wholly unfettered in his loose t-shirt with no jacket, even though it's about sixty degrees and drizzling. He's wearing his usual threadbare pants, too short for his long legs and knobby ankles, and a beanie over his head. I wonder if I would have ever looked twice at him before. But his angular jawline and long, lean body are apparently my kryptonite, so I probably would've regardless. He passes by without seeing me, and it doesn't occur to me until then that I had actually wanted him to—I was aching for it. And when he disappears, my heart sinks as the key inside it turns yet again and my stomach lurches with that morbid feeling of abysmal sadness. I wish I could throw away this key and undo this undoing. But then I think about how it had unraveled me when he kissed me, and how lovely it felt. And no, it most certainly wasn't a dream. You can't manufacture that kind of vivid, lasting impression in dreams. And how could he forget me so easily after that kind of kiss? I awoke this morning to no message, no knock on my door. He walks with the confidence of someone without a single desire in the world, who wants for nothing, let alone me.

But surely, he doesn't experience that sort of thing with every girl he kisses.

"He's cute," Stephanie remarks, drawing me out of my lovestruck daze. She must've noticed me staring out the window.

"That's him. Joseph. The guy," I intone with a mechanical doom trembling in my lowered voice, even though there's no way he can hear us.

"Are you kidding me?!" she practically shouts, and maybe I was wrong, about him not being able to hear. Because her voice is deafening. She stands up to watch him disappear around the corner. He's already got his back to us, thank god, so he can't see her shameless ogling. And didn't spot me through the window. But I feel as much disappointment as relief at his being blissfully unaware of my presence. I'm tempted to chase after him—a hideous inclination that I quickly and forcibly subdue.

"He's actually really hot, Eve."

"I guess," I finally mumble half-heartedly, and set to finishing my smoothie bowl. But the dark purple liquid has melted like my insides when he touched me, and I've suddenly lost my appetite. I'm usually never one to leave my food unfinished; chalk it up to my bulimia or my impoverished childhood. I always struggle to stop eating, even when I'm full and my stomach is distended and I can feel the food and the stomach acid creeping back up my throat, I feel compelled to clean my plate. But not today. I'm lovesick, apparently.

When I push the bowl away, Stephanie gives me a strange look. "What do you mean, you guess?" she continues to prod. "You said you were attracted to him, and that doesn't just happen every day."

"But I told you. He's not into me." I choose again not to mention the kiss. It's all just too confusing and will confuse and frustrate me further. "I don't want to talk about it though."

"You never like talking about yourself. You can't just repress your feelings forever."

"Sure I can," I mutter solemnly. She arches her brow at me.

Chapter Nine

I make a point to go in and out of my apartment a lot, just to give him the opportunity to talk to me and apologize, or rekindle things. But then I remember that it's the weekend again—I hate that I can never keep track of what day it is—and that means he won't be working, and I won't see him until next week.

So I have to distract myself and fill the rest of my weekend with activities. I go on a run through Forest Park. I go to the salon for a hair trim. I run to the bank and deposit some cash. I clean my apartment. I eat dinner. But then there are still several hours of the evening left, stretching out ahead of me intimidatingly, and I contemplate binging. And I think about Joseph. And I have an existential crisis.

But then I'm saved when I get a call from my buddy David, who runs a strip club on the Eastside, and he asks if I can come in tonight since they're short on dancers. It's just the sort of distraction I need: the kind that makes money.

The strip club is on a particularly rowdy street on the Eastside. It's lined by every sort of purveyor of alcohol you can think of—expensive cocktail bars, sketchy dive bars, trendy hipster vegan bars, dance clubs, strip clubs, liquor stores, and last but not least, ye olde Plaid Pantry, doling out tall boys and candy bars to the stoned scum of Portland.

I usually hate stripping, because it's more work than I usually have to do escorting, but nothing too unexpected happens tonight. A man gropes me, and I get bruised on the pole, but I leave with a decent wad of cash. I step out into the cold night air, and just as I start heading down the rowdy street, I see Joseph, of all people, leaning against a brick wall.

What are the fucking odds? Is this fate? Is this destiny? Are our stars aligned?

He looks over as soon as I emerge from the dark and greasy club, so he can see the front door to the strip club closing behind me, blatantly broadcasting where I've just been.

He's with a butch-looking girl dressed in the clothes a mechanic or factory worker might wear, one of those zip-up coveralls with chunky Doc Martens. But she's obviously not a factory worker. She probably thrifted them from some vintage consignment shop on Hawthorne. And I instantly judge her for this fashion choice and her stupid aesthetic, and decide that I dislike her, though it might just be because I'm jealous that she's with him, being all friendly and laughing, and I am apparently the most jealous bitch in the world.

I feel nasty after dancing for four hours. My hair is matted, and my skin is damp with sweat, and the perfume from the other dancers has imbued itself into my clothes, even though I wasn't even wearing them onstage. That locker room smells more obnoxious than a Bath & Body Works.

"Hi!" I blurt out in a disembodied voice that doesn't sound at all like me.

"Heeeey Eve," he practically sings, donning one of those infectious smiles of his. He's wearing different pants than usual—khakis—but they're still too short for his long legs. His sneakers are covered in scuffs. He's wearing a t-shirt still. It's not raining, but it's even colder than earlier today, now that it's nighttime. But I'm not mad about it. His biceps are protruding even more than usual, what with the way he's holding his arms up as he leans against the wall. I find them difficult not to stare at. "This is my friend, Yolanda," he idly remarks, not bothering to look at her. "She's rad," he adds without sounding especially sincere, as if her existence neither enriches nor detracts from his own perfect and unfettered equilibrium.

"Are you a stripper?" Yolanda asks curiously. Joseph's eyes go wide. He was wondering the same thing, of course, but her boldness surprises even him.

"No," I answer, but then quickly backtrack. "I mean, yes, sort of."

"Well, which one is it, Eve?" Joseph asks in a teasing voice, singing my name emphatically again, and my heart swells in the most insufferable way when he does that.

"Your name is Eve and you're a stripper? That's dope." She claps Joseph on the back of his arm, and whispers delightedly, "Isn't that rich?" and the blatant show of physical contact makes me feel even more like an outsider, and I wonder if they've had sex. It wouldn't be out of the realm of possibilities. At this point, I think he has sex with everyone. And even though Yolanda looks like a dyed-in-the-wool lesbian, everyone in Portland identifies as queer, even the married heterosexual couples who've actually never even kissed someone of the same sex but like to seem edgy. So it's difficult to tell what sexuality anyone is, and who's fucking whom.

"It's totally okay if you are," Joseph interjects in a suddenly sympathetic voice that irritates me. Perhaps he noticed how distressed I look. But it's not because I fear their judgment.

"I know it is," I snap. "But what I meant to say is that I don't do it a lot. It's just to help out a buddy of mine who owns the place. He's a total pig. Don't ask why I'm friends with him." I roll my eyes exaggeratedly. I'm not sure why I'm throwing my friend David under the bus, as he isn't actually such a bad guy. I find I frequently do this to my friends, even though I'd be utterly alone without them and probably pretty miserable.

"I'm not sure that you can own a strip club and *not* be a pig," Yolanda says in a condescending tone. "The whole concept of stripping is really sad actually." I wonder how she feels about sex work. She

73

probably thinks it's yet another degrading, systemic form of female oppression.

I feel a spike of hostility and say in a sarcastic tone, "Yeah. Brings tears to my eyes. Tonight I made roughly eight hundred dollars. It just broke my heart." I'm glad it was an unusually lucrative night.

I don't give a rat's ass if Yolanda judges me. But I do care about Joseph's opinion, and even as I maintain that icy, apathetic expression, I glance guardedly at him out of the corner of my eye to gauge his reaction.

"Shit," Joseph just mutters as he averts his stunned gaze, looking more than a little uncomfortable. Perhaps because he's never made that much in a day of work. Perhaps because he's reconsidering insisting on paying for our date last night. Perhaps because he kissed me and now he's regretting it. I glance at his lips. I long for him to do it again, but there's a chasm between us now, and it's as if it never happened. We could be total strangers. Just like every other man I've been with. But he penetrated me in a different sort of way, even though he scarcely touched me.

Then I realize this girl Yolanda has no clue we've been on a date or spoken more than a few times about pretty deep stuff, let alone kissed. And maybe I even know things about him she doesn't know.

"Aren't you cold?" I ask, even though he looks perfectly content in his flimsy t-shirt.

"Oh, me, I run hot," he says in a sultry voice I can't believe, as he tips his head sadistically, just to torture me with that amazing jawline and long sinewy neck with its cartilaginous protrusion I find so mysteriously erotic. *Adam's apple.* I pull my gaze away from it, hoping he'll say something or invite me to his place later, but he doesn't. And the silence is growing awkward. And it's obvious I should go.

"Well, I'll see you around," I say finally, trying to disguise how crestfallen I am that he's shown no signs of affection, because he doesn't

74

even go to hug me. I could cry, actually, and I'm wishing he would envelope me in those long, lean arms and kiss me again right in front of his friend, proudly displaying his feelings for me.

But instead, he merely replies, "See you," with that soft lackadaisical smile.

As I walk down the street, I can hear Yolanda asking Joseph how the fuck he's acquainted with a stripper, and I'm glad that I am too far away to ever hear his muffled reply.

Chapter Ten

On the bus home, I find it difficult to believe that it's still the weekend, even if it's nearly over, considering all that's happened in one day. I scroll through Instagram at the endless pictures of foodporn and Facetuned models and exotic places I'll probably never have the guts to travel to, and I feel a sense of inadequacy and that low sinking feeling unspooling inside of me as the world weighs down so very heavy and somber-like, and the rain is pouring again, gloomy to match my low mood as it beats against the window pane and the pneumatic rocking of the bus lulls me into a listless daze.

"Miserable weather, huh?" A scratchy male voice says in my ear, making me jump a little. A nervous reflex, I turn off my phone screen to hide the bone-thin models and food I'd been longingly gazing at.

The source of the voice, a man in soiled rain-sodden clothes that smell of mildew, sits down beside me. He looks like a construction or factory worker. I think of my father. I pretend to be on my phone, checking emails. I feel my anxiety spiking, replacing my former melancholy, and it sits with me until I finally get home because I hate when male strangers speak to me.

That edginess lingers as I take a Lyft to Fred Meyer on Burnside and accumulate an impressive array of binge food. My cart is piled high with Reese's, Oreos, Debbie cakes, a half-gallon tub of ice cream, two boxes of cereal, milk, Pop-Tarts, and bakery cookies. The guy at the checkout counter makes more than a couple snide remarks regarding the junk food, then I realize he's flirting with me, which is even more mortifying. That, even when I'm ordering a grotesque amount of processed food, all men notice about me is my nice tits and pretty face. As I stand outside the grocery store waiting on my Lyft home—since I can't take all this on the bus, that would be far too mortifying—I order Chinese food and pizza delivery. I've timed the two deliveries to arrive at the same time.

I always get so nervous and excited and antsy leading up to a binge as I prepare for it. And I feel like a drug addict, even though I haven't even taken my first bite, as I get into my Lyft that's just rolled up. I'm glad he can't see what's inside the paper bags.

"So, any big plans for the night?" my driver asks.

Just going to stuff my face to the point of pain, so that I'll forget my problems, then chuck it all up, I want to say. But, of course, I don't. "Nothing much. Just gonna watch Netflix and eat dinner," I answer instead.

"Netflix and chill, huh?" he asks with a laugh, trying to meet my gaze in the rear-view mirror. I'm not amused and refuse to even indulge him with a smile. "So, a pretty girl like you, surprised you're not going out on dates." I continue to ignore him, my eyes glued to the window but not actually looking at the buildings and trees we pass, and an awkward silence ensues the rest of the ride.

When I get out in front of my complex, I don't even say good bye. If only he knew why I don't go out on dates.

I've never told anyone about these episodes except for my mother, who found out while I was visiting last year and has been urging me to move back ever since and admit myself into some awful hospital or get therapy—which is totally out of the question. She'll frequently tiptoe around the subject and always try to bring it up and pester me about it on our weekly phone calls. She usually calls on Sundays, and I realize that's only tomorrow and dread pools in my stomach. I'll just lie to her, I think. I'll tell her I've been good. I have been mostly good. Better than I was at my worst. I make excuses. I rationalize it. I assure myself this is the last time.

It's just that it's so hard to be good and behave like normal people and never do anything wrong. If it's not the binging and purging, it's something else. It's like badness is ingrained in me. It's my natural inclination. I used to tell myself what I did was my own business as long as I didn't hurt anyone, but apparently that says a lot about how I truly feel about myself, because I'm someone, aren't I? And I'm hurting myself.

Once I get home, I get my computer out to load my shows and set my food up in the frenzied ritual I'm so accustomed to. My heart is racing, my breath shallow with excitement. I'm on my bed loading a show when I check my phone to see my deliveries will be arriving in about five minutes, and then see another notification appear on my screen. It's a friend request—from him: *Joseph Sheehan*. I sound out the last name more than once as I familiarize myself with it, and it feels like a forbidden realm of intimacy, this identifying factor that was previously unknown.

I scroll through his feed and the sparse posts he's made about existentialist philosophers or traveling abroad. Further down, there are several photos of him gallivanting through Budapest and Iceland and Africa, where he had mentioned he worked as a tour guide. And he's got a big smile stretched across his face in every photo. The self-assured happiness he exudes even in photos is borderline obnoxious.

In one, he's leaning out of a safari truck, shirtless, and he looks more masculine and sexier than ever. I can make out his sparse scattering of dark chest hair and, sweet Jesus, I'm in love. I stare at the pictures, hopelessly enraptured. And he's friend-requested me. I've never felt such euphoria. Right after I finally hit "accept friend request," I get two back-to-back notifications that my food has arrived, and the delivery guys are waiting outside my building. But then, I'm no longer so enthused about my binge.

I go to the lobby and see the delivery dudes standing outside.

I'm not wearing a bra, just a slip and open robe like usual. They both whirl around and look me up and down, and I say, "Hi. I'm Evelyn; y'all both got something for me, I reckon?"

One of them ogles my chest as he hands me the bag while the other remarks, "Lots of food for just you."

"I'm having a party." I yank the pizza box out of his hands and give him a killing look, then make sure not to tip either of them on the app. That'll show them. I'm the worst sort of human being, but people need to know there are consequences for their actions, which include insensitive and unfunny remarks, in addition to looking at my tits.

I'm feeling that pre-binge frenzy return as I re-enter my apartment. But as soon as I sit the food down, my phone lights up and pings. It's Joseph.

"Well, hello Miss Eve. Fancy meeting you here. I hope I didn't offend you," his message reads.

"You didn't. Honestly, I'm shocked you have a Facebook. You seem way too enlightened for all of that."

"Well, I keep it for the fam. They freak out whenever I try to deactivate it."

"Afraid you might've gotten eaten by a lion? I wouldn't be surprised. Nice photos, by the way."

"Hey, thanks. Yours aren't so bad either, Miss Eve. I have to admit, I can't stop thinking about that kiss last night."

He's still thinking about me. About that kiss, which apparently, did happen. My heart is hammering in my chest and I'm feeling that dizzying euphoria again. And the food is forgotten. Almost. But then I can smell it wafting from the boxes I've set on the coffee table. I can smell the greasy deep-fried chicken and garlicky soy sauce of the Chinese food and the salty, cheesy aroma of the hot pizza.

I don't want to binge and purge anymore. But I'm also starving.

Then a lightbulb goes off in my head. He's put himself out there, sending me the friend request, bringing up the kiss. That's a lot, for a passive, pussyfooted Portland boy. I have to take the plunge.

"Hey, you hungry at all?" I ask.

"Starving, actually."

"I just ordered some take-out. Couldn't decide on pizza or Chinese, so I ordered both," I lie, but it's plausible enough. "It's way too much for me. Interested?"

"Wow, that stripping really pays off," he says, but I can tell he's only teasing. I can practically hear the flirtatious lilt to his voice. "You're eating like a king. Err, a queen."

"God forbid you misgender me," I tut, smiling to myself at how well I'm doing, though my chest is fit to burst, and I must maintain coolness. "I also have Netflix."

"Netflix and chill? Very cliché of you, Eve," he teases. The same joke the driver made. But coming from him, it's received far differently. After a pause he adds, "Sign me up. I'll be over in fifteen, is that okay?"

"Perfect. The food will still be warm. See you soon." I add a smiley emoji and hit the send button and my heart almost bursts.

And suddenly, I'm not horrid. For once, I'm good.

And when she was good, she was very good.

But my goodness is always so ephemeral and subject to selfish whims, so it's not very good at all. Goodness eludes me. And apparently it hinges upon such a precarious thing as Joseph agreeing to come over and was precipitated by a variety of uncontrollable variables.

If Joseph had never messaged me, for instance, I would've remained in low spirits, and gone right on with my binging. Or if he had messaged me just ten minutes after the delivery man had arrived or if I'd neglected to check my phone, I would've already started the binge, and the point of no return would've long passed.

I rush to hide the other stuff I've set out—the groceries I'd bought, like the cookies and candy and other processed junk. I also tidy up my apartment, which is already surprisingly tidy, thank god. Then I look at myself and check my body, lifting my shirt and assessing my stomach analytically. After not having eaten for several hours and exerting myself on the dance floor, I am both ravenous and impossibly skinny. Relief washes over me.

This means that even if I eat a lot of food, I won't be too noticeably bloated. I put my shirt down and tousle my hair with some dry shampoo and stare at my reflection critically and approvingly in the way I imagine most vain people often look at themselves. I'm obsessing about my appearance way more than usual. Even with paying clients, I don't care all that much. Sure, I eat less throughout the day whenever I have a scheduled meeting in the evenings, but I don't fret if I'm bloated because I don't honestly give a damn what they think, because even with an extra pound or two or a fresh pimple, I'm still drastically out of their league.

When Joseph arrives exactly six minutes late, I appear at the door in a baggy sweater and night shorts. I purposely did away with my usual duster or slutty negligee get-up, and traded it in for what I hope gives off a more casual, girl-next-door vibe. He looks me over with a bemused twist of his perfect lips that is almost sardonic and that I don't know how to read, but I'm trying not to look at him too much as I let him in because I'm so nervous and excited.

I have a studio unit, so my bed and couch are in the same space, but I have an Oriental screen partition separating them. There's also a coffee table, which all the food's been laid out on. I rarely use the couch; I usually just sit in bed. I'm often not here, and both of my two best friends have larger apartments, so I rarely entertain guests besides my clients. My house is really more of an office space.

"Wow, it smells good in here."

"Like pizza and Chinese food?" I ask, hoping it doesn't smell weird or gross. "Go ahead and take off your shoes, if you like."

"Thanks, I will," he slips off his sneakers, and his socks are striped and have a hole in them, revealing a long toe with a clean toenail. Even his stupid toe is endearing. I must be a goner.

I go the kitchenette and open the cupboard and retrieve two plates, then set them out with some mason jars of water. He's already made himself comfy on the couch. He's sitting cross-legged, making him look impossibly youthful and yet more endearing. With him sitting down, I can finally get a look at his head and neck and see that he's not balding at all. And his hair is cut close in the back, revealing the nape of his slender yet strong neck, and the collar of his woolen sweater is stretched loose, revealing the bony ridges of his vertebrae. I ache to trail my tongue along that delicate spine. I force myself to look away.

I open the carboard pizza box, and he eyes it hungrily, but he doesn't make a move for a slice. Looking at his unraveling sweater and broad bony shoulders, I feel a pang of regret for not having offered to pay when we went out on our first date; he might be muscular, but he's also scrawny. And apparently, he's making me defy all my norms.

"Grab a slice," I insist, since he seems to need my permission. He goes for one reluctantly.

I set out everything and dump out some deep-fried chicken pieces laden with syrupy orange sauce and a pile of greasy noodles on our plates. "I hope you know how to use chopsticks," I say as I hand him a pair.

He finishes chewing his bite of pizza and retorts facetiously, "Please. I'm practically a chopstick expert."

"Let me guess, you've been to Thailand and China and Japan too?" I say, naming off the list that seems too far-fetched and distant to even actually exist. But then, I live in an insular bubble.

"I've been to two of those countries, yeah," he says, grinning and looking at me with his eyes twinkling. He doesn't tell me which two countries. There is something almost devious in that twinkling in his eyes. My heart skips a beat then I glance away and roll my eyes. I. Must. Remain. Calm.

"It's kinda dark in here. Why don't you cut on the light?" he asks as I sit down to eat with him. The ambient light from the bathroom and the stovetop is the only source of brightness. I've lit a couple candles, too, but it's still dim.

"Oh, that," I laugh dismissively. "It's been out for ages and I can't be bothered to fix it. Besides, it's romantic isn't it, this dim lighting, with the candles?" I joke, but secretly, I like the idea and wish he'd indulge me by agreeing and perhaps moving a bit closer so that I can feel the warmth of his strong, lean body, but of course he doesn't.

He shakes his head at me reproachfully then asks, "Can't be bothered or don't know how?" Figures. He is a handyman for a living, so he would judge me for neglecting to change a bulb.

"Both, maybe?" I crack a nervous smile.

He shakes his head again and part of me wants to shrivel up into a tiny, miserable ball, because he elicits such shame inside of me that I wouldn't have felt otherwise. And over a stupid lightbulb! And another part of me wants to giggle delightedly, wickedly at him for rebuking me, like a child that wants whipping because she's twisted and horrid, and that's me apparently, though I hadn't realized until now that I possessed this particular vein of masochism.

And watching him sitting here in my apartment, I can't believe how much my perception of him has changed since the first time I saw him that day the sprinklers got all fucky. I can't believe that, back then, I hadn't thought much of him. And now I feel an excited fluttering in my stomach at his mere presence and proximity, and my heart is lurching, anxious with expectation, and my sexuality has awoken from what feels like a prolonged—no, *perpetual*—state of dormancy.

"You could've called me, you know, that's what I'm here for," he teases. He *is* the maintenance guy. But I don't like asking for help. I'm not like his stupid friend Katy. Even something as simple as changing a lightbulb. Something about it is impossible for me. Perhaps it's because I've prided myself on being self-sufficient, when it once seemed like some insurmountable achievement. Stuck out there in bumfuck-nowhere, Tennessee.

"You were too busy helping Katy out," I say instead, my tone both wounded and incisive. I could ask him if he fucked her—now's the perfect opportunity—but then part of me doesn't want to know. So I punish him in my oblique way.

"Oh, her. Geez," he moans whilst rolling his eyes. "Don't tell me *you're* jealous of her," he says, putting stress on that particular word, and I don't understand what he means by it. He has an elusive and evasive manner of speaking, making it impossible to know if he did fuck her, or if he prefers me, or if he's annoyed by the mere insinuation. I find that silence is key, as I stare patiently at him and he finally cedes, "Look, Katy got me the job here, actually. We're friends. She helped me out."

Now I'm even more suspicious. I have to ask. The poisonous curiosity, the noxious unknowing, is unbearable. "Did y'all used to date?" I ask timidly, and my Tennessee twang slips out involuntarily.

"No, I ain't never dated her," he answers mockingly. I realize then that I should've just come out and asked if he fucked her. Because no relief comes to extinguish my nagging suspicions. Given my own past with men, I can't quite accept that he'd be capable of having female friends without having fucked them.

"And what about Yolanda?" I find myself asking. Really, I need to stop. My jealousy is becoming oppressive.

"What about her?" he chuckles, clearly amused, but I'm not amused. I just want the real truth, even if I'm by no means entitled to it. Really, I won't be satisfied until he tells me he's slept with one of them. But then I'll be gutted as well. Chalk it up to my self-destructive tendencies. "You think I sleep with all my female friends?" he asks incredulously and with a quizzical brow, as if the idea is absurd, as if I'm being absurd, even though nothing could be more perfectly obvious.

"No guy is friends with girls unless he wants to have sex with them. Haven't you ever watched *When Harry Met Sally*?"

"No. Never heard of it," he shrugs, and I gasp with horror.

I guess most people my age haven't seen it. I grew up on VHS movies bought from thrift stores, and therefore outdated, and so I've seen pretty much every popular film from the eighties and nineties. *Pretty Woman* was very influential to me during my formative years. Go figure.

"Besides, most of my friends are chicks. I prefer them—none of that toxic masculinity," he adds with all his sage wisdom.

"I mean, I agree. Men are awful," I say facetiously, giving him a dirty look, but merely sparring. I save the real venom for his friends.

"You seem to like their company," he remarks.

"Hey!" I exclaim, recoiling from the deft and unexpected blow.

"I'm kidding. I'm not judging."

"Yes, you are," I say, feeling suddenly miserable. It's easy to forget that huge facet of my life sometimes. He provokes the same deplorable feeling of shame as when I'd been so cavalier about not knowing how to change a lightbulb. "But you can't help it. I haven't explained myself," I add, but then refrain from elaborating. My evasive eyes are frantically darting around the room, anywhere except his unwavering gaze.

"And you're not going to," he says resignedly, looking suddenly sad and weary, and I realize he is in fact capable of real sadness despite that perpetual easy breezy way about him.

He gets up and stretches to reach the bulb. He's so tall he can do that. When he reaches up like that, stretching his long slender body, his scratchy sweater rides up to reveal a trail of dark hairs running down his belly. That vertical line looks sensual rather than unruly. And my eyes stalk the trail of it right down to his loose trousers that hang low on his narrow hips. I can see his pelvic bone jutting out. The desire to trace every sinuous line of his body resurfaces with a vengeance, and I feel my insides begin to unspool. I'm getting wet just looking at him. That's never happened before. I didn't think I was capable of such an animalistic response. When he looks down from unscrewing the bulb, he catches me staring and I glance away, mortified.

"Whatcha staring at?"

"I—I was wondering what you were doing," I stutter awkwardly, unable to meet his smiling gaze. I can feel my face getting insufferably hot. He knows.

"I'm fixing your light, obviously," he says, inspecting the hazy bulb.

"Free of charge?" I ask timidly.

"No," he says with a devious grin that makes my heart flutter, and reaches down to grab another slice of pizza. "It'll cost you a slice." And he takes a big bite.

"I'll be right back," he assures me, and I almost don't believe him. He's so slippery, so evasive, so difficult to catch.

He goes to get a replacement bulb, and it feels like an eternity as I sit there with my mind racing. Then he's back and we're eating greasy, MSG-laden Chinese food, and watching a shitty movie that's funny in an ironic way, and his deadpan commentary makes up for it, and I find myself summoning the courage to make a few witty remarks myself. And

I've crept gradually closer to him throughout the film, so that we're now touching legs, and I can feel the heat of his body radiating onto mine and the mere contact is electric—for me at least. But it must be electric for him as well, right? How could it be otherwise? How could I feel something so strongly and him nothing at all?

And yet, and yet, he hasn't even tried to kiss me again. He's not at all antsy to touch me like other men would have been. The movie ends, and we're both done with the food and still, nothing. I'm screaming internally for him to make a move. Goddamn him, he's unmovable. He just sits there blithely and blissfully without a care in the world or seemingly a thought in his head, and then he turns to look at me while the credits are rolling and says, "Well, Eve, that's a wrap. I better get out of your hair. It was lovely, thank you."

And that's that. But how can it be? How can he leave me like this? So perfectly cordial, so intentionally withholding of his affection? Even after changing my lightbulb and showing off all his masculine know-how.

He gets up and stretches, blatantly flaunting that stupid goodie trail again. I find myself saying, in a despairing and wounded tone, "And so that's it? You're leaving, then?"

He shrugs and laughs, but does linger there at the door, immovable still, his eyes twinkling with a spritely, almost wicked, species of longing. And I realize I haven't really looked at him since he arrived, and even then, I had been nervously avoiding his penetrating gaze. But now it cuts to the quick.

"You didn't really give me any signs," he explains rather frankly, even though his voice is suddenly meek and soft at the husky edges. And Christ, he's looking at me like a dog that's been whipped or left out in the rain with his head tipped down.

"I moved closer to you on the couch, during the movie," I reply in a feeble murmur, as I get up from the couch. I feel so stupid, having to explain myself like this. "You caught me staring at you, at your—"

"What. At my what?" he's grinning now. Mocking me.

"Stop. You're making me do everything."

"I'm not making you do anything! That's the point. I won't."

"That's not—I—" I stammer frustratedly. I'm so flustered with him being right here, so close, yet so on the verge of slipping through my fingers, yet here he is in my apartment and we've kissed before and I know now he feels the same, after meeting that longing gaze. But he won't say so. "I like men to be forward and take control," I tell him, averting my gaze self-consciously. "I never have to do anything."

"Well, you've got the wrong guy, then. That's not me. I never want to make a girl feel taken advantage of, or feel uncomfortable."

"So you wait on the girl to make all the moves?"

"Well, yeah."

That surely makes all the women he's been with feel like frustrated, aggressive creeps. Or perhaps that's how a lot of men feel, it dawns on me.

Well then, you'll never get laid, I want to say, but I know he has, and I don't want to bring that up.

"Then what're we supposed to do?" I say, my voice stricken by despair.

"I don't know, Miss Eve. I guess we'll never find out," he says, inching closer to me. We were close before, but now I can smell him. He smells piney, like the forest and hemlock trees and Christmastime.

"I guess you really do have to go, then," I ask, leaning forwards, inhaling that heady, redolent scent and feeling faint with longing.

"I suppose so," he says, leaning in as well.

"It's too bad."

"Oh? And why is that?" his brow arches with intrigue. God, I love those expressive eyebrows, too.

"Because I want you, obviously. You're making me say it," I practically whine.

He shushes me, for once, and finally submits to taking me into his arms. I fall apart in those strong arms. My limbs turn to putty in those strong arms. I realize why people go mad with lust in those strong arms. And my insides turn to liquid as his deft tongue slowly unravels me.

I don't usually like tongue. But I like what he does with his. He's patient but passionate, and his strong searing fingertips work at the curves of my body, the mounds of my breasts, he is cautious and caring and never callous. But the intensity of his ravenous mouth and hands sets me ablaze.

"I've been fantasizing about this moment all week."

"Really?" I ask incredulously, because his hesitance certainly didn't suggest that. "I had feared it was all one-sided and I was going crazy," I admit in a self-conscious whisper and he chuckles deep and throaty then shushes me again.

And then he's leading me to the bed, and I'm fussing at his clothes with a groan of frustration, and we're suddenly entangled and wrestling frantically and kissing with the same fevered and frantic passion. And then he's flat against the mattress and I'm on top of him, and I'm finally able to trace my tongue along that sensual trail of hairs on his belly to the end where his black boxer-briefs poorly conceal his erection. I pull them off and watch as it springs out with a pronounced bounce. It's long but not thick, just like his body—long and lithe and beautiful and veined like marble. A smile spreads across my face as I look at it, wholly enamored. I've never been so besotted with a cock. I usually find them revolting and odd-looking, almost alien-like. But not his; it's a continuation of himself, and it's throbbing, rock-hard—and for me.

Before he can say anything, I take it into my mouth, and he lets out a surprised hiss of a noise, then a luxuriant groan of pleasure escapes his throat and it makes my heartrate quicken with delight. I'm going to town, sucking that cock. And I've never sucked a cock so hard in all my life. He pushes my head away with a frantic moan, as he's already on the edge of cumming. "Wait—wait," he laughs out breathlessly. "You'll make me cum."

"That's kind of the point, isn't it?" I murmur teasingly, torturing him by running the tip of my tongue along the full length of his cock. He practically whimpers in response.

"Not yet. I'm not ready yet. Too soon," he says, panting. I watch his chest rise and fall, feeling the string tied to my heart wring tautly with a yearnful adoration that is almost painful. He sits up then takes me into his arms again, then he pins me down with a sudden swell of dominance that undoes me. Now he's on top of me, and I'm the one lying supine on the bed.

He's going to fuck me. He's finally, really going to fuck me.

I had forgotten about myself and my own orgasm.

"Do you have a condom?" he asks.

I gesture to the one by my bed on the windowsill with sinking shame because I'm a little too prepared. It's an indication, I fear, of my promiscuity. "Don't you keep one on you?" I ask, deflecting my sense of shame.

"Not really. I don't have sex that often," he remarks, trying to use modesty as a defense.

Doubtful.

I roll my eyes at him, but I don't challenge it. I don't want to kill the mood. I don't want to think about him with anyone else but me.

Just me and him, and him and me, in this tiny apartment, on my tiny bed, warm and naked and united.

He fumbles with the condom, and that brief separation is agony, so when it's finally on, I cling onto him and pull him back close to me so that our hot flesh is pressed together once again. A blissful reunion. How will I ever part with him? This new special discovery?

And I impatiently maneuver his cock between my thighs, but he takes my wrist and stops me again, pinning both my hands above my head onto the mattress as he kisses all my most sensitive parts, torturing me until I'm whimpering and he's whimpering too. His engorged cock falls against my thigh, and I've never wanted a cock inside me so desperately in all my life. He rubs the tip against my entrance, and it's slippery-wet and I blush, embarrassed. But it feels so good, and my desire for him eclipses my embarrassment, so I moan instead.

"Please, please," I beg when I can't bear it any longer.

He pauses right when I think he's about to end my torture, and looks at me with that searing gaze. We lock eyes and the world stops. I feel more violated by that stare than ever before, more so than any stranger's cock could violate me. And regret not having told him the truth. I can see the passion smoldering there, but he doesn't know about me prostituting myself or the countless men I've been with. So many men I cannot count, and most of them old and nasty and revolting and evil, perhaps. And I'm evil and I'm horrid and disgusting and unworthy of that lust-filled gaze and his impassioned touch. If he knew the truth, that lusty spark would surely die like a flame snuffed out. He'd wouldn't want to be with me anymore. He'd be disgusted. He'd think I am vile and horrid.

"Hey, are you okay?" he asks, pulling me out of that dark train of thought. I look at him and his searching eyes and realize I've completely zoned out, away from this moment I've been so ardently longing for, because of these insecurities, which are, admittedly, not totally unwarranted. "Do you want this? Because if you don't..." and then he's starting to withdraw and recoil. And that lusty light has died from his eyes just as I feared, but for a different reason. But Christ, it's all so fucked up. And he's the pure, unpolluted feminist, ever-enlightened, ever-cautious.

"Yes, of course I do. I want it more than anything. You have no idea," I plead, my heart wrung tight and voice stricken. I meet his gaze and caress his bearded jaw to reassure him, and then I kiss him deeply until we're both gasping for air.

When he pulls away and looks at me, and his gaze intensifies.

And then he slowly, carefully, caringly, as if I'm some virgin—a laughable idea—penetrates me, and I cry out from how good and fulfilling it feels to finally have it inside of me. I'm so close to coming already. And he's delving into my soul with those grass-green eyes and delving into me literally.

And he's thrusting slowly at first, but then his pace quickens as I urge him, beg him, to go faster and harder, and then we fall apart together. It's no mistake. I know by his strangled moan that follows immediately after mine, and that noise that, in any other context would be laugh-inducing, is possibly the hottest thing I've ever heard.

He leaps up to go to the bathroom and take the condom off, and I lie there with a warmth spreading through me as my orgasm wanes in dissipating waves of pleasure, but a mournful sadness replaces it, because he's left me, and I'm vacant now. Then he returns and spoons me tightly, but not as tightly as I crave. But I can't allow him to know the full extent of my obsession. Because there's still the fact of my escorting that I'm reminded of as we lie there awash with pleasure. Then I see my phone go off beside me as a regular client messages me and I pray he doesn't see, then he speaks, and my heart seizes with apprehension.

"I was thinking," he begins tentatively. "If you don't mind, maybe I could stay the night." His soft voice breaches the dark air and I feel a spike of anxiety at his simple question.

"Oh, well, I guess you could if you wanted. Sure," I say through gritted teeth.

"Wow, the enthusiasm. Don't sound so excited about it!" he says, and regret wracks my conscience. But so does guilt. He doesn't know the truth about me.

If he stays the night, what does that mean? What could this lead to? The thought of us being a couple does initially make my heart flutter with excitement, but that's delusional—it's not logical. I can't have a boyfriend. I'm a prostitute. And he doesn't know. I can't let him stay the night without knowing. I have to tell him. But I can't. I can't bear to do it and ruin this—but I'm ruining it anyway, right now. But this was inevitable, and I should've known that, and now I have to suffer the repercussions.

My silence is full of conflict. But he doesn't know that. To him, it's only silence. And that doesn't bode well. "Oh, so you just wanted to use me for my body. I get it."

But he's got it all wrong, and my heart cries out in despair, and I cling onto him like a baby sloth clings onto its mother.

"No! No, I do want you to stay. Please do," I whisper, my voice muffled against his back. I want to beg him, burrow myself inside of him. "It's just," I falter, still conflicted, "I don't want you to go—I don't." I've never had to be vulnerable before, and ask someone to stay or to love me, and the mere idea is terrifying, enough to make me a trembling, incoherent mess. "I wasn't sure if you really wanted to, or if you were just saying it to please me. Most men never like staying over." This is, of course, a generalization. And I'm usually the one kicking men out.

"I'm most men now? Do you think I'm like most men?" he says with the edge of spite sharpening his tone. "Though you women are so impossible to please—so maybe I am," he adds snidely.

"Yes, you're right. I didn't enjoy myself at all," I say teasingly, trying to draw him back, but he's already escaped me, I can tell. He's not looking at me, just staring out at the door in obvious disconnect. I can't continue to try drawing him in, as I don't want to sound desperate. To be desperate, for some reason, seems worse than anything.

"So, will you stay?" I ask anyway as a final plea, but I'm not going to be reduced to begging again.

"Well, I don't want to keep you, Miss Eve." He says with a smile, all venom gone from his voice, but so is the passion. Then he stretches and gets up. And all of a sudden, he's placid and cool and utterly aloof. I let my eyes stalk his chiseled edges and masculine lines unashamedly as he dresses, and I feel my heart wrench at his beauty I so long to capture and keep for myself, and a morbid agony at having let those long lovely limbs slip through my fingers, and how his going is irreversible now, and the chasm that's stretched out between us is untraversable. I can't get up and demand he return to the bed and fuck me again and stay the night. That would be pathetic. But I'm already halfway there, and I wonder how it came to this. It's because he has that good dick. Even though I've had sex countless times with countless men, I've never had that good dick. Sex has never been a revelation. Sex has never wrecked me. Not until now.

"Sorry, I'm bad at this," I say, bringing my knees to my chest as I sit in the bed and watch him gather his wallet and his keys and his phone and put them in his pockets.

"Bad at what?" he chuckles, and adds in a flippant tone, "You have men over often enough, right? Though I guess they never do leave in the morning, do they?" He smiles as if he's teasing me, but he can't hide

94

the vitriol in his voice, no longer so light and aloof, and it cuts through me.

"How do you know that?" I blurt out, affronted. There's no denying that I have men over. That cat's been out of the bag for a while. I draw my legs closer to hide myself, as if it will somehow protect me. I want to re-erect my walls now, but I'm naked, splayed open, defenseless. The soreness from him inside me is still lingering like a wound now rather than a lovely reminder of the pleasure he fleetingly brought me. How dare he violate me like that then not love me? My heart seems to cry out. It's stupid. I don't want to act like a stupid emotional woman. I had once thought I was icy, frigid, and inviolable. "Well, it doesn't matter. It's true," I state frankly, and I want to add despairingly: "but I thought it was different with you." But I don't.

Then my phone goes off with another text from a regular, and reminds me that this is likely for the best.

He doesn't say goodbye, and the sound of the door shutting echoes odiously throughout my silent lonely apartment for what seems like an eternity.

I text my client back to tell him that unfortunately, I can't meet him tonight.

Chapter Eleven

The next day, I wake up to an empty apartment, and my phone is lit up only by notifications from the escorting site. For some reason, I had hoped to see something from Joseph. But that's foolish. I feel an abysmal dread as I open up my messages from prospective clients. And then I remember I turned down money last night, and I try to tally the bills in my head, and how much I need to cover next month. I breathe a sigh of relief when the rough mental sum reveals I'm good and therefore don't need to earn a single penny for the rest of the week, but I can't get stuck in this mindset. I still need to make money while I can because this isn't sustainable, I always remind myself. One day, I'll be too old or too ugly. Beauty and youth are such ephemeral things I can't depend on. And so I can't get in the habit of turning down work.

The pale tendrils of dawn spill in through the blinds covering my window. They illuminate the things I do not want to see—the dirt on the floor, the dust on the tabletop, the boxes and dirty dishes from last night, as if I need a physical reminder of it. Joseph ate from that plate. Joseph licked that fork. Joseph drank from that mason jar. Joseph's used condom is in the trash can in the bathroom, filled with his cum. And Joseph's gone. My heart twists at the mere thought of him.

He hasn't messaged me on Facebook. He never asked me for my phone number, so of course he hasn't called or texted. I race to the bathroom and look in the trashcan at his used condom with a pathetic swelling in my chest, tempted to save it somehow, but that's ridiculous. I really am going crazy. If this is love, I don't want any part of it.

I have to get him out of my head. I have to distract myself.

So after getting ready and having my first cup of coffee, I take a walk through Forest Park, which is a vast public park consisting of thousands of acres of forest with multiple trails running through it, and happens to be a fifteen-minute walk from my apartment. I go to try and soak up that sweet damp air and cleanse my anxious thoughts and rid them of *him*.

I've read articles online about taking hikes and being in nature and meditating in the woods, and how it's meant to cure depression and decrease anxiety. Of course this is on my mind as I go down the well-trodden path sludgy with mud from the rain and breathe in deeply the cool damp air that must be the cleanest, purest air in all the world. Here in the forest, the trees are all covered in thick swathes of moss that absorbs all the rainwater and purifies the air while also making it perpetually humid.

I've gone here with the purpose of meditating, but I suck at meditating. And this is how it always goes. It always feels too willful, so that it isn't relaxing, and instead, my obsessive-compulsive nature is triggered into a neurotic self-awareness where I second-guess and pick apart not only my deliberations, but the very cadence of my breathing. The inhale, the exhale, the inhale, the exhale—I find it maddening, and I end up feeling like my breathing isn't natural or easy, but a laborious task, and there is a tightness in my chest, and I feel an oncoming panic attack. But then, at least the trees and the moss and the bubbling stream of Balch Creek are pretty. There is that. And if I focus on the nature around me, I can forget about the other stuff, perhaps, and truly let go, and perhaps not think of anything, not even my breathing, and perhaps that is what meditation truly is. Perhaps it's just letting go. But the trouble is, I don't like letting go or losing control. And I don't know how you're supposed to change something that seems ingrained in you. And I don't understand those mysterious parts of myself, nor do I have a desire to know them.

After walking long enough down the trail alone without a tourist in sight—because it's far too early and it's not as popular lately, now that it's gotten chilly and the leaves have fallen, their autumnal colors still vivid as they rot with the other detritus on the earth, or choke the glassy streams—I enter a somnolent sort of trance, and everything becomes meaningless and vacuous. Lonely strolls in Forest Park often do this to me. The mere act of walking alone amid this cathedral of ancient trees makes more of a nihilist of me rather than uplift my spirits. I always think it's going to make me feel better, but it never does. But I like the trees, and maybe I like being sad. Maybe I'm addicted to sadness, if such a thing is possible.

And inevitably, my thoughts return to Joseph. I could only distract myself for so long. I can't just willfully shun him from my mind by staring at moss and ferns.

I should've let him stay the night. But no, no, it's no good. Why are you so stupid, Eve?

I return to my apartment building, my mood grayer than before I left, and grayer than the sky outside. I still hope to see him sitting in the lobby with one of his books, but he isn't there, and if he was, what would even be the outcome?

So there're other things to do to distract myself, the same sort of things I always do to break the monotony and fill my day. I go to my regular coffee shop by my apartment, and Ricky's working, thank god, so I can chat him up eventually, when he's not bombarded by customers and the morning rush has simmered down. And perhaps that will lift my spirits, as well as the caffeine.

As I wait on my latte, I see a copy of *The Oregonian* sitting on the counter and while I'm not usually a reader of newspapers, the headline captures my eye: PORTLAND-AREA PSYCHOLOGIST SUED FOR $10 MILLION AFTER HAVING A SEXUAL RELATIONSHIP WITH HER YOUNGER PATIENT.

Apparently, she was married and significantly older, and they had an affair and took long walks in Forest Park. The intimate details about their unethical relationship I find a bit unsettling (says the prostitute), because it's clear the therapist didn't approve of this article being written, and its likely sabotaged her. But what's particularly unsettling is the bit about them taking long walks together in Forest Park, where I just was. Perhaps I walked down the same trail they did. And perhaps I breathed in the same damp air their intimate whispers polluted. A shiver crawls down my back as I continue reading about how the therapist eventually cut it off when he told another therapist about it. The other therapist reported it, of course, so her license was taken away in the end, and her marriage was probably ruined. And then the boy had a mental break when she ended things, and went to her house and strangled her. She didn't die, but still. "Wow, this story just gets wilder the longer I read it," I mutter in disbelief.

I catch Ricky staring at me from across the counter.

"Daydreaming, huh?" he asks with a smile, and slides my steaming latte towards me. "So, this might sound like a random question, but what is it you do for work, Eve?"

I freeze at the unexpected question—the last question I ever want asked of me—and my mind goes blank.

I really ought to be more prepared for this question. It's not all that uncommon. People ask it on dates, at parties and, apparently, in coffee shops. I ought to have a good cover story. I just don't meet new people outside of the site all that often, nor do I interact with strangers much when I can help it beyond what's necessary and polite, so I don't worry about people finding out. But Ricky exists in that dangerous, gray area between acquaintance and friend. So it makes sense that he'd be curious. This is why I can't make friends.

"Huh?" is the only noise I'm capable of emitting in that anxious moment as I frantically try to figure out what to say, and if I should lie and I realize how unprepared I am for the judgment of my favorite barista at my favorite coffee shop. "Why do you ask?" I chuckle nervously.

"It's just, I notice you come in during weekdays, in the mornings and afternoons, and you hang out for a while sometimes. And you've never mentioned your job, and that's one of the first things people usually mention. So I was just curious."

"I guess it's fairly obvious I don't work the typical nine-to-five," I say in a feeble and shaky voice, my heart sinking as I resign myself to the fact that I can't lie and I'm not going to—had Joseph asked me the frank question directly, I probably would've divulged the truth as well, but he didn't—and I'm about to risk this friendly repartee we've established. We both moved here from Tennessee, from abject poverty. We both like similar restaurants and have shared the same rants about passive-aggressive Portlanders. He's even opened up to me about his struggles in the city. But now I'm hit by the harsh reminder that we don't really know each other at all, and we're not truly friends. And would he even want to be my friend if he knew the truth?

I feel a sudden but deep, consuming shame at what I do for a living. This happens now and again, especially when such a seemingly innocuous question is posed to me by a stranger or an acquaintance like Ricky.

"I'm—I'm," I stutter and hesitate, finding it exceedingly difficult to utter those killing words that will ultimately decide the future of this precarious acquaintanceship. "I'm an escort. Well, a prostitute, pretty much," I finally state as bluntly as possible, trying not to show any emotion or look around at the people I fear have heard this admission and are staring at me. "Escort is just a euphemism."

I'm wondering for a moment if Ricky heard me at all though, because he says nothing for quite some time and just stares at me blankly with his mouth slightly agape. Then he smirks slightly in disbelief and laughs, "What?" incredulously. He doesn't think I'm serious, and he's waiting for me to tell him I'm kidding, of course. Because it's all a funny joke, and I certainly feel like a joke right now and wish I could be swallowed up by the floor.

The longer we both stand there in silence looking at one another, the more awkward it becomes, as the realization that I'm not kidding settles over his stupefied expression. He's waiting on me to speak, to say that I'm actually a trust fund baby or work remotely or something else just as common in this city and far easier to digest. But I've never been easy to digest. I'm not palatable. I'm crude and I'm crass, I'm cruel and I'm cunty. And to make matters worse, I'm a sex worker.

The sense of shame that comes over in a wave of anguish triggers a childhood memory I had forgotten about:

I'm standing in the cafeteria line in elementary school. And for the umpteenth time, I'm having to tell the lunch lady that I haven't got any money to pay for lunch. And she chides me, she judges me, she pities me. Then she reluctantly, ever-so-graciously, hands me a tray.

I guess the stain of poverty is not so different. And in the same way, I thought I could discard that feeling once I had money, once I had a different life with nice things, but the stain had imprinted itself deep inside me, like an indelible mark I'd never be able to get out. And now there's another irremovable stain.

I could've lied to Ricky, I could've erected that confident pretense, but the lesson would've been the same. I'm different from him and everyone else. The sense of otherness would've been just as stark, it just would've remained my own internal struggle.

"Oh, shit. I thought you were fucking with me. That's great! I mean, well, you know, no judgment. That's actually really brave of you," he finally responds, his awkwardness palpable as he tries to seem cool about it, but it's obvious that something's shifted between us. He adds, because he likely can't bear the silence now, "Hell, I'd probably do that if I was female. Alas, I was bequeathed a more abysmal fate," he says in a deep, morose voice, and I'm almost convinced by that bit of self-deprecating humor. I appreciate the effort, at least. "I'm not gonna lie, I have a ton of questions." He smiles to further assure me of his acceptance, and I feel some relief. The anxiety from before has dissipated, but there's still no denying the shift that's just occurred. A shift in the carefree dynamic. I can no longer casually walk in every morning or afternoon for my 12oz triple-shot oat milk latte and make idle conversation about the weather or fuckall. Now he won't be able to see me the same. He'll envision me committing those illicit acts and wondering if I'd just been with a client, or how much money I make a week.

Fortunately, it's not that way with my real, tried-and-true friends. They know the truth, but they don't see me that way. They see me as Eve and that's all. Like Stephanie, who's known me since before it all started. Or Gertrude, who's always been secretly envious of me or cheered me on in my pursuit of exploiting the inferior sex. I suppose I just won't make any new friends in order to avoid this painful, mortifying experience altogether

"Well, thanks a latte," I say to Ricky with an ironical smirk and leave the coffee shop. There are a multitude of coffee shops in Portland, four within five blocks of my apartment. But I liked that one the best, I think mournfully as the rain starts falling and I down the last dredges of espresso, and feel the foam coat my upper lip.

I think of Joseph again, resigning myself to the bitter fact that if I continue down this path, prostituting myself for a living, my love life will be just as bleak as my social life. I had known that; I had sworn off romance and been satisfied with my meager circle of friends. But that's not realistic. Life isn't insular. People come in and out. Interactions lead to inevitable entanglements.

Next morning, and the one after that, and then the one after that, I resort to the same bad habit of checking my phone as soon as I wake up. It's like this every morning without fail. Hoping to see something from Joseph. Anything. But all I've received are notifications from social media or from the escorting site or from regular clients texting me asking to meet, which only fills me with dread at this point. Another day of disappointment and having to distract myself from my depression. I really ought to fill up my week with dates or meetings with current clients. But I just haven't got it in me lately; I hardly have the motivation to live. I feel sluggish and heavy, and my brain seems to move as slowly as my limbs. Sure, I've suffered from the odd temporary depressive bouts before, but nothing this pathetic.

It's all very ridiculous and childish of me. I've been through tragedy and trauma far worse than a broken heart or dumb crush, and I overcame it all with more ease. Rape, my father's death, illness and poverty and strife. All like water off a duck's back. But then, maybe I was just better-equipped at repressing the pain. That's why I ran away from home and moved across the country and started a new life. I think of my father, and the abysmal dread in the pit of my stomach deepens, and my already-leaden heart grows heavier.

I'm on the cusp of giving up when I receive a call. It's not Joseph, but at least it's someone.

"Hello?" I answer in a groggy voice.

"Hiiiii." My friend Gertrude's nasally voice is far too jarring to hear first thing in the morning, especially with my nerves so fragile. "Why haven't you answered my texts?"

"It's eight o'clock in the morning. I haven't had a chance to look at them," I lie. I didn't see her texts, but not because I haven't had the chance; it's because I silenced them. I've been trying to gradually get rid of her, but narcissists like her believe the world orbits around them, and are difficult to drop. They don't get the hint because they always assume everyone likes them and will do what they say. Never in a million years would someone be actively trying to avoid them. But I guess I don't hate her that much. She is one the few friends I have, after all. And these days, I'm feeling increasingly isolated and undesirable. And hell, I'm a narcissist too. Takes one to know one.

"Late night with some handsome stranger?" she asks teasingly, but then recants, "Well, I guess your clients aren't usually handsome." That is some underhanded jab.

"There has been a handsome one recently, actually," I find myself remarking. "But he wasn't a client."

"Wow, that's unlike you. You're so hard to impress," she replies, sounding genuinely surprised.

"He's a fuckboi. It doesn't matter," I mutter, feigning aloofness, but then grimace at my unconvincing tone. I feel horribly transparent. Also, why did I just call him a fuckboi? He isn't, but he is. All Millennial boys are by default, even if they strive not to be. They're a product of their environment. A product of internet porn and option paralysis and individualistic entitlement and a myriad of mental disorders induced by modern society.

"Ah," she says, probably unconvinced as well. I'm a bit unconvinced myself. "Listen, are we still on for today or what?"

"Huh?"

"We're supposed to meet for tea today, remember? I wanted to confirm with you," she explains with increasing impatience. "I texted you last night, too."

"Oh. Shit." I'd forgotten all about it. Silencing her texts certainly didn't help.

"Ugh," she moans, frustrated with me, and I can't blame her. And I suddenly feel like a child being scolded. She has that maternally condescending way about her. Maybe that's why I hate and love her at the same time. "I've got a meeting with my editor on the Eastside later.

If you don't want to meet, I'll just head that way earlier. That'll make things easier for me, at least."

"No!" I cry out with a note of despair I hadn't intended. I don't want to be alone today, so I'll take any company I can get, even from a friend I claim I don't particularly like. "No, it's okay. I'll meet you on the Eastside. I haven't been there in ages, and I need a reason to get out. I've been wallowing in self-pity the past few days. Please," I beg her. I've really hit rock-bottom.

"Okay," she responds, unfazed. "How's the teashop on Belmont?"

"No, anywhere but Belmont. God," I moan, feeling suddenly ill as I recall running into Joseph on that same street while leaving the strip club.

"Damn," she remarks at my probably slightly over-dramatic reaction. "What do you have against Belmont?" she asks.

"It's just—" I falter self-consciously, "It's where the strip club I sometimes work at is." I neglect to add that I suspect Joseph might live on that street as well.

"Oh, god. Okay." I've ranted to her before about all my stripping fiascos. I seem to encounter more bullshit and hooliganism stripping than in prostitution, and I make less doing it, generally. It seems the less a man pays, the more he expects, and the harder he is to deal with. And pervy, stingy old men that lurk around strip clubs are the worst customers on the planet.

"I could meet you at the teahouse on East Burnside?"

"Tea Chai Te? Even better," she chirps happily. "That's close to where I have to meet my agent. I have to go over my upcoming book launch with her," she adds nonchalantly. She loves humblebragging about all of her success as a published author, and pretending to be annoyed by all of the pains of the publishing world.

But at least she's someone who accepts me for who I am.

Chapter Twelve

And when I get off the phone and pull myself out of bed to get ready, I realize my limbs are not so leaden or my heart so heavy as they were. My spirits have lifted at the prospect of something to do and someone to meet, even if it is Gertrude. And I don't have to risk running into Joseph.

But then, of course, I also want to—I want to run into him and see his beautiful face and for him to see me and be forced to resolve that which feels unresolved and has formed a tight knot in my chest. And all these conflicting emotions are thanks to my female hormones and the vast amounts of oxytocin I apparently released when he fucked me with his magical cock, and in that moment, a switch went off in my heart or my brain, or maybe it was my pussy, that said "Oh no."

My eastbound bus is ten minutes late and drags ass on the way, too, much to my frustration. So I'm pretty late when I finally arrive to the teahouse. I see Gertrude before she sees me. She's sitting by the window, and it's apparent she's been there quite some time preoccupied by her writing, as she's got her laptop in front of her and is clacking away at the keys in a frenzy, either immersed in a pivotal scene or firing off a livid email to her editor or PR guy. Beside her is a pot of tea and a half-eaten cookie, and she looks as cozy and frumpy as always in her thrifted bohemian clothes, a mismatched layering of shawls and scarves and ponchos and multipatterned skirts. Her aesthetic is like Free People, except neither sexy nor expensive, to match her frumpy, old-fashioned name. But then she wouldn't be Gertrude, were she any other way.

She looks up from her computer and finally sees me and peers through her thick librarian glasses to scrutinize my outfit, which is considerably less layered than hers. I've thrown on a satiny dress that could pass for a negligee and a motorcycle jacket and platform boots and lacy tights. Needless to say, we make an odd duo sitting there by the window, framed by the cascading leaves of philodendrons hanging from the ceiling.

"I thought you were trying to avoid the strip club," she states sarcastically. "Did you get mixed up again?" she lowers her thick glasses critically.

"Ha ha. You should give up your writing career and go into comedy."

"People laugh at me enough already, thanks," she quips with a smirk as I sit down. The rare bit of self-deprecating humor makes her slightly less insufferable. "You're late, by the way," she says in a tone that's positively reprimanding. I notice now, looking at her scowling mouth, that there's a cookie crumb hanging on the corner, which is creased by years of practiced frowning. I decide not to mention it.

"By twelve minutes! I can't control TriMet, sorry," I exclaim. She huffs in exasperation, then shuts her laptop dramatically. "Are you in a mood?" I ask warily, but secretly I'm slightly relieved that I'm not the only one.

"No, I just have a lot of shit to do and deadlines to meet with this new manuscript," she sighs, and I deflate. She always likes to broadcast that she's a writer and insert it into conversation whenever possible. "And I like it when people respect my time," she adds, shooting me an icy glare. She is a formidable creature, for being so small and formless. I, on the other hand, look like a giantess beside her. She is overweight, yet still more petite than I am. Yet I'm reduced to a witless and spineless child when she tenders those cutting remarks and that condescending wisdom. "But I'll live. I've just got to sort out this character that can't decide which love interest she wants to fuck because they're both rich and dashingly handsome," she explains coolly, and just like that, she's over it and calmed down, the smooth planes of her pale face more placid than ever.

"Poor her," I say sarcastically. "You can always kill her off. Or one of the men—even better."

She stares at me with a vacant expression, clearly unamused.

I go to order my chai at the counter. While waiting in line, I think of Joseph again, goddamn him. And I'm tempted by the pressing urge to check my phone—which I've already checked an embarrassing number of times—to see if he's texted me. There's nothing to see, of course. But then I'm up, and I order my chai and practice self-restraint as I wait for them to steep the tea and froth the milk. I go back to the table with my steaming mug and glance out the window and emit a trembling, tragic little sigh like a woman in a romance novel pining for her lover. That's me. I'm that girl now. *Pining.*

I think I see him walking down the street through the window. My heart catches in my chest. It starts beating excitedly. The pulse of it is in my throat. My stomach flutters almost nauseously. But through the waxy leaves of the philodendron, as green as his emerald eyes, I see that it's not actually him. Just another tall skinny hipster boy. So this is what it's like, to see one's lover in a thousand faces with that pathetic, angst-ridden yearning that grips at one's heart. When I return my gaze to the tea and Gertrude, I find that she's staring at me.

"Something's changed with you," she remarks, her eyes narrowing suspiciously. As if that schoolgirl sigh wasn't enough to tip her off. Then she coolly observes, "You're quieter than usual. You've got this glow. God, don't tell me you're pregnant with this fuckboi's evil spawn. Or a client's. That'd be incredibly sad. I'll go with you to the abortion clinic—"

"Pregnant—no! God, no." I snap, cringing at the mere thought. I've always been adamant about not wanting children, and therefore also incredibly diligent about condom use—which is especially important in

109

my vocation. And Joseph had been very respectful about the whole thing. But then, as I think about the possibility of it, of Joseph impregnating me, with the last dredges of tea fragments swirling in my mug, something lovely swirls inside me too. It feels as if my womb is unfurling at the mere thought of bearing his child, something containing his stupid fuckboi DNA. Then suddenly, pregnancy and motherhood—things that, before, would've filled me with utter distaste—don't seem so terrible. And suddenly I understand the hysteria of women, scorned or lovesick, and I realize I probably need to be admitted into a mental institution.

"I'm done for, I think," I whisper to her self-consciously. "This guy. I've never felt this way before. I'm in love," I say in a trembling voice, as if I'm telling her I have a terminal illness.

"Does he know about your job?" I'm sure she has a million questions. But she asks that one first. It's particularly cutting. There's something insidious in that watchful look of hers as she awaits my answer.

Sometimes, I get the feeling that she resents me for my job, and all the attention I receive from men as a result, and the opportunity I get to exploit them. But the funny thing is, I resent her for having an actual career, one that's not only sustainable, but socially acceptable, if not considered a little cliché or unserious. At least it isn't illegal and publicly shunned.

"No," I cede, slumping down in my chair. "I couldn't tell him."

"So what makes this guy so different from your clients?"

"Well, I find him attractive; there's a start. And we had the most mind-blowing, passionate sex. The kind of sex that—that—"

I stumble at a sudden loss for words, when she cuts in dryly with, "The kind of sex I've certainly never had." And I remember that I actually feel a bit sorry for her.

Gertrude is in a loveless and sexless domestic partnership with a deeply-closeted gay man. He doesn't actually know he's gay—that's how closeted he is—but everyone else does that's met him. And he and Gertrude make the most awkward couple I've ever seen. Even Gertrude knows, I think. She's never actually said the word, but she's the one that refers to their relationship as a domestic partnership. They just do it for the financial convenience. It's hard to pay rent on your own, and she uses his health insurance.

"It's the sort of sex described in my books," she continues. "The sort of sex that doesn't actually exist, honey." Even though she writes and peddles romance novels full-time, she's as jaded about love as I am.

"That's what I thought. People always told me it did, I just hadn't found the right person yet. But I never believed them."

"By them, you mean Stephanie," she remarks, her voice dripping with derision because she and Stephanie used to be friends—that's how I met Gertrude, actually, through Stephanie—but then they had a falling out because Gertrude can't stand Stephanie's high energy, and frivolous, weepy antics, and love for all things spiritual and supernatural. But Gertrude clung onto me, and I let her because I have a habit of hanging onto things I don't need or want, like the dozens of clothes in my closet that no longer fit or books from thrift stores I'll probably never get around to reading, or the creased paper envelopes from past clients that once housed the multitude of loose bills, but are now useless and I really ought to throw them away, but I don't and I'm not sure why.

"Well, yeah. She's done her card and tea leaf reading on me and says there's a lover in my future," I say melodramatically, letting her know I don't actually believe that shit, though I'd like to.

"I'm sure she always says that to you. But then, you're gorgeous," she says frankly, not as a compliment, but as a simple truth, one she no doubt resents me for. "I don't need tea leaves to know there's no steamy romance in my wake," she states scornfully, and I can tell she's referring not only to her depressing, sexless arrangement with her partner Colin, but her own lack of attractiveness. But then, maybe she's more idealistic than she lets on, and has too high of standards. I know I do.

"Well, there's something to companionship, and having someone to come home to. Trust me, the life of a perpetual singleton is a lonely one."

I'm almost tempted by an unexpected wave of empathy to touch her hand, when she looks up suddenly and her eyes brighten behind those squarish, bottlecap glasses. She's looking over my shoulder at someone coming into the teashop. "Well, hello handsome," she whispers emphatically.

I turn around to find out what she's drooling over. At first glance, I see that it's just an attractive man that's walked in. Tall, blond hair, broad shoulders but very slender with narrow hips that look good in those business trousers. But nothing extraordinary. He's no Joseph. He's wearing glasses too, but they give a Clark Kent effect rather than Gertrude's frumpy librarian aesthetic. But then my eyes zero in on his actual face and I let out a gasp.

"What, he's not your fuckboi is he?"

"No," is all I'm able to utter. I feel suddenly out of breath and speechless from pure disbelief.

He finally notices us staring, then turns and meets my gaze. A grin stretches across his face as he recognizes me as well. "Austin!" I call out at the youthful face which has changed so much but is still so keenly familiar. I suppose men change a lot during their early twenties.

"Evie!" he shouts excitedly as the recognition lights up his face. He bounds towards me like the puppy-dog-Austin I remember. "I can't believe it! How long has it been?"

"Three years." I knew him shortly before I discovered escorting, when I worked as a waitress in a Japanese izakaya on the Eastside. He doesn't know anything about the escorting, I realize. When I left, I recall jokingly telling all the waitstaff I'd found a sugar daddy, but they didn't take me seriously. And back then, Austin was no more than a gangly, broke, malnourished pothead who lived off frozen pizza and couldn't get laid to save his life, and frequently confided in me, bemoaning both his financial and dating struggles. We'd been great work friends, and I saw him as a little brother. We never even flirted. I've never had a friendship like that with a member of the opposite sex before, or since. But that was what feels like a lifetime ago. "You've really cleaned up. Look at you!" He's put on about twenty pounds, and most of it is muscle, and his face is less boyish and more masculine. But maybe it's the beard. An optical illusion. He certainly didn't have that before.

"I know, check this out." He digs in his coat pocket. It's a nice coat. And he proffers a business card with his name and photo. And beneath it reads: "Frazier Marketing Solutions." I guess that's the firm he works at now.

"Damn. So fancy. Quite the step up from bussing tables," I remark, handing him the card back. "And you look like a different person. Like a real adult. Frankly, it's creepy."

"Yeah. It's crazy what money will do. Now I can afford proper food and a gym membership. And clothes not from Goodwill."

"And hair product. And a barber." He leans down and I touch his smooth coif of silky blond locks.

"You look great, too," he says breathily and my heart flutters a bit with fear that there's something behind that innocuous compliment. Does he like me? I'd always feared that. He's the only male friend I've had who didn't try to get into my pants, which is why I generally avoid male friends.

Gertrude interrupts our reunion by loudly clearing her throat. I'd forgotten all about her. "Oh, this is my friend, Gertrude. Gertrude, Austin," I introduce the two. Gertrude's wearing this sly, insinuating smile, and I find it mildly infuriating, especially with that cookie crumb still trembling on the corner of her lips.

"What are you doing for work? You didn't go back to waitressing, did you?"

"No. Never," I laugh. And it's true—I'll never be reduced to that again. Funny that I felt more abused, misused and exploited waitressing than stripping or whoring around.

"I've been thinking about you, you know," he says, and my heart clutches anxiously again.

"You have?" Gertrude blurts. I hit her foot with mine beneath the table and shoot her a reprimanding glare. Usually, she's the one doing that to me.

"Yeah. The office could really use your kind of energy. It's a great gig, but the work culture's a bit…lacking."

"Stuffy in there, huh? I'm actually unemployed at the moment." I pause to glance at Gertrude and make sure she's behaving. A faint smirk plays at the corners of her mouth. "But I'm not looking for work."

"Well, take my card anyway," he says, pressing the card into the palm of my hand. His hands are damp and warm like I remember, and not fondly. "Think about it. The guys in the office would get a real kick out of you. If you change your mind, just give me a call." He winks like he means to be cheesy, and I groan in mock-disgust, but take the card anyway. It's crazy that he has a business card now.

"Thanks," I chirp, and the air is suddenly tense as we glance at one another with nothing left to say, and he begins to chuckle awkwardly.

"Well, I guess I'll leave you two ladies to your tea," he finally says. He orders, then quickly heads out.

When he's gone, Gertrude looks at me again with that same maddening, insinuating smile.

114

"Why are you looking at me like that? I hate that look. Stop," I whine, shifting uncomfortably in my seat.

"Why don't I know about this guy?" she demands.

"We drifted apart when I left waitressing. It was years ago. And he certainly didn't look like *that*."

"You need to set us up," she whispers insistently, pointing to herself.

I don't have the heart to tell her she's not exactly his type, but then, I also don't have a clue what his type is. Three years ago, he'd probably fuck any female within his age range that bathed at least once a week.

"I barely know him anymore. Besides, you're coupled up."

"Unhappily," she reminds me. "And maybe we're in an open relationship."

"You and half of Portland. And I know you're not." Her SO probably wouldn't care if she did cheat, though.

"I think he likes you anyway," she remarks sadly, her shoulders slumping as she admits defeat, and I almost feel sorry for her. "I saw the way he looked at you."

"It's not like that," I say, though I'm not so sure. He had said my name with such cloying fondness and had maintained eye contact just a little too long during certain points of conversation that left me feeling vaguely disconcerted. But then, most men make me feel that way. If they don't, they're either very happily married or gay. "He's like a little brother to me." If I recall correctly, he's two years younger than I am, which makes him 25.

"Fine," she digresses, rolling her eyes. "So, about this fuckboi—"

"Joseph," I interject, regretting ever calling him a fuckboi, because now Gertrude isn't going to let it go. And as I'm forced to say his name, a fresh wave of pain sweeps over me. Even saying his name causes me pain. And the agony is probably visible on my stricken face, too. "His name is Joseph."

"Joseph, my bad. You were the one that called him a fuckboi though. Is this Joseph as attractive as that friend of yours?" she asks.

"I mean, *I* think so. But then, maybe I'm biased. I've got these stupid chemicals in my brain controlling me. So I don't know." I take out my phone and show her his Facebook. "He isn't very present on social media. And takes terrible photos of himself, if any." I reluctantly yield my phone.

"How edgy," she mutters, then begins scrolling. The anxiety mounts as I watch her scrutinize him behind her glasses and await her opinion, which I care way too much about for some reason. In that moment, everything seems to hinge upon her approval, even though he doesn't even reciprocate the way I feel, even though he hasn't messaged me, even though her opinion doesn't matter. But she has a certain manipulative power over me, one that allows her to influence, denigrate, and disempower me, and it always leaves me feeling bad afterwards. That's why I've been trying to distance myself from her and ignore her texts. But she always reels me back in. And in person, she's not so bad. She has a way of growing on you, like an invasive plant. Choking in a quaint sort of way.

"Not bad," she says at last, though I feel like she's holding back just to torture me, then she adds, "But nothing special. Honestly, I'm surprised. I thought you liked more clean-cut guys. He looks a little homeless."

"I did too," I remark dryly. "He's a little skinny, but he's strong, trust me, and he knows how to..." I stop as I realize I'm about to yield up too much information. Her eyes go wide, and a bemused smile stretches across her face. Meanwhile, mine colors in mortification. "I mean, maybe looking a little rough around the edges is part of his allure," I mumble and shrug, looking down so I don't have to bear that patronizing smile of hers. I feel my face growing uncomfortably hot.

"Wow. So he's that amazing in bed? I insist you divulge the details," she demands. "I need to live vicariously through you." I act reluctant at first, pulling a grimace. "Come on," she whines, "you can't *not* tell me now—that's just cruel—"

"Fine!" I relent. And secretly I'm dying to tell her anyway. "He was amazing. *It* was amazing. I practically ascended to a higher plane of existence when I came. The way he touched me and moved inside of me and looked at me with these searing eyes. And he was so agile and strong. And he has these grass-green eyes. And he's the perfect balance of gentle and rough and witty and handsome and playful and serious."

"And his…?" I realize she still has my phone and is staring at it, perhaps straining to picture him in the act. I tear the phone out of her hands with an exasperated sound.

"It's the perfect size. It's perfect. He's perfect," my voice quivers. "Except that afterwards, after giving me this mind-blowing orgasm, he just up and left." I don't mention the other details that complicate things, because I have a way of complicating things. "And he hasn't contacted me since and it's been days. Like the typical player. But it didn't feel that way in the moment. We came at the same time, for Christ's sake!" I cry, my tone rattling with despair. "And he gazed at me the entire time. How can someone do that, then just forget about you?"

"Ugh, men," she groans wearily, then remarks in a dry tone, "In another life, I was a lesbian. At least as a writer, I can pretend there are perfect men and portray them in my novels, and pretend they're besotted with me—err, my protagonists." Then she digresses to the matter at hand with a no-nonsense expression. "Anyway, that's how players are, making you feel special and blessing you with their amazing cocks. But then, they're able to magically turn off that convincing façade. That's how they become true masters of the game. How do you think they get all that pussy in the first place?"

"Ugh, don't say that word."

"I'm just telling you like it is. They're fucking psychopaths if you ask me."

"Players, or all men?"

"Hmm, good question," she mutters. "The latter, probably."

"But it just felt different with him," I sigh sadly, unable to accept the fact hanging in the air, unspoken yet perfectly obvious: he's just not *that* into me. But my feelings and those stupid chemicals released by my spellbound brain are tricking me into believing otherwise. "It felt like we ascended to a higher heaven or opened a seventh chakra or some shit. I just don't get it."

"Sounds like Stephanie talk," she says with repulsion, triggered to the point of looking ill.

"Yeah, well, I'm really done for then, ain't I?" In an odd show of vulnerability and desperation, I look at her and ask, "What do I do?" She does give scathingly honest advice, at least.

"Well, you know what they say," she says with a conspiratorial smirk, "The best way to get over someone is to get under someone else."

Chapter Thirteen

After leaving the teahouse, on the bus ride home, I consider taking Gertrude's advice and downloading Tinder. I hesitate with my thumb hovering over the little pink flame of the app's logo. Here I am, a prostitute, contemplating installing Tinder again after swearing it off years ago, because I went and fell in love like a miserable fool, and I'd rather not drown the sorrow with alcohol or food. Sex, for once, seems preferable.

I feel as if I'm on the cusp of either a downward spiral, or some transformative revelation.

In the end, I decide not to download the app, and instead, cling onto the pitiful shred of hope that something, anything, will happen with Joseph, even though, in the pit of my stomach, I know it's doomed to fail. But never seek logic in the human heart. That's what my mom once told me.

Instead of swiping away my troubles, I check my email. I have a new one from the nursing home I'd applied to as a volunteer. Apparently, I've been approved, and can show up on Tuesdays or Thursdays whenever I like.

I decide to go the next morning. It's perhaps not as exciting of a distraction as online dating, but it's something. I even make an Instagram post about it—because one can't simply do good deeds without broadcasting it, obviously. I wonder if there is a single human capable of being that humble. And then I think of Joseph, and his being so eager and willing to help me with my light long after he'd clocked out, and the time he abandoned me to help the Katy girl down the hall with the fridge, whom he supposedly didn't have sex with, and then his absence on social media, the primary platform for humblebragging, and

I wonder if perhaps he is just the sort of guy who would do good deeds unselfishly, without telling a single soul. But I feel such a sting of rejection towards him that I can't believe he's that pure or wholesome or definitively good. If he is, I hate him more for it. And sweet baby Jesus, I do love him, I think with despair as my heart both swells and sinks, all wilted and deflated, at the thought of him.

For the nursing home, I've dressed in heeled penny loafers and a camel-colored coat that reaches past my knees. I'm impressed with how well I match the fall foliage outside. Most of the leaves have changed by now and blaze in the mid-morning sunshine or have been stripped off their arboreal skeletons and blanket the streets in shades of gold and red.

I'm just then leaving my apartment feeling not only beautiful and very well put together but also a little morally superior, given where I'm headed, when I bump into Katy and experience a violent shift in my mood. I feel dumb in my color-coordinated outfit, which I selected so painstakingly, the effort of which is humiliatingly obvious beside her. She's dressed in a loose hoodie and tight leggings and messy yet cute bun I've never been able to pull off myself. But then, she's so petite anything looks cute on her.

"Oh, morning," she pipes up. "Eve, isn't it?"

"Yeah. How do you know my name?" I say, not exactly intending to sound so defensive.

"I know everything," she replies in a teasing voice, then smiles, and I reluctantly smile back, unable to confront her and instead complying with the usual insufferable social niceties. I hate that she knows anything at all about me. I hate that I haven't the capacity to be cruel to her. "Have you seen Joseph around?" she asks suddenly. The question totally throws me off guard.

"You don't know where he is? I thought you knew everything," I say coyly, my smile insincere.

"You're funny. I see why he likes you. I'll just text him." My chest burns with anger. Of course she has his number and I don't.

"He's a slippery one, isn't he?" I mutter, unconvinced by her remark about Joseph liking me. How would she know? And why would she just casually relinquish such knowledge? Does she see me as competition, or not? Doesn't she like him?

"You have no idea," she replies in an insinuating tone that increases my confusion and anxiety. I can't stand that cute little smile on her heart-shaped face either.

"Later." I quip and turn to leave before she can say anything else that will leave me feeling even more unsettled.

"See you around!" she chimes back.

I want to holler back that she won't, but unfortunately, since we live on the same floor, the odds are not in my favor.

My spirits aren't as lofty now as I step into the cold, damp gray and actually start walking to the nursing home.

Then the middle-aged lady at the front desk of the nursing home is rude and unfriendly when I arrive, and looks me over judgmentally, which I'm used to, but it still doesn't exactly make me feel welcome. She seems dubious when I explain to her that I'm a new volunteer. Then she calls a nurse to come and give me the tour.

The lady shows up, looking just as frigid and formidable as the receptionist. This whole volunteer thing isn't doing much for my ego so far. I should've just downloaded Tinder.

"Cynthia," the nurse introduces herself in a curt, no-nonsense voice before ordering me to follow her.

"The volunteers here usually work in the cafeteria serving meals," she turns her head and tells me as she rushes down the hallway and I hurry to keep up with her. "Or in what we call the recreation department—that's where you'll be—though it's a bit…"

The hesitation in her fading voice doesn't seem promising.

She leads me to a tiny closet of a room which only has a little hanging lightbulb with a feeble, sporadic light to illuminate it, and only succeeds in making it look more ominous. There are no medical supplies or pill bottles lining the janky shelves, but instead, there are board games and cardboard boxes and dusty paperback books, covered by cobwebs.

"This is it, then? I guess entertainment for the patients has been pushed to the wayside."

"Well, we just don't have the funds for it, that's why we have volunteers run it usually, and we have more important things to focus on, like patients falling and breaking their hip or going into cardiac arrest," she says bluntly, and I feel put in my place, even though I never had a place to begin with. To think what legitimate emergencies comprise her job and must fill her day makes my life feel wholly inconsequential, not to mention lucky and undeservedly so. She probably has to put up with way more bullshit and harassment than I do. "But, nonetheless," she chirps curtly, "the patients do need something to take their mind off things. Most of them have been dumped here by their families and rarely get visitors. And the volunteers come and go. I doubt you'll last a week," she concludes cynically.

I'm tempted to concur then leave. "Everyone needs human company," I say instead, trying to muster whatever vestige of empathy I still possess within my shriveled soul. I think of my male clients who come to me sometimes not only for sex but simply for female intimacy, the feeling of a warm body beside them, a comforting voice or a listening ear.

"Ain't that the truth," she concedes wearily. She's about to say something else when the phone strapped to her hip starts going off. "Shit," she hisses, then barks into her phone, "What?"

"We have a situation in Room 102," I hear a portentous voice whisper through the hiss of static.

"Jesus Christ," she groans irritably, and I wonder who shit in her cereal this morning. I guess that goes for all the workers here, but it seems like an abysmal place to work, and I'm already dreading the prospect of volunteering a mere two days a week for what will feel like a hopelessly long time, not a mere couple of hours. I doubt I'll last a week, just like she said, as much as I hate to admit it.

"Bob left his room and got caught with Marty again, didn't he?" Cynthia replies to her colleague.

My eyes widen at that last bit.

When she gets off the phone, she tells me, "Marty has a broken hip. And Bob has TB. They can't be having sex."

I tremble with horror. "So Bob and he…"

"Yep," she nods soberly.

"Does that happen often?"

"Oh yeah, this place is a page straight out of *The Notebook* by Nicholas Sparks. And the spread of STDs is rampant in nursing homes like you wouldn't believe," she vents.

"Good book," I remark nonchalantly, hoping she'll crack a smile for once. "*The Notebook*, I mean," I add meekly.

She doesn't smile.

"Maybe you can read it to one of the residents," she recommends bluntly, then hands me a clipboard sitting on the shelf, covered in a thin film of dust.

"Everything in this room is at your disposal. Here's the list of all the patients in the home accepting visitors. Watch out for Bob though. I wouldn't visit him if I was you."

"He's not gay?"

"Honey, people here go all sorts of ways. Good luck."

I'm left alone in the dark room to contemplate all my bad decisions, this one being by far the worst. The whole risky ordeal of prostitution. That seems like a walk in the park compared to this.

And to think I had signed up for this with the idea that it might somehow atone for all those illicit acts.

I decide to visit only female residents to begin with. I pick one on the top of the clipboard named Charlotte Theriot. I look at the titles crammed on the bookshelf. I see that *The Notebook* and *A Walk to Remember* are on it and chuckle idly to myself. But I take *Rebecca* by Daphne du Maurier instead. Nicholas Sparks seems too corny and sentimental for a place as bleak as this. And gothic classic literature is more up my alley.

I'm even more uncertain of how selfless and good this volunteering venture really is when I get to her room and open the door and get this overwhelming feeling of being a creep violating her sacred space. These are her private quarters. Or the most privacy she'll ever know again. And she is sleeping in her bed, completely vulnerable. And here I am, thoughtlessly encroaching. She awakens right after I've opened the door, making me feel even worse for barging in. I realize then that I haven't even knocked. I can't imagine someone doing that to me, but I guess when elderly people get left in nursing homes, they are forced to relinquish all control and freedom, resigning themselves to their interminable imprisonment.

As she sits up on her stack of pillows, she looks impossibly diminutive and brittle, not only thin but having a very petite frame. Her skin is olive-toned, and her hair is dark brown except for the ribbons of white streaking it. She mutters something in a foreign language I vaguely recognize the flowery flow of. Then I recall her name, Charlotte Theriot, and wonder how it didn't occur to me earlier that she might be French. "Who is it? What do you want from me?" she demands in a slurred accent, sounding rightly assaulted, and I step back and cower behind the partially opened door.

"I'm a new volunteer here. I'm sorry for disturbing you. I'll go if you like. I'm sorry," I say in a meek and disembodied voice that quavers with embarrassment. But beyond that is the unfurling of something novel and exciting. Just hearing that odd bit of French has awoken a childhood fantasy of mine, to go to Paris. I had forgotten all about those dreams in the wake of a sordid and sobering adulthood.

"Who are you? What do you want?" she asks brusquely, then mutters something under her breath in French that I'm sure has curse words in it. Then she peers at me through her narrowed eyes, wreathed by a multitude of fine wrinkles that cover her face, which I can tell might have been quite beautiful once. Her lips are still full and sensual, even in such advanced age. "Collette? *C'est vous?*"

"No, I'm not Collette, sorry," I whisper tentatively, and watch as the hope in her narrowed eyes is extinguished. I wonder who this Collette is—but that's a question for later. "My name's Evelyn. I've come to read to you. I'm part of the recreational department."

She scoffs in disgust. "No reading, Evelyn," she says my name as if it tastes bitter in her mouth. "I find it tedious. Even more so when it's someone else doing it for me."

"All right. No reading, then."

Before I have a chance to run away, sufficiently discouraged, and leave this terrible place, she beckons me towards her, "Come over here. Sit with me and talk. I am lonely and bored in this odious prison." She speaks in such a brusque and commanding manner, I can't refuse her, so I silently obey. There is a chair right beside her bed and as I walk towards it, I also see a shelf against the wall with framed photographs on it.

"Is this Collette?" I ask, pointing to one as I sit down.

"*Non, ma cherie, c'est moi.* Once I was almost as beautiful as you," she says with a mysterious and self-conscious smile. Even at the odd bit of French, I feel my heart flutter again with excitement.

"So who's Collette? You're daughter?"

"Oui," she says, a little somberly, her eyes cast downwards. I wonder what became of Collette, but then I determine it couldn't have been anything good. She's not here, after all, and her mother's in a nursing home, alone. So she either outlived her daughter or was deserted by her. "Every woman is another woman's daughter," she seems to answer my thoughts, but has only succeeded in confusing them more, as she speaks in riddles. Or maybe it's just the French accent. "And you have a mother, do you not, Evelyn?"

"Well, yeah."

"And where is she? Where is it you come from?"

"Tennessee. That's where she is."

"This Tennessee is far away, *non?*"

I nod solemnly.

"Why did you come here?"

"Why did I come where?" I ask, wondering if she's referring to the nursing home, because I certainly don't have a good answer for her. To feel something, I suppose. But then suddenly I'm having a full-blown existential crisis. Love those.

"To Portland! To this godforsaken prison where old people go to die..." she gestures vaguely in the air with a bony, trembling hand.

"Shouldn't I be asking you those questions?" I ask, feeling suddenly defensive.

"What is this attitude?" she demands. "Why this hostility? I am a poor decrepit old woman!" And suddenly she's the victim. I feel bad, but I don't show it. That would be an admission of guilt. Here I am,

126

harassing an old woman in a nursing home, as she says, but I'm simply asking questions. Tit for tat. We make quite the duo.

"Are you always so evasive?" I ask with an insinuating smile that she doesn't react well to.

"I do not know this word! Get out!" she shouts, her mood worsening. "Out with you. Let this poor old woman live in peace." She begins muttering again in French in that cantankerous tone that sends me rushing out the door. If she could get up and walk, she'd be batting me out with a broomstick. Still, I can't help but smile as I rush out of the room.

"I'll be back in a few days," I call back.

I ought to feel awful after that shitshow. I was sent to entertain and comfort the residents, not harass them. But instead of feeling any lasting guilt, I feel a spark of energy and something akin to inspiration.

My heart is racing excitedly, and I can't stop smiling as I go down the hall to return to the closet and scout out some other diversion for the next tenant, but also to be alone with my thoughts for a moment. Because she's reminded me of the child I used to be. With all those childlike dreams, mesmerized by the flowery French language and the idea of Paris and all its pastel-colored and sepia-toned romanticisms. Paris seemed so remote and exotic and luxurious to a small hillbilly girl from the rural mountains of Tennessee. I had watched the film *Amelie* for the first time at the age of fourteen, and before that, I'd watched Disney's *The Aristocats* and *The Hunchback of Notre Dame*, and even before that, I'd fallen in love with the *Madeline* picture books, which made even orphanages and boarding schools in Paris seem glamorous. The illustrations depicted were, in fact, far more beautiful than the trailer-strewn Appalachians I grew up in. As a child, I had fostered the farfetched fantasy of traveling there, but never truly believed I could. I'd dreamed of seeing the Eiffel Tower lit up at night, or eating a fresh-baked croissant in a boulangerie, or strolling through Montmartre in the afternoon.

But then there were all the obstacles, which only increased with age. There was the airfare and the accommodations and the necessary travel documents and the fear of the unknown and most importantly, there was the language barrier. The French language was as intimidating as it was intriguing. I'd tried learning once, but I simply hadn't had the resources to learn, and somewhere along the way, I lost my desire to even try, to travel, to experience novel things.

Because when you grow older, you get more content, and less inclined to take risks, and your zeal for life and adventure fades. And all that childlike wonder is replaced by jaded cynicism.

And here I am, 27 years old, wasting away in a darkened nursing home closet too afraid to truly live. I should sign up for a French class, I decide. Because I really don't have anything holding me back any longer. Rather than let some stupid man constantly intrude into my thoughts, I ought to better myself. So I resolve to actually try and learn French, and plan a trip in the not-so-distant future, and do something interesting for once.

After leaving the sanctuary of the closet, I make a couple more rounds. But after having one of the especially crotchety male patients throw a book at me, I decide to call it a day and go home, feeling sufficiently dehumanized.

I stop at the coffee shop on the way home, but thankfully it's Ricky's day off, so I don't have to deal with that awkwardness. I take my laptop and sign up for a French class while sipping my latte. The espresso is so smooth it soothes my rankled nerves after being more or less assaulted at the nursing home. But I also made one of the patients smile while playing cards with them, and I met the passionate and mercurial Charlotte, who inspired me to finally go to Paris and learn

French. So all of that atoned for the less enjoyable experiences, I suppose.

The French class is six weeks long and has two classes a week. It's a stepping-stone towards going to Paris, and I feel I've made a lot of progress today and I haven't even thought of Joseph that much. I'm bettering myself and enriching my life and all that, and even though this sense of accomplishment feels a bit manufactured and fleeting, at least I've not been rotting in my bed all day wallowing in self-pity, binging and purging in an endless cycle. And now that I'm on my computer, I can go about my usual routine of checking emails and setting up meetings with prospective and current clients, which isn't as agonizing as usual, and I've gotta make that rent. Knowing that I have other things going on in the week ahead, like the volunteering and the French classes, makes me dread the prospect of work a little bit less.

And it'll give me a break from thinking about Joseph incessantly. But inevitably, like always, here I am staring down into the last dredges of espresso and semi-coagulated milk, pining for him with an abysmal feeling swirling in my empty stomach. Or maybe it's just hunger.

I ought to eat something. But I'm afraid to go down that dangerous path. That's why sometimes I just don't eat for several hours on end, until I'm ravenous and the urge to binge has surfaced, exactly the predicament I've been trying to avoid by not eating, because when I eat, the beast of my appetite wakes up and is fathomless. Then I'm in an even more perilous spot than before.

"Wanna go to Harlow?" I call up Stephanie. My saving grace. If I eat with a friend, I won't let myself go crazy and overeat, which will surely trigger a binge. And she likes healthy food too.

After eating dinner with her and venting to her about the nursing home experience, I feel effervescent, lighter, and validated.

I don't tell her about fucking Joseph or signing up for the French class because, for some strange reason, I want to keep those things secret, even though I told Gertrude about the fucking.

Sometimes I like to be secretive and mysterious. But I'm not good at keeping things to myself, especially when pressed for information, because I do want people to know about my actions and my achievements. Doesn't everyone? No one's really humble or selfless. Like when I insist on paying for her meal, even though it's only to boost my own ego, to make me feel not only generous but also superior. And I was in sore need of an ego boost.

Chapter Fourteen

Returning to my apartment, I hadn't expected to see Joseph. For once, I'm not thinking about him. And it's way past his usual working hours. I almost bump into him as I hurry in from the chill of the autumn night—a crisp forty-eight degrees, and there he is.

"Hey!" he shouts.

"Hi!" I echo in a disembodied voice. Like an idiot, I almost believe he's there to see me. But then I see how surprised he is. So obviously he's not.

And then the truth occurs to me, and it hangs palpably in the fraught air, as my brain connects the dots as to why he's here at nine o'clock at night, coming from the end of the hallway, where Katy's apartment is. I remember our chance encounter that morning and how she'd nonchalantly remarked she would text him, and I'd wondered why and if he'd be here to visit her, and here he is leaving her apartment. I feel ill as the food I've just eaten turns in my stomach. I wonder if he gave her as transcendental an orgasm as he gave me, and I feel sick inside—more violated and corrupted than with any client, no matter how perverse or foul-smelling.

"Wait. What are you doing here?" I blurt, and my voice trembles at the end in the most pathetic way imaginable. I know the truth. But I need to hear it. But also, I don't want to hear it. I can't bear to hear it. But apparently, I couldn't bear to pass by in silent ignorance either.

He doesn't seem to notice my inner turmoil though, and he certainly isn't about to give me closure. "Nothing, just hanging out with a friend," he says with his usual insufferable vagueness.

"Oh, and you weren't going to call on me, I reckon," I laugh, the bitter tears burning my eyes and causing that laugh to catch in my throat.

"No. I didn't know you wanted me to," he says matter-of-factly, and for a moment it does make perfect sense, and I feel like an idiot for having wanted him to in the first place, and I'm ashamed for all my feelings and my pining and toxic jealousy. I ought to be cool and unfettered like he is now.

"Well, of course I did," I confess in a quiet whisper that turns to a tremble. The tears are about to come, but I can't let them surface. I can't let them expose my emotions in their full and ugly rawness.

And to think I felt fine only a few seconds ago—a new woman—and now here I am reduced to a fragile, tearful, quaking mess. I want so badly to ask him if he had sex with her, accuse him even, but my body won't let me utter the formidable question.

"Hey," he says, his cavalier tone suddenly softening as he stares at me with concern. "Come here, you. What's with the long face?" I'm rigid when he takes me in his arms, determined to be as aloof as he's been, but then, as soon as he shows the smallest bit of warmth and affection towards me, I instantly melt. I relax in his embrace, and it feels just like that night. I breathe in his scent and I turn to putty as he draws me tight against him, my whole soul unfurling and sex awakening as the key in my heart turns with a resonant click I swear is almost audible.

"I've always had a long face; it's my bone structure," I murmur against his hard chest, wanting to dissolve into it, laughing even as I sob and come undone.

"Well, will you have me then, Eve?" he asks, feather-soft but husky and guttural just the same. That sultry, deep voice with its high, honeyed tones, my kryptonite just like his unraveling touch.

"That's all I want; you should know that," I say, my tiny and tearful voice quivering emotionally. To say those words is so degrading, but

I'm weak. He has a way of tearing down my walls so that I readily give myself over to him.

"I'm fairly oblivious, though," he remarks, his calloused hands moving up my arms and leaving goosebumps in their wake.

I haven't the willpower to ask him about Katy anymore. Because now he's holding me. And who cares? Ignorance really is bliss, for a time. And I'm truly convinced there's no way he could hold me like this only moments after sleeping with someone else.

"I've gathered that," I say, calming down finally.

But he's not as obtuse and careless as he lets on—it's an expert façade. I can see that now in his intelligent eyes, gentle yet sharp as they meet mine again. This time the pupils are dilated because we both know now what's about to happen. And those ruthless eyes undo me, cutting into me uncouthly. They tear me down. And it's just what I long for—to be annihilated.

And when I'm with him again, my fixations about myself and my body and all my problems dissolve. It's all just me and him and all the world can go fuck itself for all I care. And the world really could be ending when we're naked together, reunited as one, and it's just as good as I remember, and far better than I could've hoped for. He's thrusting with the same soul-crushing passion and vigor, upturning waves of pleasure inside of me. I'd opened up for him like a flower blooming the moment he touched me with those long electric fingers, undoing me in their wicked way. Now I'm unraveled again, and aching around his hard cock, hard for me. I can't believe it. I could cry out from pure joy and exaltation for that cock alone and for him, too, as he gazes at me all the while with every slow and soul-crushing thrust. "God, you feel so good. It's never felt this good before," he whispers to me, and I believe him, because in this realm of intimacy and vulnerability, he cannot lie. Lying is not feasible. But maybe it's because I am a woman, and this is what it means to be a woman, finally, with my soul splayed wide open like a pulsing wound. Believing every lie.

He prods at that wound, he penetrates it and violates it and I beg for more. "Go deeper," I beg and whimper, and he holds me closer so that he can, and I want to cry out that I love him. The need to say it presses heavily upon my heart, so that it is painful not to, and I almost say it as it shudders through me, but I hold back. And so my heart aches with every thrust and as I gaze into his eyes. And the aching builds and becomes blurred with pleasure, and I feel my orgasm budding as he thrusts harder and breathes in shallow little pants until he whispers, "I'm going to cum," and mine sweeps over me just as he falls apart with a thrust so deep that I can feel it in my womb, and the pleasure swells around him inside me and he lets out a shattered moan, and I know this is the best feeling in the entire world.

But it's so fleeting, and I'm already mourning the culmination of it all. And then he slips out of me, eliciting a feeble whimper. He's soft now, and his condom is full of cum. I wish it were inside of me, I think, then regret that crazy thought, and silently rebuke myself for it and what's become of me. Weak and irrational, dumb and hysterical.

"That was incredible," he says breathlessly, and I almost can't believe he's saying it out loud, and his words make me feel validated. But they ought not to. The dangerous seed of doubt is an ever-present whisper in the back of my mind.

"It was amazing," I agree, feeling my heart swell as the pleasure dissipates, the pulse dying to a sweet numb nothingness. And then there's other sensations flooding my consciousness. It's probably just the oxytocin. But the fact that I know the name of the hormone causing these emotions doesn't seem to lessen its power over me. But it does cause me to resent the fact, and if I was otherwise ignorant, I would've simply been powerless and disarmed. The resentment gives me some mirage-like sense of control, at least. "Is it usually like that for you?" I ask, unable to quell the curiosity as that resentment subsides, and is replaced by a sickening curiosity intermixed with jealousy, and it eats away at me. I want to know, at least, that it's better with me, that it doesn't feel as good with the other girls. Like Katy.

"Never," he says, and I believe him, the sappy and lovestruck fool that I am. But then I really do believe him when he adds, "You've got some crazy power over me. You're like a witch. I told you."

"Really?" I say, not sure if the idea pleases me any longer. I've been told I'm like a witch by more than one client. Though I'm not sure it's a good thing. I like to think I have some seductive sway over the male sex when it comes to escorting. But with Joseph, it's different; it makes his attraction towards me seem insincere and involuntary, like it's against his better judgment. And I want him to want me willfully.

And yet…if only I possessed the power to make him fall in love with me. Or at least to make him stay.

"I'm gonna get this thing off of me," he says, getting up and bounding from the bed with acrobatic nimbleness. I watch the muscles in his back and even his buttocks ripple as he moves.

He's in the bathroom washing his hands, then surveying all the walls with my paintings I've collected from thrift stores and IKEA, and as he stands there in his full shameless nakedness, I'm able to survey every inch of him. He's so beautiful—the hard lean lines and his still semi-hard cock. He's not aroused, only alert, every fiber of his being so healthy and strong and vibrating with masculine vigor. I never understood male beauty until now. But then, I'd never encountered a truly beautiful man before. His lines look as though they might've been chiseled from marble like a Greek statue.

He catches me staring, and even though he was inside of me a mere minute ago, I feel ashamed that he's caught me, and I blush.

"Come back here, handsome, and stay a while. Hold me."

"If you insist, missus. I'm at your service." He obliges and spoons me, and it's even more delicious than the sex, I think.

After some time, he says with a yawn, "I really ought to leave soon." But he doesn't budge, but I know it's an imminent thing and will happen soon. Too soon.

"Wait. I have to tell you something. A secret."

"Oh?" he asks, intrigued.

My stomach flutters nervously. I have to tell him. Basking in the afterglow of sex, he cannot hate me. Even if he doesn't have the same flood of hormones surging through his veins like I do. While gazing at him, I've resolved that I'm not going to tell him about all the sex work. No, I'm going to quit all of that. I can do anything. I can be anything. As long as I'm with him. And I earnestly believe that in this golden moment. But I have a different secret to tell him.

"You're going to think I'm crazy."

"Go on, don't increase my suspense," he says, his eyes twinkling as they gaze into mine.

"I love you, Joseph. I really think I love you and I don't know why, but you do something to me."

And then that lively loving twinkle dies.

"You're right, that is crazy," he agrees in a chipper voice that is actually quite taciturn, given the context. His muscles tense around me suddenly, then he begins to retreat. "You really should stop that, Eve."

"Oh, right, I shouldn't have feelings?" I say defensively, already irreparably wounded. I regret everything again. How could he be so cruel? After fucking me like that and telling me those things?

"No, those are the worst. I never signed up for those," he chuckles.

I'm speechless and I'm shattered. But more confounded by this level of cruelty.

He glances at me, and I see pain and regret pass across his face at seeing me so devastated and knowing it's his doing. "Maybe I shouldn't have come over. It was a bad idea. I should leave," he announces abruptly, standing up and jerking on his clothes. His words only do me more damage. Digging the knife deeper in my open wound.

But I'm still desperate. Desperately in love.

"Wait. I—I'm sorry if I scared you. I know it was really sudden and came out of nowhere…"

"Look," he stops me. "I can't commit like that. I'm shit at relationships. They just aren't my forte. I can't give you that much," he explains, his voice fraught by something akin to angst.

"I don't understand. You wanted to have passionate, mind-blowing sex with me."

"Well, I didn't exactly want that. It's complicated. Like I said, you've got this power over me. And I certainly never signed up for love or a relationship, so you can't put that on me." He acts as though he had no power over any of it, as if he was just an innocent bystander, even though he did all the fucking. As if I lured him magically into my bed with some hypnotic spell, totally against his will.

"Well, you should know the consequences of having sex with people," I whisper.

"And what about all the people you've had sex with? Huh?" he demands defensively, and I'm caught totally off-guard by that incisive question. "Don't act like you get your feelings hurt so easily."

"But it was different with them. It was all mechanical," I mutter in a tiny voice. "You don't understand," I say in frustration, but he can't help it. I've told him nothing. So how could he understand? "I'm allowed to have feelings," I whisper in a trembling voice, sounding like a pitiful weepy child. Then I state even more quietly, "You don't know how it is."

"No, I don't Eve, but why don't you tell me?" he recommends in a sarcastic voice that is far louder than my own. He puts his hands on his hips and stares at me pointedly, and I have to look away.

He knows. He's has some inkling, at least. Now I'm the one that can't meet his stare.

"Well, with the others, we didn't have eye contact the entire time, or come at the same time. I've never had good sex until it was with you. We didn't have that bond. And with you, it was mind-blowing. So, yeah, forgive me for being a stupid emotional woman and catching feelings." I conveniently leave out the part about them paying me, even though that might make him understand.

"I'm sorry. I never meant to lead you on."

"It's not your fault. It's mine. Like I said. I'm the stupid one that caught feelings." The last words stick in my throat, and the tears of self-pity that've been brewing there for quite some time finally come pouring out of my eyes.

He is disarmed by the sight of my tears. "Hey. Don't do that," he whispers anxiously and kneels down on the floor, and rather than return to the bed and comfort me, he pets the side of my head awkwardly. His hands are trembling, I realize. "Hey, now," he says.

"Why?" I sob suddenly, exhaustedly, recoiling from the touch of his trembling hand. It's not the kind of comfort I want. "Why, Joseph? Why can't you just love me?"

"I don't know. I'm stupid like that. Men are stupid. We really suck. I'm sorry," he states with genuine regret. As a supposed, self-proclaimed feminist, he's resigned himself to the fact of how universally, indisputably awful men are. At least he's sorry. But sorry doesn't solve anything. His apologizing only makes me feel worse, because it confirms my fear. Saying sorry is an admission of guilt that he doesn't love me, that he can't reciprocate my feelings, and that all I'm left with is his guilt, which is no real consolation.

"Why did you have to get it all started? Why do you get involved with anyone, if you're just going to..." My voice trails off confusedly, and he sighs a heavy sigh that seems as though it's been pent up for years, and his whole body deflates.

"I don't know. I don't know. Like I said, men suck. We get bewitched by women like you and all the blood leaves our brain and goes to...well, you know the rest. And I probably need therapy. I mean, it's hard not to be involved at all. Dating is fine every now and then. But I'm fine with the way things are. With being single, I mean. I didn't know you'd catch feelings."

"That's what women do. Haven't you done this with women before?" I can't imagine him being with another woman intimately like he was with me and her *not* catching feelings. I've been with so many men...countless, in fact. So I feel like I am an authority on the matter.

"This kind of thing rarely happens, to be honest," he mumbles, gesturing vaguely at the bed and at me. So I take it he means hooking up—or sex in general—is a rare occurrence for him, which doesn't make sense at all. He's certainly alluded to the fact before, but I didn't believe him then and I don't believe him now.

"Bullshit," I quip bluntly.

"I'm serious. Before you, it'd been...three, four months maybe?" His heavy brow furrows as he tries to think hard about it. So it's been *that* long. I'm not one to assume people are generally lying outside of my vocational activities—in the realm of sex work, all bets are off—because I don't see the point to lying in the real world. But four months? With someone so handsome and charming and virile as he is, with the most beautiful cock I've ever seen and a collection of friends so diverse and vast, he ought to be able to meet anyone he'd like, or walk into a bar and use that endearing, convivial aura of his and have his pick.

"Impossible!" I exclaim incredulously. "What? Since getting laid?" He nods solemnly and I sit up in disbelief. "No way. There's no way."

"It's true," he shrugs simply, like it doesn't matter and hasn't even bothered him that much, the whole not getting laid, even though every other single and remotely healthy male on the planet would be on at least one dating app if not lurking in bars to get his fix, had he been without sex for that long

"But why me?" I ask, suddenly incredibly flattered in spite of everything, if it is in fact true that he hadn't had sex for such an inordinately long time, and not for lack of options or some inability to do so.

"You were different," he says with a shrug.

"I was?" I ask as my heart, that funny finicky organ, stutters ecstatically at the statement that seems to hold some intangible form of hope. But god, even as it does, and that dangerous train of thought begins again, another thought supersedes it: I'm a fool. He doesn't even know the worst thing about me, I remind myself. He doesn't know me at all, and he doesn't really care about me anyway.

"Yeah. Like I said: you're a witch. Plus, you started it," he blames me in a childlike tone.

"I did?"

"Yeah, you flirted with me first."

"I did not!"

"You totally did, man."

"Don't call me man!"

"I'm sorry, missus," he corrects himself in a facetious, over-obsequious tone just to mock me. And now everything's chill. But not really. But I'll let him off for now.

"Well, then, if I did, I wish I hadn't," I mutter sullenly like a child.

"I'll be around, don't worry," he assures me, stroking my face then standing up again. "Well, I ought to get going," he says. His voice rings sadly, but not because he's sad to leave me, but for a different reason I can't quite explain, except that it's something to do with my obvious unhappiness with him. But he's itching to leave all the same, so that he can return to his free and unfettered, natural state of being.

And this time, I know he really will leave, and there's no chance of keeping him, and I know it with that same sinking sadness, that familiar and mournful feeling of loss as last time, but there's no clinging, no desperation, even if the despair wrenches at my heart. I resign myself to the sadness and watch him go silently. But we both know this time it will be the last time, no matter what vacant assurances he's made. I ruined it with that single, cloyingly sentimental word: *love*.

I can't bear to watch him dress or gather his things. As I turn and look away at the wall, trying not to cry again, I can feel his eyes on my curled back. Because however aloof he is, he craves others' approval, I can tell. That's why he has so many friends and is always doing random things for them. But he doesn't actually want to give himself fully to anyone, or perhaps he doesn't have the capacity to do so because, like he said, he's fucked up and needs therapy. And don't we all? But then there are certainly lies mixed in with all of that. The same vacant and vague reassurances.

He doesn't need me. But I hadn't needed him either. I had secretly craved the whirlwind romance and falling in love, like any female who grew up on thrift-store Harlequin romance novels and Disney movies and Nora Ephron. But I had been just fine. I was untouchable when I was that frigid ice queen. Why did I have to go and ruin it?

After Joseph leaves, I only wallow in self-pity for about an hour. The tears are cathartic in a way, and then I'm able to move on to some other distraction with surprising mental clarity. And that newfangled chip on my shoulder is oddly motivating as I scroll through my phone and install Tinder.

Chapter Fifteen

So it's Tinder, then. That's what I've been reduced to. Tinder, with its infinite array of choices and endless swipes and crippling option paralysis. I resolve that surely there's a guy out there in a city of one million who is as good as Joseph. Or better, even.

After installing the app, creating a profile is necessary of course, before I can start the hunt for someone I've convinced myself exists somewhere in Portland, in some trendy neighborhood I've yet to explore, waiting for me just like I'm waiting for them, with the very same impatience and expectation. Someone who can help me totally forget about Joseph.

Naturally, I have to make sure I portray myself not only flatteringly, but also comprehensively and accurately, if I'm to have any success. So I go about the whole thing very pragmatically, and select close-up and full-body photos wearing minimal makeup and minimal clothing, to give the men on the other side of the app not only a good idea of what I really look like, but also how good I really look.

I'm rather cocky while setting it up because, after all, I get paid usually to have sex with men, and here I am advertising myself for free. So I don't think I'll have any issues finding someone as attractive as Joseph.

The mere thought of him causes my resentment to fester and increases my determination to extinguish him from my heart. But the truth is, if he came knocking on my door right then, or weeks later, even, I'd likely let him in with open arms and open legs. He might've broken my heart, but he didn't cut the string attached to it. If only I could willfully yank it out.

Tinder's fun at first—perusing the plethora of profiles and swiping through a colorful blur of faces in my frenzied pursuit—it's like some sort of game. Even the bad profiles are amusing, at least. And when I do match with someone, I feel a spike of endorphins at the validation it provides, and my heart races with exhilaration at the possibilities. So it's not only a source of entertainment, but an ego-boost as well. I can see why people get addicted to this shit.

I send Gertrude several screenshots of the more cringe-worthy men I find amusing, some dressed in furry costumes or fedoras, and others simply with ridiculous, misogynistic profile descriptions requesting only hookups and "no fatties," who will likely die horny and alone.

"You've really got the pick of the litter," Gertrude replies via text, but then adds, "At least they're straight." It's not often she actually alludes to her partner's closeted homosexuality. She must be feeling particularly deprived lately. I wonder if they've ever had sex at all.

I would broach the matter, but the subject seems too delicate, even for someone as frank as Gertrude.

So instead, I just reply, "Litter is a bit too on the nose, because they are all no more than infantile dogs."

After texting her, I sit back against my pillows and contemplate binging. The endless swiping has lost its allure after a couple of hours, and the threat of Joseph plaguing my thoughts again is imminent. And there he is. In my thoughts. My heart sinks abysmally.

I could just binge until I'm numb. The blackout that occurs while shoveling food into my mouth and preparing meals—as if on autopilot—provides a sort of bliss even Tinder cannot supply. A binge sounds good right about now, actually, since this swiping is taking too long, and the only attractive men I've swiped right on are catfishes, I think. Because they haven't even messaged me, even though most of them matched with me, and it's been a whole hour, and I'm beginning to second-guess my attractiveness. I'm certainly not messaging them first, but given how passive men in Portland are, I might be going through menopause by the time they ask me out, and this app will be obsolete by then. So I'm contemplating what else I could do with my night, and all the restaurants and stores that are still open where I could amass the perfect binge based upon what I've been craving lately. But the only thing I crave is Joseph.

Then something fortuitous occurs.

One of my regulars, a fifty-something-year-old, retired financial advisor stuck in a sexless marriage, texts me. Swearing off escorting was abandoned the moment Joseph rejected me.

"Can I take you out this evening?" he asks, always a true gentleman. And he pays me five hundred every time, no questions asked. He's one of the few that likes it to feel more like an arrangement than prostitution, and I'm happy to oblige. So we always go to dinner or coffee and brunch first, depending on the time of day.

I readily agree. Because I've been so distracted by Joseph lately, I've really slipped on the hustle, which would be the perfect form of distraction, were it not such a chore—erecting that façade and performing for those endless hours, suffering their agonizing company, when all I want is to be with that beautiful bastard Joseph.

And I know tonight will be harder than ever after seeing the light with him. But if he had stayed, what then? I couldn't just quit the hustle, however much I want to, because how will I continue making a living?

I'd been so deluded earlier, eager to abandon it all, if he'd only consented to love me.

But now I see some logic, at least. I see how illogical that desire was, is, and will be, knowing too that I'm still not off the hook.

Of course, the hustle can't continue forever. But I had hoped for more time to figure shit out. Like by thirty-two or so. A few more years to save and procrastinate until I'm too old. I'd never counted on wanting to stop, and I'd never been so captivated by a man before now. I'd never known what it meant to have good dick like that. It ruins a person. That good dick ruined me.

And my regular client, Roger, looks as old and ugly as ever when we meet for the date. His sagging face is speckled by age and white hair so thin it's semitransparent, revealing his smooth skull speckled by age spots beneath. He's a far cry from Joseph, that's for sure. And not only in age and appearance, but disposition as well. He's a Republican and misogynist who gets off on paying women almost a quarter of his age. Despite this, we have a nice cordial dinner at his favorite restaurant in the Pearl District, which serves tapas infused by truffle oil and squid ink and other stupid things I've never understood people liking, even after my assent from trailer trash to semi-bougie trash.

When the waitress brings our check, nausea pools in my stomach and I wonder if I'll be able to keep down the rich, buttery risotto I just ate, especially if he expects me to suck off his withered worm of a cock. I've been dreading this moment the whole time, like when I go to the doctor and have to get my blood drawn, and they're cleaning the spot of skin they'll pick, then poise their long, insidious needle, and so I lead him back to my apartment to get pricked by him.

The pricking is not as physically painful in an immediate way, like the doctor's needle, but it lasts far longer. Roger might have the urge, but he's not particularly virile, and he takes eons to finally cum, and the feeling of him inside me, and his wrinkled skin and slobbery, puckered mouth against me, feel sacrilegious after being with Joseph not even 24 hours before. I can't bear to look at him as he thrusts inside me, but he must notice I'm more deterred than usual, because he takes my chin in his hand and jerks my face towards him, so that we're looking at one another as he commands, "Look at me when I fuck you," his voice so raspy and inordinately cruel that something inside me quakes with fear. And I had thought he was a gentleman. But I'm a fool to think he's genuinely kind, when I really don't know anything about him except that he's married and inclined to cheat on his wife, and pays significantly younger women to do so, which doesn't exactly speak well of him.

I look at him obediently, though it kills me inside, and have to watch this stranger using me like a disposable and utilitarian vessel until he's done, and I'm rubbed raw inside so that the stray tear that's rolled down my cheek isn't from the worthlessness I feel or the inner turmoil, but from the pain he's unknowingly inflicted. This does happen sometimes. But usually, it's not as hard to take.

I've conditioned myself with all my flawless pragmatism to view myself as some utilitarian thing when I'm with him and with others, because if I didn't, I wouldn't be able to continue doing it for so long. It is necessary to detach myself from my own body and view it as a sort of object immune from desecration, because it isn't some sacred thing. It's the same as when you work for a company that abuses or underpays you, and you have to just accept it. You are the cog in a giant wheel, necessary but disposable. To degrade yourself as such allows you to keep clocking in every morning, to suffer the majority of your life there, to follow this routine so diligently without the slightest hint of rebellion for years and years and years on end. It's a wonder people don't crack more often. Some do, but most don't. And it's because of this mental conditioning.

I couldn't last long in all that again. I've tried my fair share of working class and service-industry jobs. I'd seen escorting as a form of temporary escape. But even now, I'm still a cog, and I'm realizing it now as brutally as ever when he finally gets ready to leave and hands me the cash, all in twenties, then plants a slimy kiss on my lips.

"Drive safe," I say sweetly as he goes, but really, I mean, "Get into a fatal car crash." I don't think I'll see him again. There are other fish in the sea. And they'll be waiting. But for now, I really need a break from all that.

"I can't do this anymore," I text Stephanie after I've showered to cleanse myself of his germs, and stripped my bed and gone through the usual cleansing routine. "I'm seriously so done," I text again after she doesn't immediately respond, much to my annoyance. This breed of fatalistic talk is not like me. Usually, she'd be the overdramatic one, saying tragic things about her relationship with Stephen or her business, only to bounce back in true Stephanie fashion the next day with an overly-optimistic mindset, and then only to come crashing down again some days later when all her vision-boarding didn't realize itself or tarot card readings come true. For the first time, I consider getting into that stuff I usually mock. Maybe a crystal, a deck of cards, a journal will solve all my problems.

"Hey bitch," she calls me up shortly after I've sent her that dramatic text. "What's going on? What can't you do anymore?"

Tears are already gathering as I try to form the words. "The site. The escorting. You know," I say feebly, trying not to crumble completely. I've always been the ice queen, the calm, cool voice of reason.

"Did something happen? Are you okay?" Typical Stephanie, to be concerned about my well-being. It's nice, though. I wish I could vent like this to my mom, because that's what I realize I crave. That maternal concern. Stephanie is the closest I can get for the time being. So I resolve to use her for that purpose, using her again. Just using, using, using for my own selfish and lonely needs. But now I understand how important friends are, and I want to do good by them more than ever so that I can keep them. And I feel a sudden outpouring of love for her that swells in my chest. And the same for Gertrude—I really ought to treat her soon; I have the money to do so now, I think, staring at the cash on my table. "You want to come over and talk about it?" she asks, and my heart swells with yet more love. I hide the cash after counting it, because the longer

I look at it, the more tainted-looking it becomes—the green ink lurid and the printed faces unsettlingly malevolent.

"Yes, please. Thank you," I sigh, and make the short trek to her apartment, where she's burning sage to cleanse the space of bad juju, I guess. Maybe I should ask for some and add it to my routine.

Stephen is sitting in his old man chair with his laptop and headphones on, likely listening to TED Talks or a stale documentary or whatever nerdy smart people watch in their free time.

"Smells like Thanksgiving," I say fondly but with a pang of sad nostalgia. Another reminder of the things I've sacrificed to forge my independence. I'm always alone for Thanksgiving unless a friend invites me to theirs, but it's not the same, and I feel like an outsider or orphan encroaching on another family's intimate gathering. But then, when I do go back home for Christmas, I feel like an outsider there as well. Like a misshapen puzzle piece that doesn't quite belong anywhere.

"My favorite holiday!" she brightens, but then her face darkens and tone shifts. "When it's not celebrating the mass killing and consumption of animals or glossing over the genocide of Native Americans. Fucking white people," Stephanie—a white person herself—adds, her voice dripping with self-righteous disgust. "And it's coming up soon!" she says, tone immediately brightening.

Stephanie always does a vegan shindig with all her other edgy witchy friends I don't fit in with. I think of Joseph and how nice it'd be to share the holidays away from home with him and how nice it must be for couples to have that sense of security in never being alone for anything, and I suddenly understand why most humans are so codependent. Before now, I used to just think they were all pathetic.

"Will you come?" she asks with earnest concern, because I know she wants me more than anyone to be there. She sits down and clasps my arm and looks into my eyes. Her big, blue, doll-like eyes are trembling with emotion, and I wonder where she gets it all—it seems exhausting. I'm emotional now, sure, but that was a recent thing, and I don't call myself the ice queen for nothing. "You're invited, of course."

"Oh, I don't know," I mumble noncommittedly, because the idea of a crowd and a party and all the jovial festivities seem suddenly horrible and terrifying. And then I'm unable to conceal the emotion in my fragile voice as the weight of the recent events suddenly crashes over me. I settle into the couch, feeling suddenly weak and on the verge of tears again.

"Hey! What's the matter? Is this about what you said on the phone? About the sex work stuff?" she says, lowering the volume of her voice to a clandestine but melodramatic whisper, even though we're in the privacy of her home and Stephen can't even hear us as he's got headphones on, and he knows about me prostituting myself anyway.

"I—" If I say it all, I know I'll cry. But she's staring at me and gripping my arm again. And this is why I came over, isn't it? For sympathy and consolation. To not feel so lonely, to not be left alone with the heavy darkness festering inside of me. To vent. "The guy I told you about. The guy I like. Joseph," I say in sentence fragments as I struggle to form the words, because the tears have already come pouring out. Sobs wrack my body, making it even more difficult to speak as I feel short of breath. "We slept together. Twice. And it was fucking incredible. But he doesn't actually want to be together. He—"

She's been following my every word with wide and frantic eyes up until then. "He's trash. Men," she grumbles in disgust, eyes narrowing hatefully, and I can tell she's only getting mad on my behalf, even though she doesn't even know the dude. And part of me is comforted by that.

Stephen looks up from his laptop when I fall apart because it's impossible to ignore. If I am an ice queen, then he is like a cold jellyfish, and my crying seems to both confuse and disconcert him. After staring

149

and blinking at me for a few seconds dumbfoundedly, he gets up and leaves the room.

"See?" Stephanie scoffs. "Men, I tell ya." Then her voice softens again. "I'm honestly surprised though. No one impresses you. I mean, sure, he was hot, but—"

"I didn't want to fall for him. I hadn't planned on it," I blubber irritably, more so at myself than her. "Someone in my position isn't exactly a good candidate for a relationship, you know. So I never seek it out. I can't afford to. Now I can barely stand to let my clients touch me." My lip quivers as I recount my evening with Roger. I've told her about my dates before, and how I go about escorting, because her curiosity was insatiable when I first started doing it. But now it just disgusts her, and I think she feels sorry for me, deep down, even though she's never said so.

"I guess there's no rhyme or reason to whom you fall in love with."

"Also, I downloaded Tinder," I confess, a deplorable feeling spreading through my insides.

"No," she says in a hushed whisper, she's so filled with disbelief. "Wait—" she says, sounding suddenly worried. "You didn't see me and Stephen on Tinder, did you?"

"God, no!" I say, cringing. "Not yet." It hadn't occurred to me that *that* was a possibility until now. It makes me feel creepy just thinking about it.

"Well, the door's always open," she says, wriggling her eyebrows lasciviously. She's always looking for an opportunity to implicate a threesome.

"Thanks, I think I'll be going now," I say with an exasperated chuckle.

"No, don't go yet. I was only kidding. Stay longer. Stephen's such a stick in the mud lately." I didn't know there was a time he wasn't a stick in the mud. "He won't fuck me."

"Maybe you should create a separate profile on Tinder just for yourself. You'll have more luck," I recommend.

I know from her venting in the past that the search for a unicorn is a largely unsuccessful one, hence why they're called unicorns by the polyamorous community.

"That's not funny," she remarks, utterly deadpan, turning suddenly cold towards me. "Stephen and I do everything together."

"Well, off I go."

"You don't have to," she says, warming up to me again at the prospect of me actually leaving.

"I know. But, really, thank you so much, Stephanie." I smile at her and take hold of her slender wrist. "You're a good friend. I'm lucky to have you." I state with newfound clarity, the headache from crying beginning to dissipate. "I mean it." She might annoy the hell out of me sometimes, but I'm still grateful to have her as a friend. "I'll visit you again soon, okay? Is that okay?"

"Duh."

"Bye, bitch," I chirp, now that I'm not a sobbing mess and can joke with her like we usually do.

"Byeeeee." And we're back to the way we were. But it takes an additional five minutes to actually get out the door. It's difficult to extricate oneself from her.

Chapter Sixteen

I think of how Joseph last extricated himself from me as I leave Stephanie's apartment complex. And the sinking abysmal sadness returns. But I don't need him, I tell myself resolutely. I have my friends. I have myself. I have Tinder. And apparently, I have a new match, I realize when I get home after stopping by the store to obtain some fancy expensive food with my latest earnings: vegan cupcakes, dark chocolate with rose petals and lavender, a salad box that looks like alien bunny food, and a latte from the coffee shop across the street, of course. I foolishly tell myself I won't purge this time because the food is far too aesthetic and high-quality.

It's cold now. It's not just all fun and games and apple cider donuts and colorful dead leaves anymore. The leaves are rotting, and the trees are skeletons, and Halloween's come and passed. And the sun has gone into hibernation until spring. People have retired their sailboats and jetskis and hiking gear and bathing suits and kayaks, and the waterfront is no longer filled with festivals and farmer's markets and festivities. And cuffing season has just begun.

My match has a handsome enough face, though I do find myself comparing it to Joseph's in spite of my resolution not to. He has a strong jawline, at least, and deep blue eyes. And on his profile, he claims he's 6'7" so I agree to go on a date with him tomorrow night. I can't to do tonight because I've already committed to a mini-binge, which will likely lead to a downward spiral I'll need 24 hours to recover from. I've never had sex with a man that tall, I realize, and the novelty of it alone appeals to me. I think to myself, maybe this is the one hot enough to magically extinguish Joseph from my thoughts.

A prospective client has also messaged me to meet tomorrow evening around the same time, but I try to schedule with him at a later date because I can tell from his single, blurry photo he's ugly and enormous and thirty years my senior, and I just don't have it in me at the moment.

The extremely tall man and I agree to meet at a restaurant in town famous for its Thai food, even though the owner is Caucasian in a city full of authentic Thai restaurants run by actual Thai people. But its kitschy hip décor and overpriced food seems to be more palatable to white Portlanders, and apparently to my date.

He isn't there when I arrive, wearing my skimpy dress which could easily pass for lingerie and a trench coat and thigh-high boots, because it's colder than a witch's tit right now. I had expected to feel unwaveringly confident during this date—and that I was doing this nonpaying but obscenely tall pedestrian a favor just gracing him with my presence—but he's late. And I'm in this skimpy sexy getup waiting on him in the freezing cold, and I feel even more self-conscious than when I've waited on my clients on street corners and people look at me strangely. I know what they're thinking, the people passing by; they're thinking I look like a prostitute, and they're wondering if I am one, and I feel like I'm getting those same looks now, and he's not even paying me for this. Tonight, there will be no solicitation.

When he finally arrives, he is very tall, I'll give him that. So tall that people stop and turn to get a second look at him as he breezes past. But he isn't nearly as attractive as his profile picture deceptively suggested, and I realize he must've gained at least twenty pounds since posting those photos. His formerly defined jawline has converged with his soft neck.

I'm fit and slender, so I like men who are fit and slim as well. Sue me. And Joseph was so lean, his face so chiseled and body so lithe as he moved against me and held me close—but I can't think of that now. I have to be civil with this Tinder date, even if he was deceptive.

I compose myself and go to meet him. He recognizes me instantly and his face lights up. "Eve!" he greets me, and then my heart plummets to my stomach as I realize with doom that I haven't the faintest memory of what his name is. He pulls me into a side-hug I think is a smidge too familiar, considering we've only just met, and I'm definitely not attracted to him, and I'm already contemplating my escape, and also need to figure out his name, probably.

When we get our table, I don't sit down. "I need to run to the restroom to wash up real quick. I'll be right back." I give him the same coy smile I give my clients, which is pitiful—I'm fake-flirting when I ought to be genuinely attracted to him and having a good time. And I certainly shouldn't feel pressured to act like I like him, considering I'm not being paid.

On the toilet I pull up his Tinder. I guess that the name is something common like Mike or Andrew or John, but then gasp with horror when I read that it's Gerald. What kind of name is that? It almost makes me feel sorry for him. Then I scroll and I find I do actually possess empathy, because when I re-read his bio, I recall how he's looking for a serious relationship, and complains about being stood up or flaked on and ghosted, which is really pathetic, actually, that he'd admit to that on a dating site for thousands to see. And it makes me reluctant to flake on him, to fulfill that complaint written with such resigned and passive-aggressive exasperation. Even though I don't know this man and he means nothing to me. But I find that I can't muster the courage or the cruelty to leave the restaurant through the back door and abandon him as I had planned. And when I return to the table, I don't come up with some excuse to flake because he looks so hopeful when he sees me, even if he also looks a little cocky, this fool named Gerald.

"Gerald!" I repeat the awful name.

Then he begins asking me the usual loathsome laundry list of questions like what my hobbies are and where I come from and what I do. When he gets to the subject of my employment, I lie and say, "I'm actually in between jobs right now, so I guess I'm technically unemployed." I pull a pained, wincing look as I say this. Being unemployed is, after all, perceived negatively by society, so I have to pretend the fact is disconcerting, or embarrassing. Even though if I told him my real occupation, he'd likely be far more disconcerted, if not repulsed enough to walk out himself, and that would solve my problem, wouldn't it? But I find that I'm actually worried about his perception of me, even though I don't want to have sex with this dude. I don't want to be judged. I don't want to relive that experience with Ricky.

So I lie.

He orders the fish sauce wings the restaurant is known for, and I almost gag as I watch him eat them like an animal and catch a whiff of the fishy aroma. I try to daintily tackle the khao soi I ordered, but I probably look just as uncultured as I struggle to slurp the soupy noodles. We eat mostly in silence.

"Wanna go Dutch?" he casually remarks when the check finally arrives, whilst sucking on one of the bones from his chicken wings, so stingy he's determined to suck off every spare ounce of flesh.

"Say what?" I blurt without thinking, staring at him as he continues to suck. I don't know which is more confounding.

He had said he was a software engineer—which means he makes more than enough to take a girl out on a date at a mid-range restaurant. And he had even suggested the place. And he had asked me out. And the nerve to suggest that I pay for my dinner while knowing I'm supposedly currently unemployed is heinous beyond belief.

"Oh, you don't know what that is?"

"Umm," I mutter, stalling because I realize how strange my reaction probably just was if I do in fact know what going Dutch means.

I should've flaked while I had the chance, and now I understand why he's failed in love. "No," I giggle innocently, feigning ignorance. "What is it? Some kind of sex position?" I ask with a shaky laugh.

"No," he laughs with ease, and how dare he, I think, as my anger rises behind my innocent, unassuming smile. "It means we split the bill. It's usually how I go about it; takes away the awkwardness."

"Does it?" I chirp in a strangled whisper as I look at my bill, which totals almost twenty-five dollars—which won't exactly break the bank, but it's enough to make me feel both offended and swindled, considering I've basically had to pay to not enjoy myself. Besides, I ain't Dutch, and I'm pretty sure Dutch people would take offense to the phrase commonly used in America.

And then, as we leave the restaurant and stand outside awkwardly on the cold street, and I'm already gripping my phone in my pocket with the intention of checking the bus schedule or ordering a Lyft, he has the nerve to suggest, "So, do you want to go back to my place?" in the same idle yet brazen manner he suggested we split the bill.

"What?" I stammer. And again, I'm just so dumbfounded by the nerve of this entitled tower of a man. "I—no—no thank you," I state, nearly wavering. To be so confrontational as a woman takes some effort, and I can feel my heart pulsing in my throat, all my wit suddenly failing me. I must strive to summon it so I can drum up some cruel remark.

"Oh, well, okay, that's cool. Just wanted to offer."

"I'm sure it would've been a huge service to me," I find myself retorting sarcastically, then add before he has a chance to respond. "I'll be going now." And make sure to walk away in the opposite direction he came from when he first arrived, ten minutes late. And I make sure to unmatch him before he can do the same.

I do reap some pleasure, at least, from that dumbstruck look he'd worn on his stupid face after my cutting riposte, before turning to leave him. And the drama of it is somewhat exciting. But not as exciting as receiving five crisp Benjamins for lying naked in the comfort of my own bed.

While the thrill had certainly waned the last time I met with a client, and the inner turmoil had increased, the money no longer seems as tainted as it did. I much prefer the solicitation, rather than wasting two hours of my life with some average Joe I'm not attracted to either. It hardly makes dating seem worthwhile.

But at least dating offers some fresh perspective. After Joseph, I needed something to get me back on track and realize how good I actually have it. But I'm still spoiled and discontent. I still want to find someone to fuck that I'm actually attracted to. I feel owed that, as an attractive young female in her prime.

But there are more matches and dates to go on, and I find the endless swiping oddly addicting. The longer I swipe, and the more dates I go on, the more I suspect the app is built to keep people single rather than in a relationship and therefore off the godforsaken app. It's a great marketing scheme. Most people seem to use it for hookups and finding friends or another partner to join their polyamorous circle anyway, so they have no intention of getting off the app. And Portland is the perfect cesspool for the online dating industry.

"It's called option paralysis. I read about it in a book once," I inform a guy I'm on a brunch date with one lovely Saturday afternoon. Since my first debacle of a date, I've resolved to make it clear who's paying for whom from the get-go, and if they don't like it, they can unmatch with me and fuck off. It's a certain kind of male I'm looking for anyway. One that can afford to pay and wants to—and also wants to open doors and take control and fuck my brains out. Otherwise, I'm not remotely interested in them, and it's best we don't waste each other's precious time.

The only reason women need men, after all, besides their vital sperm, is to dominate and provide for them, to use all that muscle and strength which we females were (usually) deprived of evolutionarily. Otherwise, they're obsolete.

And this guy I'm currently with has all the muscle and, in addition to being tall, has long beautiful hair, even more beautiful than mine. He looks a bit like Tarzan all cleaned up, with his sharp jawline and long chin and brooding brow and just the barest shadow of stubble that I long to graze my hand against. I'm getting excited.

I can feel myself becoming aroused again as I take him in in quick, flirtatious glances, and I feel my sexuality gradually awakening from its dormancy. I wasn't sure if it'd be in a perpetual hibernation, given the seemingly endless string of disappointing dates I've been on. This must be the tenth or eleventh date. And what's more, it's retreated further and further inside of me with horror. There was the guy with body odor, and the other with hideous breath, and both kissed me at the end without me giving any indication that I wanted them to, and I almost retched during both tortuous experiences. And there was yet another that asked me about my sexual preferences before the appetizers arrived and bragged about his sexual prowess despite being shorter than I was, and totally out of shape, which meant he couldn't run a mile let alone possess the stamina to satisfy a woman.

You might think all these contemplations are sexist—and they are—because the bottom line is, men suck, but we need them to some extent, obviously, and really, they can't help it. But I can help getting in unnecessarily taxing scenarios, and I've strived to do so after one too many disappointments. Now, I also make sure to ask their height before meeting them, which takes some degree of finesse because it's perceived as rude and superficial to fixate on height. And I can screen them by hobbies, too, and make sure they like outdoor activities or lifting or running so they don't have dad bods without having children—another thing I screen for, because I hate children.

"Option paralysis?" he asks confusedly with a quizzical brow and open smile that reveals his perfectly straight, white teeth, and my heart flutters, even though he's obviously not very bright. This bemused smile of his, as charming as it is, has appeared several times already every time I use a word over three syllables.

"Yeah. It's only a recent phenomenon of modern society that we as humans are faced by seemingly endless options. But our brains didn't evolve to make decisions that way, so instead of it being useful or advantageous for us, it results in us not being able to make a decision, so we're paralyzed by that indecision. And then we refuse to settle because of the delusion that there are all these other potentially better options out there waiting for us." I have been reading more lately. I've been doing a lot more things lately. Including visiting Charlotte at the nursing home, who really gets a crack out of all these horrible dates I've been going on.

"But don't you think it's for the better?" he asks after some deliberation. "I mean, the opportunity of finding your soulmate…"

"You believe in soulmates?" I ask, leaning back and smiling at him, amused by the quaint concept. I think of Joseph, and my heart wrenches in spite of myself, but he wasn't my soulmate. Even with him, I'm a staunch skeptic. We weren't destined to be together. We weren't tied by some inextricable red string of fate. Divination and horoscopes aren't real. Otherwise, it might've worked out between us. Otherwise, romance wouldn't seem so illusory and simultaneously contrived, and like it only exists in fantasies and romantic comedies.

"Yeah, maybe, I guess. I'd like to," he says noncommittedly, but maybe it's because of the incredulous, judgmental look I'm giving him. He laughs self-consciously, and I feel suddenly guilty for being so cynical and making fun of him.

"That's pretty optimistic of you," I remark, modulating my tone to not sound so judgmental, and more impressed instead. I hold his gaze and I see that he is a good person. And I know then that I do want to fuck him. Even if he's not the brightest bulb on the tree. And I also wonder at what brand of conditioner he uses. If we fuck at his place, I can look in his bathroom and find out. "You said you live around here?"

"Yeah, just around the block," he says, smiling.

"We're practically neighbors then." I deepen my voice so that it sounds sultry and intriguing, and I try to communicate with my eyes my intentions in that implicating tone.

"I noticed when we matched that we were only a mile away from each other."

"Stalker," I tease, playfully nudging his leg with my foot.

"Yeah," he chuckles, holding my gaze again, and his pretty blue eyes practically twinkle. I can see the dark of his pupils dilate as we stare at one another, and even though witty retorts seem to elude him, and though our conversation is staler than old bread, there is something about those smoldering eyes looking into mine that unravels me. A man need only a hot body and piercing gaze, no wits necessary. Joseph just happened to be graced by all three. And that's probably what made him so slippery and insufferable, too, plagued by existential angst and commitment issues and a jaded mentality when it comes to romance.

"Well, I can't promise I'm your soulmate, Daniel. But you do make me feel a certain kind of way…"

"Oh yeah?" he responds, a little taken aback. But not in a bad way. His eyes light up and he leans closer to me from across the table, then reaches for my knee beneath it. He traces his hand up my thigh, along the line of my inseam, until it's only inches from my crotch. Even through the thick material of my blue jeans, the sensation makes a shiver of pleasure inch up through me down to the wick. It's burning now. "Would you like to see my place? I can at least make you some coffee."

"I've already had too much caffeine. But I'm always up for more."

We both seem to be coffee addicts. Maybe we *are* soulmates after all. I begin to fantasize about all the possibilities. I look outside the window of the brunch restaurant we're at on Alberta and wonder what it would be like to walk down the street with him, arm and arm, after a late lazy Sunday morning, watching the women passing by with their jealous looks and the smell of sex still lingering on our skin. I realize I haven't entertained this sort of fantasy since Joseph.

"Me too," he says, lifting his brow as if to imply something more. And then I quickly realize coffee has become a euphemism for sex.

He takes care of the check without question, without any awkward pause, without any quibbling. I could scream with happiness. "You ready to head out?" he asks, standing up and towering above me.

I've never seen myself as all that sexual. That might be surprising, given my vocation, and the fact that, currently, sex seems to be my sole impetus. But it wasn't always like this, before I'd known how nice it could be, even after having hundreds of sexual partners. Then I got ruined by that good dick. It was better when I was a frigid ice queen. I was more powerful and controlled then and could exploit men much more easily. My mind was more lucid and focused, my pussy a dry and unsacred vessel, and my heart a frozen desert which could not be penetrated.

During our walk to his apartment, once he's let me inside and given me the tour—it isn't that big, but still much larger and nicer than my own—and guided me to his kitchen, where he actually does start assembling a pour over, right down to grinding the beans, I feel a sense of urgency and anticipation. Will this actually happen? Will something go wrong? Will the outside world disturb this intimate yet fragile bubble we've somehow magically created within an hour-long brunch date?

He turns on some music. Soft, lo-fi jazz starts playing, thrumming through us, reverberant and intermingling with the rainlike trickle of the steam filtering through the coffee grounds. The aroma fills the room. I feel my limbs slacken and anxiety dissipate. He hands me the mug and I grip the warmth in my hands, and he sneaks a hand behind me and traces it up my back, and his brooding eyes look so sultry all of a sudden. The thrilling sensation his touch elicits snakes up my spine and lingers long after he moves away from me and goes to the living room. And I follow as if in a trance. He looks good barefoot, with his pants riding low on his narrow hips, and his shirt hanging off the muscles of his brawny back, only just barely clinging to them to tease me. I kick off my sneakers and sit down beside him, and when he finally looks at me, filled with purpose, and kisses me, we both taste like bitter coffee, and we both seem to unravel, and I wonder if he craves this release as much as I do. He seems to suggest that he does in the deep and throaty moan that escapes from his throat, into my own, and echoing through me like the delicious pleasure that throbs even deeper within. This is it. Every fiber of my being seems to awaken and vibrate.

Then he hitches me up around his waist, stands, and carries me to his bed. I've never been carried before, probably because the vast majority of my clients and men in general lack the strength to do so because of my thin but not-so-tiny-frame.

And to be carried by a man is unbelievably hot. I'm learning I have all sorts of kinks I never knew about. Adam's apples, arm veins, clavicles and scratchy woolen sweaters being a few others, thanks to good ole Joseph.

He urges me out of my clothes, and I let out an impatient noise, akin to a petulant child, at his still being dressed. I help pull his t-shirt over his head. He's got a six-pack. Even Joseph didn't have a six-pack. And his dick is huge, and beautiful, and rock-hard. It's perhaps not quite as beautiful as Joseph's, but that's only because I, admittedly, still haven't quite gotten over him. But maybe now I will.

When I'm fully naked, I feel suddenly self-conscious.

"Hey, you okay?" he asks.

"Huh? Yeah. Of course. Why?"

"You just looked distracted all of a sudden, like your mind was somewhere else."

"Sorry. Work stuff. Been a bit overwhelmed." I saw a client last night, and the sordid act feels too fresh and palpable on my naked skin. And then there's Joseph looming in my thoughts. But he doesn't have to know about that.

"I thought you were in-between jobs," he says with the barest hint of suspicion creeping into his interrogative tone. Shit. I had forgotten what I told him when we first started messaging weeks ago and went through the usual tedious introductory questions.

"R-right, I'm stressed about looking for work, I meant."

I am stressed about work though. That wasn't a lie. Most of my regulars have gone suddenly MIA—though it's no surprise, as I've cancelled on them repeatedly and don't put on such a convincing façade anymore. The last few times I moaned only halfheartedly and didn't even pretend to come. The last client was even reluctant to give me my money, I gave such a shoddy performance. And the site's hit a bit of a lull, and likely will until December.

After an awkward silence follows, he says, "Hey, if you're not feeling into it, it's perfectly fine if you want to stop. I won't be mad."

"No. I want this. I do. So much," I exclaim, pulling him back towards me and down onto the bed. But the action of saying those words in an attempt to convince him makes me realize I'm trying to convince myself even more. I keep reassuring myself of his hotness—dwelling on it—and how having sex with him will cure me of Joseph once and for all. And the knowledge of all that seems to deflate my arousal. And then there's something else that deters me. Something about him claiming he won't be mad, as if he ought to—the implication alone bothers me. I'd have more patience for that sort of remark with my clients because they can say or do whatever tickles their pickles, short of physically hurting me, so long as they pay.

And then it all goes downhill from there. He doesn't kiss me or touch me much before putting a condom on and prying my legs open. He doesn't even ask me what I want besides, "Are you sure?" a couple more times, like that makes him an honorary feminist or something. Then he's thrusting inside of me with a vengeance while gazing at me with those searing ocean blue eyes, and his long beautiful Tarzan tresses draping over his shoulders onto me. It helps that he's gorgeous, but something's still off. He's not passionate or caring or sultry like Joseph, whom I try to put out of my head to focus on Tarzan, I mean Daniel—that's his name, I think—but just as I get going and try to adjust to his erratic rhythm, he thrusts very hard inside of me as he orgasms and stays there buried deep inside, his cock so huge it feels like he's perforated my insides. It's painful. And I'm fairly certain it's not been two minutes since we took our clothes off.

Well, good for him.

He gets up, and his cock slips out of me so suddenly the effect is jarring. He goes to the bathroom without saying anything, so I'm left lying in the bed sore and alone, wondering when he'll be back, and what's supposed to happen now. And as I lie there, trying to work up the resolve to put on my clothes and leave while he's still in the shower, I find that I can't, and I'm rendered immobile by pure shock. He hadn't even tried to make me cum. He hadn't asked if it felt okay, or given me warning that he was about to cum. Even after having asked more than once if I wanted this. Well, now I regret it.

I begin to cry as I sit up and try to gather my things as quickly as possible. I don't want to cry at first, but I feel so pitiful, and the tears are pressing insistently at the rim of my watery eyes, and as I bend down to get my panties, the downward force seems to finally wring them out of me. I miss Joseph. But then, even Joseph had discarded me. And now

I'm worse off for it, trying to get my fix, only to be yet more disappointed and unfulfilled.

I'm embarrassed about the crying, at first, but quickly resolve to let this Daniel guy see me in this wretched state when he does finally get back from the shower, which I hear running in the next room. I want him to see at least how bad it was for me so that it will hopefully take his ego down a few notches. There must be something emasculating about a man failing to fulfil his sexual partner and making them cry afterwards, so I am compelled to throw it in his face.

"Hey," he says, coming out of the bathroom with stringy wet hair and a towel around his waist. I realize then how rude it was of him to abort me so suddenly like that. He doesn't notice me crying at first. Oblivious idiot. "Sorry, I always have to shower right after. I don't know why. Weird habit." Then he actually sees me as I sit at the bed in my bra and panties, half-dressed, and searching ineffectually for my shirt on the floor with tears staining my face. "What's wrong?"

"You just left. You fucked me then got up and left. And you didn't even ask me if I was enjoying it."

He finds the shirt I've been searching for beside him, hidden beneath the comforter that's spilled on the floor.

"Well, I figured that was up to you. If you want something, you have to tell people. That's generally how it works. It's not my fault you weren't communicative," he states logically, as if it's perfectly sensible, and without an ounce of defensiveness, because he is somehow utterly convinced he's not to blame.

"Seriously?" I bark back, my lip trembling, and feeling smaller and sillier than ever with my wet red blubbering face, and the fact that I haven't got a good riposte. Even if what he's said does sound logical, he still sounds like a jerk, but saying so would only sound juvenile. A wise man once said that when the debate is lost, slander becomes the tool of the loser. Well, I guess I'm a big fat loser, because as I stand up and slip

165

on my clothes, I say, in a voice dripping with venom, "That's a very eloquent excuse for not being able to get a woman off. I bet you don't even know how." Of course my resentment also stems from feeling as if I've been cheated—I'm accustomed to being paid for sex, after all, so the fact that he got something from it, and I didn't, not even an orgasm, is especially infuriating.

"I think you should go," he says solemnly, and I leave, feeling as if I've been kicked out. As I sit at the corner, waiting on the bus, his musky sweat still a dewy mist on my skin, I feel tears threatening to discompose me again. I look over sullenly at some broken furniture that's been thrown out on the sidewalk and left to be rained on, and it does begin to rain, and I feel an outpouring of sympathy for the furniture, and pity for myself, and I feel more discarded than ever.

Chapter Seventeen

There were more dates. There was more disappointment. There were far too many futile attempts at feeling something—anything—in blind encounters and mindless hookups. But these fruitless endeavors did teach me something, so perhaps they weren't so fruitless after all.

Other dates were simply lessons of really how worthless the men in Portland—or perhaps men in general—are.

On one particular date, the guy shows up twenty minutes late, just as I am about to throw in the towel and angrily storm out. I'm at the bar waiting on him, and I'm forced to buy a drink and start my own tab in his absence.

I could stall, but then the bartender would know I was waiting on someone, and if that someone didn't show, it would be obvious I've been stood up. I'm just not in the state to deal with that kind of humiliation.

When he does finally arrive, I regret waiting for him and ordering the drink. He's shorter than I am, even though he told me he was 5'10" and was pictured in group photos with much shorter friends. Apparently, he's an excellent curator.

I don't understand why he wouldn't be upfront about his height online, as it probably leads to a lot of rejection and wasted time in the end, regardless. But then, perhaps, it's a more nuanced technique I'm not aware of. A game of numbers and blind chance.

When I stand up reluctantly to greet him, my head towers above his. I must be at least three inches taller than he is, and I'm not even that tall.

"Hi, sorry I'm late," he says, looking up at me, and seeming both relieved and excited as he takes me in. He doesn't seem to notice my unimpressed expression.

"It's no big deal," I answer brusquely, then find myself muttering snidely, "let's just get this over with." Usually, I wouldn't be such a cunt right off the bat, but my patience has worn so thin and my frustration so ripe, I've lost all motor control of my big fat mouth.

"Umm, wow, okay," he mumbles with an affronted look, sitting down reluctantly as it dawns on his face that this is not going to be a fun time for him. "Did you already start a tab?"

"Yeah," I say, then realize I closed it out already because I was about to leave when he showed up. But I decide not to mention this, thinking it unimportant, and hoping he'll at least have the manners to spot me another drink.

The bartender comes and asks him what he wants.

He glances at the food menu then says, "I'll take whatever good IPA you have and a burger."

He reaches into his pants then looks at me anxiously, but there's something about it all that feels oddly rehearsed. "Oh shit, I forgot my wallet. Can you spot me this round? I'll get you next time." He puts his arm down and smiles at the bartender, who's wearing a kill-me expression and doesn't care where this conversation goes one way or the other; he's probably just counting the minutes until he can get a smoke break. And I'm shocked and offended that he'd so readily assume a lady would spot him. Doesn't he know anything about the gender pay gap or male chivalry? But this is Portland. This sort of situation was inevitable, and I was too naive to think otherwise.

I waver for a moment, but not for long. "No. I don't think so."

"What?" he says with as much shock as I felt when he had the nerve to ask me to pay. He had expected me to eagerly oblige him. He didn't count on me being a prostitute though, so I'm not accustomed to this sort of thing, nor am I obliging. To be fair, I've neglected to put certain information on my profile as well.

"There's not going to be a next time," I tell him in a clipped voice, gathering my things and standing up.

By now, the bartender has snapped out of his Zoloft and weed-induced fog. He glances at the dumbfounded Tinder idiot and then back at me fixedly, waiting to see what I'll do next. The power I wield in this interaction feels good, at least.

I recall once again that I've already closed my tab—how convenient—and get up to leave him there. I hope that he feels mortified and hungry.

But as I leave, that power-high quickly fades, more ephemeral than my morning caffeine fix. And I'm still out five bucks for the beer I'd nursed, and the twenty or so minutes I lost. But it won't happen again, I resolve, and delete the app with a feeling of resigned finality.

"I've discovered I'm fucked up," I tell Gertrude matter-of-factly one day not long after that last failed date, which made me swear off dating once and for all.

"Wow, and it took you this long to figure that out?"

"Hey!" I shout because of that smug, omniscient look she sometimes gets on her face.

"What? We're all fucked up, honey."

"I've realized I can't get off with anyone, or even like anyone, because I'm wired to view sex only as a means for money, and love seems like a waste of time. So I can't even enjoy sex."

"Maybe you're just picky. You enjoyed it with that Joe guy," she points out encouragingly, but I can feel the doubt creeping into that hopeful tone.

"Joseph," I correct her, nausea pooling in my gut at the mere mention of his name, even still, over a month later. When we'd met, it was barely fall. Now the trees are stripped bare, the world desolate. I watch a man outside scraping his windshield. We're in a residential neighborhood in a coffee shop in an old craftsman home decked out with Christmas lights already. I always hated Christmas. I hate things most people associate with joy and fun—like children and holidays and musicals. So I had figured I would've gotten over him by now.

"I had known there would be consequences to all my shenanigans. I just hadn't accounted for this one."

"What—falling in love?" Gertrude asks.

"Well, yes, it's a complication. But, more so, the inability to. I can't be falling in love with people because of the sex work stuff. And also, because deep down I don't want to get hurt. Maybe I only fell for Joseph because I knew he would never reciprocate."

"Whoa, that *is* fucked up. Hey, maybe that's what I was doing with Colin, but for a different reason. I knew he was gay, and so I knew he could never truly reject me, even if he's not actually remotely attracted to me, it's not the same rejection of a heterosexual man."

"You fear rejection too?" I say, hiding the fact that I'm shocked she's finally said it out loud—Colin being gay, I mean. Maybe she's just recently accepted the fact.

"Well, yeah." She stares at me blankly, blinking in shock at my own question, as if it's the stupidest question in the world and the answer is crystal-clear. "I'm not good-looking. Of course I fear rejection. I've gotten too much of it in my life already," then she looks away, because suddenly everything is too real. And I realize then how we rarely actually talk about her feelings. I'm usually just venting about my own, too selfish to truly look at my friend. I feel a sinking guilt in my chest at having neglected her in some capacity. But I'm also realizing she doesn't like talking about herself. I'm like that too with some people, but not her. It's like a surgical extraction when I go on my rants to her, painful but necessary, and which I'm compelled to do for some reason.

"Let me buy us another round of lattes," I offer, trying to make up for my past negligence. "What do you want? Or if you're hungry, I'll treat you to lunch," I offer with an outpouring of affection for her, and a pressing need to show it.

"That's sweet. I have to head out, though. And don't you have a meeting?"

"Oh crap!" I had forgotten it was Tuesday. I always forget the days. On Tuesday, I go to visit Charlotte at the nursing home, which is on the other side of town. Part of me doesn't feel like rushing over there, but then I imagine the fiery little French woman's disappointment, and it twists at my conscience. "You're right. Thank you," I say as we both gather our things. "Next time, then?"

"Can you afford it?" she asks dubiously, and I remember how I texted her yesterday about not making much money lately. And it's true. I've been struggling not only to get clients but to force myself to meet them. I've resorted to stripping more, but only once every couple of weeks, and even that has become such a chore, I can hardly muster the motivation to do it. Crawling onto a stage in front of dozens of ogling spectators is no easier than crawling into bed with a stranger.

"I really should've gone to college," I mutter to myself jokingly as I leave the coffee shop and head to the nursing home. Charlotte is sitting up in her bed. She seems to have improved since I started visiting her more frequently. She sits up more and looks more alert. And whenever I arrive, her face visibly brightens.

"Any exciting new dates?" Charlotte asks excitedly as I close the door behind me.

"None. Only the same disappointments. And mediocre sex."

"The men here, they are mediocre," she says with a derisive noise. "I never told you about Thomas, did I?"

"*Non. Dites-moi, qui était-il?*" I ask, blushing. I still feel self-conscious speaking what little I've learned in my classes around her. She's fluent, after all.

"Ah, your enunciation is much improved," she tells me, beaming in an almost maternal way. "He was *l'amour de ma vie*," she says nonchalantly, perhaps because she wants to seem cavalier about such a bold statement. It only makes it all the more intriguing. "I met him here. In Portland. I was traveling around all of America by myself. During that time, I was a bit of a gypsy. But I guess it was during the hippie days. Free love, so they called it," she says fondly.

"We happened to be sitting next to each other at a bar and I realized I didn't have enough cash for the food I ordered."

Funnily enough, the opposite of what happened to me at my last comedically catastrophic date happened to her. When it's the man spotting the woman, it's so much more romantic. "So he paid, and even ordered me a slice of pie and another glass of wine. We made love that night."

"So risqué."

She waves her hand, giggling, and she looks suddenly youthful in spite of her wrinkles.

"Next thing I knew, I was pregnant. We were very negligent then about contraceptives. Then he told me his family would never accept an outsider, let alone a moneyless, pregnant one."

"But *he* knocked you up!" I say incredulously, getting angry on her behalf, even though this was technically over fifty years ago.

"*Oui.* That was how it was back then. It was shameful for the woman but not the man, even in the sixties. Contraception wasn't so easy then. Abortion...next to impossible." She gestures vaguely as she pronounces the word in French. "But I got my Collette out of it at least. She is old now, like me, but I forget sometimes. When you came in that first day, I thought it was her," she says, smiling at me fondly. Since that first day, she's told me all about how Collette decided to move to Paris when she came of age and bore resentment towards her mother for not taking her there as a child, because they were French and there was nothing good for them in America—her father had deserted her after all before she was even born.

"You kids now practically live in an amusement park with no consequences. Complicated!" she scoffs at me again, refusing to let that remark I'd made go. "It's too easy, if anything. Far too easy. You have the world at your fingertips and for what?"

"For what?" I repeat, mulling over those two words as I balance the phone in my hands. That comforting weight and sleek rectangular compactness. "We're worse for it." She hums in agreement, and as if on cue, my phone vibrates with a new text from my buddy David, asking me if I want to reserve a spot on the stage tonight. Tuesday, not the most happening night, and I'm guessing he's low on dancers because of that. But I need the money, I remind myself as I hesitate with my phone clutched in my hands.

"What's wrong?" she asks.

"A lot of things. But right now, I'm debating if I should go into work tonight. I need the money."

"Work?" she asks inquisitively. She's let me come in here and invade her privacy. She's practically divulged her entire life to me. And I've told her nothing. "You know, I've never asked you about what work you do."

"You don't want to know."

She waits patiently anyhow.

I sigh deeply as I decide to tell her—not the whole truth in its ugly entirety, but the half of it, at least. "I'm a stripper," I state in a voice leeched of feeling. I watch as her delicate, creased face remains as serene as ever. "And, sometimes, I also sleep with men—for money. Lots of money, actually," I add as the urge to tell her the whole truth suddenly weighs upon my chest irresistibly and comes pouring out in spite of my previous resolution not to tell her. But I still haven't told her about Joseph, and don't plan to quite yet. Because, for some reason, the ideas of rejection and failure and vulnerability are more humiliating than the shame of prostitution.

"Well then, my dear," she begins resignedly, and then in a soft, sad voice whispers, "you're smarter than I thought. But you are very lonely, aren't you?"

Chapter Eighteen

Now picture this: I'm on the stage and it's 6:00 p.m.—as slow as it gets—only a couple trucker-type guys sitting bleary-eyed in the back, nursing their Rainiers, watching me, wearing sullen yet depraved expressions. The low bass music is thrumming and thudding through my leaden body as I move up and down on that pole sticky with the fingerprints of countless girls turning their tricks and spinning their vacant dreams. Me—I have none.

Now that it's December, it gets dark at four o'clock. The only other dancer on the floor is a strung-out girl named Peaches with a juicy booty curdled with cellulite that customers gag over. If she stays on her pills long enough, though, it'll probably get not-so-juicy. I've noticed she's already dropped about ten pounds since getting hooked on fentanyl. I was never one to get into all that stuff—though I've got my own host of addictions—likely because I approached the field of sex-work with pragmatism and intention. I didn't resort to it out of desperation for my next fix, whether it be pills or booze or weed or coke. But coked-out, strung-out girls like Peaches make better strippers, and men love their frantic prancing. Meanwhile, I've gotten even less motivated lately.

And with a night as slow as tonight, I predict I'll leave with four hundred, if I'm lucky.

At least my buddy David has good taste in music. Half the reason he opened the place up was so he could play DJ. He winks at me from across the expansive room, all dark and sinister-looking behind the bar, beyond the men sitting nursing their beers and leering at us. I can see David tampering with the music and lights. The music switches to "my boy" by Billie Eilish as the lights change color, flickering from fluorescent blue to a deep magenta. He knows this is my type of music. He wants me to try harder.

I do a slow, deep-squat to the floor. I can't twerk like Peaches, so I gyrate to the beat of the music with a coy smile that inspires a catcall from the audience. I can even do a few pole tricks when I have enough energy. But tonight, I feel frail and weary. I do a half-hearted twirl around the pole.

Then I freeze when I look out at the audience and see him: Joseph. But my eyes must be playing tricks on me and giving me illusory visions. Or perhaps it's the exhaustion from dancing on an empty stomach. It can't be him.

I dare to look again, my heart racing even faster than before. It's pounding in my ears as I meet that piercing gaze. His eyes penetrate the magenta darkness, and the sharp planes of his face are etched by shadows.

It takes me a while to get past the initial shock. But then I am filled with confusion at why he's here in this sleazy establishment—he must be here for me. He's not the type to go to a strip club. He sticks out like a sore thumb amid the foul-smelling truckers and foreign businessmen.

I don't know what to do, frozen up there on the stage, but I have to keep dancing. I can't stop. I do a trick on the pole that prompts a few men to edge closer and throw their five- and ten-dollar bills at me. There's a vent on the edge of the stage that makes the loose bills flutter like butterflies around my silhouette, slick with sweat, clad in black velvet lingerie that makes me feel sluttier than ever. I might as well be on full-display in a brothel window. When I dare to look over at him again in the far corner, and meet his penetrating gaze, he holds it so sternly that my soul quivers and I feel utterly naked—I practically already am, but I've never felt so self-conscious. I've made myself become so detached and mechanical and logical about the whole thing. But there's no logic in the human heart, and he's infiltrated mine.

For some reason I decide to show off in front of him. To show him what I'm made of. I steadily ascend the pole, greasy with lotion, using all my core and arm strength to lift myself up. Then I spin down it slowly, legs splayed open obscenely as the song finally ends, both to my relief and dread. Dread, because I now have to confront him. Relief, because after all, this is the moment I've dreamt of, longed for, fantasized about. I've looked for his face a thousand times on the street, in strangers' faces, and especially at my apartment building, where he seems to be avoiding me like the plague, since I never see him around anymore. But not here. I never dreamt in a million years I would see him here.

David has no clue what's going on, of course, and he switches the music during our brief intermission to "interact" with customers on the floor to try to get them to buy lap dances or private sessions before the next set.

I stand alone on the stage for a while, breathing heavily from both the exertion, but also my mounting anxiety. Peaches descends the steps before I do, and sure enough, goes directly to Joseph. And just like that, my anxiety transforms into jealousy and outrage. Of course she's going straight for him—he's the most attractive person here by far; she'd be an idiot not to.

"Is it your birthday, big boy? Special occasion? Wanna have some alone time with me to unwind? I could give you a lap-dance or a private sesh," she says in a seductive voice. She's really laying it on thick. She must really need her fix tonight. I have a good mind to let her have him, but I don't think he's here for that.

Joseph, on the other hand, looks utterly bewildered. I can't tell under the pink lights if he's blushing, but I'm sure he is. He seems flustered as she puts her leg over his, practically straddling him.

When he sees me over her shoulder, he looks relieved and my heart swells. What an odd setting this is for our long-awaited reunion.

177

"Hey, Peaches, why don't you go take a walk or entertain one of our other customers?" When I glance behind me, I see that the other attention-starved men are gazing at us with both longing and resentment in their hungry eyes.

"I got to him first, sug," she snaps possessively, and I feel a fresh flare of jealousy in my chest.

"I'm here to see her," he speaks up finally. "Not that you're not very lovely, Peaches," he adds with a genial smile, suddenly reclaiming the charm he'd lost somehow in these strange environs.

"Funny seeing you here," I remark lowly, trying to summon the courage to look him in the eyes again.

"You know her?" she asks in surprise, still unwilling to give up. She really is thirsty tonight. I've never seen her this stubborn. But strippers can be prone to catfights and backstabbing, so I have to tread lightly.

He nods solemnly.

"Fine, what's her real name?" she barks as a final act of desperation.

"Eve—Evelyn."

She pouts and tramps off, submitting defeat.

"Thank god. I thought she'd never leave," I mutter nonchalantly, restraining my emotions. I don't want him to think I'm actually glad to see him.

"So, you have a different stage name? Isn't Eve sexy enough?" he asks with a wry quirk of his left eyebrow, which I'd love to trace my tongue along. I'd even pay him to do it, here and now. I really haven't changed. I'm just as crazy as before. "What's your stage name?"

"Lilith. I thought it was clever. You know about Lilith in Jewish folklore?"

"Nope. Sorry, I'm just a worthless gentile."

"So am I," I retort in a teasing voice. We've somehow fallen so effortlessly into our old banter, even in the grimy darkness of the strip club. How is it so easy? But it isn't easy. I feel oddly weak and frail, like he's taken the lifeforce out of me by just being here. But maybe it's because I haven't eaten much lately, and I'm physically spent. The past three days, I've been stuck in a vicious binge-purge cycle. And today, I consumed nothing but lattes.

"I have to go back up for the next set soon," I say wearily.

"Oh. Okay," he states with disappointment, but making no effort to stop me.

"Why are you here, Joseph?" I say, my patience wearing thin. I had somehow forgotten about that stupid frustrating aloofness that seems to radiate from him.

"I was in the neighborhood," he remarks matter-of-factly with an aloof shrug. But then I realize it's at least partially a show. He probably had to pay the $10 cover fee, and he probably asked the bouncer if I was working tonight.

"This *is* your neighborhood, isn't it?" I ask him, still unconvinced. "Why haven't I seen you around the complex?"

"I don't work there anymore."

"Oh." There's a sinking feeling in the pit of my stomach. Is it nausea or regret?

I have so many questions swirling around in my head then, like if he left the job because of me, or if he was fired, or if he misses me, or if he has any regret about the way we left things.

"Well, if you'll have me, I'd love to see you again," he digresses, and it only serves to further my confusion. I thought he didn't like me that much. I want to believe that I was wrong.

"Preferably somewhere else?" I say flirtatiously, afraid to interrogate him because it might shatter this impossible dream.

"Well, yeah. Let's have tea or something," he says, and my heart wants to swell with excitement, but something's weighing it down. The pain he brought me, and the distrust that pain has born. So I am the jaded one that's shattered this thin and friable veil of intimacy. He looks so nonchalant as he shrugs and says, "Or not. Whatever, it's up to you," even though he's the one who came here out of his way to seek me out in this dark and dodgy establishment. Yet he still acts so noncommittal.

He had regretted getting involved with me, though. He had rejected me. He had left me. I remind myself these things so I won't crumble again.

And I feel my annoyance growing at the way he's just barged into my life like this with the same cool apathy. "Look, what do you want, Joseph? Like what do you want with me? I thought you weren't that into me. And now you're here. And I'm confused."

"I know. I really suck," he admits guiltily, turning his eyes all downcast. I wait for him to say more, but he doesn't volunteer anything else, and it certainly doesn't lessen my exasperation. It has the opposite effect.

He doesn't resolve to change, so I should know what that means for our future. It'll just be the same vicious cycle. I so long to get wrapped up in it again.

But I can't stay and flirt with disaster any longer. David is motioning for me to go back to the stage and the music has switched. I really don't wanna go for another set.

"I have to go," I resign with the same weariness from before. "Watch me another set?" I ask, offering that at least. I doubt he'll linger long. He's too slippery. "If you want, I mean. Whatever," I say, mirroring his apathy in a mocking tone.

"I could book you for a private sesh, like your friend Peaches was talking about," he says idly, jokingly. I know he's not sincere. "Then we could talk more."

"She's not my friend," I reply curtly. "And besides, you can't afford it, baby."

He looks as if he's been slapped, wearing that instantly wounded expression. Part of me regrets saying it. But then my petty logic assures me that I was in the right. Because it's true and I'm injured as well, so what does he expect? I have to defend myself. I can't let my walls down again. But they are fast-crumbling.

I turn away from him and head to the stage. I drag myself and my heavy platforms up the stairs, feeling weaker than ever. By the time I've made it onto the stage, the world is dizzily spinning, my heart is racing like it's about to burst from my chest, and my vision is failing. Joseph's handsome brooding face is a distant blur. But in my memory, it is permanently impressed, gazing at me, sad and stoical. Then everything fades to black.

Chapter Nineteen

I awaken to the smell of food. There are several plates in front of me. Plates of scrambled eggs beside several rashers of crisp bacon and piles of fried hash browns and triangles of golden toast and a sad-looking side salad and, most impressively, a short stack of enormous, steaming hotcakes. They're topped with thick slabs of butter steadily melting off the sides. The fat glistens under the amber-tinted glow of the diner's hanging lamplight. It smells like grease and maple syrup and nostalgia, and it's so warm in here. Joseph is here in front of me, and we're alone together. I realize where we are. It's the hotcake house on Powell Boulevard: one of the only joints in Portland open 24 hours.

"Sorry, I can't afford a nicer meal for you," he says with a surprising amount of venom in that injured tone, that is destitute of any actual remorse, but then he admits emphatically. "I am pretty poor. And not many places are open right now." I remember now as my head throbs that I had told him condescendingly that he couldn't afford me. Money always was a prickly subject with him.

"I'd been resentful, that's all. It was mean though, I'm sorry." I sound genuinely remorseful at least. I have to be though. He saved me, I think. "I love this place. It reminds me of the Waffle Houses back home," I say fondly, then ask, "What happened?"

"You fainted and nearly fell off the stage. And I caught you."

Then I remember. He caught me with those strong, sinewy arms of his. I look down at his bare biceps, then realize he's given me his jacket. I'm wearing it, which is probably for the best, because underneath it are my stripper clothes. He probably got a lot of strange looks coming in here with me slumped against him. Or maybe he carried me through the door. I can't actually remember that part.

He's all muscle and bone, but he was so gentle when he grasped hold of me—I remember now—and he carried me out to his tiny truck from the strip club with his jacket wrapped around me. I had asked him where he was taking me. "To the hospital," he'd said.

"You insisted I take you somewhere to eat instead. You said you hadn't eaten, that's all, that's why you fainted," he explains. He looks at me concernedly, and I wither with shame. I did this to myself. I've subjected those around me to this dangerous cycle of mine. It had once seemed so innocuous, so private, so personal, so protected from others and the outside world. All mine. And no one had to know. But now that's all changed. I shift under his gaze, the truth as well as my guilt utterly transparent.

"Yeah. So." The words catch in my mouth, strangling in my throat. I don't want to say it, every fiber of my being is resisting. But I'm weary, and I'm already mortified and exposed, so I say it anyway. "I'm kind of…well…bulimic." The word sounds so clinical and severe, so jagged and jarring, but maybe that's just because I'm the one afflicted.

"What?"

I shrug as tears fill my eyes, but I haven't the energy to cry. "Yeah. It's this thing I sometimes do. I don't know why. But sometimes I get caught up in it and can't stop. The past few days I've been really bad. Anyway. I don't want to talk much about it. You must think I'm disgusting."

"No. I don't know much about all that. But I know you should eat."

I nod solemnly in agreement and look down at the feast in front of me. "All this, for me?"

"Well, I figured we could share. I just wasn't sure what kind of food you'd want. So I ordered everything."

"Fortunately, I love breakfast food." As I tuck into the thick hotcakes, he goes for the large disc of hash browns that take up an entire plate. When he sets his fork into it, the crisp, lacy edges crinkle and crunch. When I swallow a few bites down, the warm food hits my stomach and it growls hungrily for more, like I've woken a beast. I really was famished.

"I did notice you looked thinner," he remarks with his mouth full.

What really sucks is that I almost reflexively thank him for saying I look thinner, as if it's a compliment. And I worry about how bloated and distended my stomach will be after this feast. God, I'm fucked up in more ways than one. I hadn't cared as much that one evening with the pizza and Chinese food. But I've reached a darker place since then. It's weird how fragile my mental state is, how changeable my body image can be.

"Thank you for saving me," I whisper feebly.

"Oh, that. It was nothing. Any time," he sings nonchalantly. God, why does he have to be so fucking aloof?

We don't talk much after that. We just eat and savor the food. He's probably starving as well. He doesn't look like he eats enough either, but I don't remark upon that. He doesn't make much money, and he's been in between jobs, so he might not have money for food sometimes. The thought fills me with shame. I regularly chuck my food up while he's out there, struggling to get by, spending what little he has on me at the hotcake house.

Then we leave and he takes me back home in his little red pickup truck. The truck is warm and noisy and smells of gasoline. When we get back to my place, I give him back his jacket. But I don't want to leave and go out in the cold darkness, or back to my lonely apartment and lonely bed. I don't want him to leave me either. But he will. Maybe not right now, maybe not tonight even, but he will. He will most certainly, because he's the leaving type of man.

But I'm weak and powerless around you. I wait for him to ask to come inside. But he doesn't and he won't. He's not the asking type of man, either. Not that he doesn't want to. The air is tense with his longing as well as mine. But still, why must he subject me to the degradation every time?

"Will you come inside?" I ask.

"You sure?" he asks back.

"Don't ask me that," I say in a voice feather-soft and quivering. It breaks as I confess, "I want you to more than anything in the world, you know that."

Why does he have to make me say it? I suppose it is a small penance for all he's done for me tonight.

My eyes finally flutter up to meet his because I've been avoiding them since we parked.

He's gazing at me with the same intensity as when he first made love to me and I can't stand it. His self-assured but sympathetic smile kills me as he says matter-of-factly, "Then I guess I have to."

He draws me close to him, and he's as hot as a furnace, and his lips feel like heaven, and I've found religion again. I practically whimper— maybe I do. He gathers me up back in his jacket then rushes me inside, carrying me like his new bride through the threshold. But my rose-colored glasses have been lifted. Everything is now wreathed in pain and sadness as I surrender myself to him. The sex is more tender this time. He moves with a tortuous slowness. Each thrust aches through me, pulling at my heartstrings. He gazes at me, angst-ridden because he knows this all will end soon too, and somehow, he's also regretful of it, and with that same searing gaze with those soulful grass-green eyes, he comes with a shattering moan. He unwinds against me and I hold him close. All his vigor was lost in that vulnerable moment. I didn't come this time, but I also didn't try to. I was far too enraptured by him. I just wanted to treasure every second. To soak him in. To hold onto it with all my willpower.

"You didn't come?" he asks concernedly as he gets up to discard the used condom. I avoid looking at his flaccid manhood, because there is something so pitiful about the way it looks when it's spent and deflated. He returns and lowers himself beside me. I remember the recent shitty hookup where the guy didn't even care. In another swell of love for him, for all he's done for me, for all his chivalry and compassion and the outpouring adoration that consumes me, I cuddle up to him, pressing myself against his sweaty chest that smells like soap, spearmint, and pine trees intermingled with that musky scent of his sweat I would bathe myself in, I'm so crazy for him. And he puts his arms around me, and I thread my legs through his, and his body is my shelter.

"Is it all right if I stay here for the night?" he asks softly, whispering because it feels like we're inside of a secret. His words are like music to my ears, and I can't believe this is happening. Everything I so mournfully yearned for these past few weeks in his absence has finally come true. Now that I think about it, two months have elapsed since I first met him. And it's been the most agonizing two months of my existence. Especially the duration where he was absent.

I wish I could stay up all night and be totally cognizant during all those precious, quiet hours while he's here, his long, lovely limbs loosely entangled with mine, watching him sleep like a creepy stalker, but I fall asleep far more quickly than I'd like.

I slip away, then so does he, evaporating into thin air some unknown hour before dawn when I awake and find him gone. No note. We still haven't exchanged numbers, so no text. And certainly no message. And there won't be. I remind myself this with that same sinking sadness from before as an even more mournful sadness takes residence in my heart. And I resolve to let it dwell there forever.

Chapter Twenty

Then, once again, I'm back to feeling shitty and abandoned, my heart broken open to bleed at that same mournful absence. Always the same. It's not unlike the whole bulimia bullshit—the endless cycle from which I cannot seem to escape. First there's the urge, then the sweet surrender into food-induced euphoria, and then the regret that mounts into fear and anxiety coupled with that extreme physical discomfort. And the inevitable purge, the moment of degradation. And then swiftly comes the abysmal, all-consuming, sinking dread, and deplorable guilt, and insufferable shame. But I don't remember well enough to not repeat the same mistake. I forget all about those bad things as the cravings magically re-emerge, clouding all sense and logic, but still not as intense as the urge for him.

That cycle has also been my crutch in times like these. When I don't want to think about how pathetic I am, obsessed with this inscrutable man who's content to flicker in and out of my life according to his own passing whims.

I'm still full from the grease-laden feast last night. I feel nauseous when I get up and try to down some water. Even breakfast sounds disgusting, so binging is impossible. Besides, what would be the point of it all? What's the point to anything? I don't even have the desire to partake in my worst addiction and favorite coping mechanism—the Band-Aid to all my deep-seated wounds—and if that ain't depressing, I don't know what is.

But coffee. Coffee could do me good, I realize. It's one of the precious few comforts I have left that won't ruin my health or put me in the poorhouse or conflict with my work. Speaking of work, I need to get back in the swing of things.

When I get to my usual spot, Ricky's working. When I go to pay, he hands me my card back with a pained expression.

"Uh oh," Ricky says regrettably. "Your card's been declined."

"What?" I blurt in disbelief, temporarily stupefied. "Run it again," I say, but even as I do so, I second-guess myself, and doubt creeps into my voice as I realize I haven't made a bank run in quite some time, and I've been burning through what little cash I've made, using it on groceries and eating out and shopping and what have you, seemingly oblivious to the automated bills draining my account in the meanwhile, like rent and utilities and my cell phone and bus passes and credit card payments. It makes sense that my checking account would've been depleted by now. Meaning, I haven't saved a dime in two months. And I'm suddenly mortified as I watch him running it with a pained expression and I feel my body heat up.

"So, it's giving me the same thing. You got another card?"

"No. But I'm sure I have some cash—" I start to fumble through my bag with mounting desperation, realizing I don't, when he stops me.

"You know what? You're a regular. We like you. Don't worry about it this time," he says with a dismissive wave of his hand. "You've given us enough of your money."

"Really?" I ask in a trembling voice as a confused mixture of both anguish and relief sweep over me. I don't like people giving me things. The only people I accept handouts from are my clients, because I get off on exploiting them, and depleting their endless funds. But with other people, it feels like I owe them something. It feels like I'm genuinely stealing and taking and mooching. Maybe because I objectify my clients as much as they objectify me. That's the only way you can make it in my line of work.

I take the coffee with a little reluctance, feeling like the act is illicit, not to mention humiliating, then take it to a corner table with my head lowered in mortification.

Luckily, I've brought my laptop with me, and now I can focus on pulling myself up by my bootstraps. First, the issue with my account. I have a setting that prevents me from overdrawing. I made sure of that when I opened it. So no overdraft fees this time, luckily. And I have savings. Plenty of savings to give me enough time to get my fucking shit together. Stop moping about this dumb fuckboi who doesn't love you back even if he has a magic cock. You've got to *survive*.

"You're a Capricorn. You're resilient. You're a survivor. You will get through this," Stephanie texts me when I rant to her via text about my predicament, and how stupid I am.

And at least I've got the savings. I'm not completely irresponsible. But I've never had to eat into my savings before. The act of transferring two thousand dollars—not an insignificant sum—kills me a little bit inside.

It's enough to motivate me to get back on the site and hustle harder than ever. But first, most importantly, I need proper background music to hype me up as I do a complete makeover of my profile. So I search for a perfect song. I settle on "Desperado" by Rihanna. Well, that was twenty minutes down the tube. I post new updated pics that are sexier than ever. Add more info. Be flirtier with my language. Feature bullet points. Change my profile caption. Sex it up. And tweak my filters to be less selective. Before, I'd been picky because I could afford to be. I was younger then and it came easier. Now I'm a true desperado. I catch my reflection in my computer screen and despair at the creases that have suddenly materialized below my eyes. Time to go get some night cream, and start eating smoothie bowls every day again, and actually drink water. I'm dehydrated after all the binging and purging lately. And what I have managed to digest is processed shit deprived of all nutrients. My body is practically screaming for a salad and some nut butters, or a vitamin, for fuck's sake.

As soon as I update my pictures, the new messages come flooding in. I'm shopping in the downtown Target for supplements and creams and other beauty-related accoutrements, when my phone starts vibrating reassuringly. I'm getting a lot more traffic on my profile it would seem. My new and improved profile is really paying off.

I check my phone after making a purchase in the Starbucks downstairs.

Someone wants to meet tonight, and the sense of urgency to replenish my funds pressures me to meet not one, but two men today. One I've scheduled to meet for dinner at 6:30 at some fancy restaurant nearby that he's kindly suggested.

The other man asks to meet very late, at 11:00 p.m., which is annoying, but also more promising than the former, since it means he definitely wants sex. And he'll probably pay whatever price I name. In these dark times, I'd easily agree to 300, but I'll ask for 500 to start. If I'm lucky, I'll make one thousand tonight and, worst case, I'll make nothing and waste over three hours of my life. But I wasn't doing anything else worthwhile.

"Where? And can you please send me a nude photo of yourself?" one of the men messaging asks. When I click on his profile, his age listed is 60. My skin crawls. At least 500 for him. And absolutely no nudes. And if he asks anything else problematic, I'll block him.

"I'll send you a full body, but I'm not sending you nudes," I reply curtly. One has to be curt in this cutthroat business. And you've got to hold strong to your personal boundaries. Any show of weakness is like a slippery slope.

"Fine," he says, and I send him a full body shot in bra and panties. Calvin Klein. Casual but still sexy. He replies, "Very nice. I can't wait to fuck you." The presumption and directness of that last statement, and the vision it conjures, makes me tremble with revulsion. But hey, it's promising. My eyes flash with dollar signs at the prospect. "Meet me tonight?" he asks.

I pause in indecision. I guess it will be a three-date-kind-of-day.

"I can't tonight. But I could meet for a late lunch." That means all my food for the day will be paid for and I'll hopefully have leftovers, so it won't all be for naught. "And who knows, if I like you enough, I can cancel the other dates," I add with an alluring winking emoji at the end just to enthrall him. Men really get off on that coy flirty shit. And I've got to lay it on thick. Desperate times call for desperate measures. I kind of like it though. I like the hustle when the stakes are sufficiently high.

I name the place I want to meet for lunch, along with the time. Usually, I'd let them pick. They prefer to be in control, these rich, sexist bastards with their tiny, shriveled dicks. But I have those other two dates lined up, so I have the freedom of being somewhat selective. And besides, I'm really craving a smoothie bowl. "Perfect. See you then," he readily agrees, much to my surprise. I'll need lots of concealer though for these dark circles under my eyes. Hopefully, in a few days, enough smoothie bowls will amend that. I throw some into my basket and head for the checkout line. I have two hours to get ready before the date.

At home, I attempt to resurrect my former self with some success. My creases are no longer so visible, and my bloat from yesterday's gluttonous dinner has mostly gone down, and I've washed all that sex and strip-club stink off of me. I emerge from my apartment like a butterfly from its cocoon, transformed.

The date goes as well as it can. I take the streetcar there and he appears, looking very much his age. The smoothie bowl place in the Pearl is filled with fit young people in active wear and women in crop tops with dreads and ripped abs. I catch him gawking lecherously at a beautiful girl behind the counter.

"You have no shame, sir," I giggle in a tone that's both reprimanding and flirtatious, batting his arm. I've slipped on my usual pretense so effortlessly.

"Excuse me?" he asks almost defensively. He's unaccustomed to being chided.

"I saw you staring at her," I murmur, batting my eyes. We go to our table, and then I wonder why I insisted on smoothie bowls in the dead of winter.

"Well, can't blame a man for looking," he says with a lascivious smile. "I just appreciate beauty. And you're the most beautiful of all." His eyes rake over me for the fifth time. He likes what he sees. That's as plain as day on his wrinkled face. I ought to be flattered, but it's a struggle to restrain my revulsion.

"Why, thank you," I whisper demurely.

"Ah, you've got an accent!" he says, that lecherous grin deepening and beady eyes brightening.

"Sure do, hon." I make sure to lay it on real thick after that. I like to test the waters first and gauge whether or not it will be in my favor to employ it.

And then he puts his gnarled and leathery paws on me first chance he gets. I find myself glancing around to check and make sure no one is staring. But they're not, even though he does stick out like a sore thumb here. He doesn't seem to mind though.

We get a table. We eat our healthy frou frou vegan food. We talk about sex and he gets all hot and bothered. I flirt and I tease and I bat my lashes and suffer his persistent groping, despite the overwhelming revulsion, which I must repress along with all the other trauma. Just fun girly things. He names 300 per meeting, and I immediately write him off with a feeling of disdain. But then he hands me a 100 for just meeting him for lunch as we leave, and he grasps ahold of my arm. "So, can I come to your place?"

"So, here's the thing. I always do five hundred," I lie, because I won't accept less from him; he's too lecherous. "I know it's high, but it's what I'm used to."

"That is higher than what I've ever paid. Like I said, I always do three hundred. And you're far older than the girls I usually pick."

"Excuse me?" I say, reeling. It's as if I've been slapped on the face. For the first time, I'm not only offended, but speechless. He's still clutching my arm, but I wrench it free.

"My age range is eighteen to twenty-two. You're twenty-seven, aren't you?"

I'll be 28 in less than a month, but I don't tell him that. He really ought to be ashamed of himself. He's 60, after all. I wonder what poor struggling college students were willing to accept such a measly sum. He did say he always does that amount, so there must have been several others.

I recall now seeing on his profile his age preference with mild incredulity. He'd initiated, so I figured he'd seen my age and simply been so drawn to my photos he'd wanted to meet anyway. I didn't think my age would come up. But now he's weaponizing it against me.

"Well then, I suppose we're at an impasse," I state bluntly, hiding how furious I am beneath this cool veneer of mine. But my ego's been wounded, and I'm even more determined not to budge. Even though, beneath that thin veil, my anger increases the longer I look at his surly, sagging face. "It was nice meeting you." I go to leave but he grabs ahold of my arm again. I almost gasp in outrage.

"Wait, fine. Five hundred it is," he says with a note of desperation I do find mildly appeasing. So he really does want me. He was just hoping to haggle with me first and try his luck. Nasty old cheapskate.

I had almost hoped that he would let me go. That I wouldn't have to fuck him. It's demeaning when he does consent to open his wallet in my apartment and slowly, reluctantly shell out the bills consecutively into my outstretched palm. He acts as if it's agonizing for him, and he's doing me some outrageous favor. My outstretched hand feels like a beggar's hand. And he had said he was involved in the stock market. He had said he owns a mansion in the Northwest Hills, where his wife lives, blissfully unaware and probably equally decrepit. She's just not interested in sex anymore in her old age, he had explained to me perfunctorily. But I can't see how she'd ever be into sex with someone like him.

When he goes to kiss me, his tongue comes out long before his lips ever reach mine. It takes a great deal of restraint not to automatically jerk away as that slippery wormlike tongue wriggles inside my mouth, prodding at the teeth and gums like he's performing an invasive dental procedure.

He pulls away from me after what seems an eternity, and a string of his spit falls across my chin. I have the intense urge to scream in utter horror.

"Take off your clothes," he commands, and I do so obediently, wiping my mouth as he looks away momentarily to take off his own clothes. I survey his naked body in my peripheral. He's all saggy skin and balls, but I hadn't expected less.

During the god-awful sex, I focus on a spot on the ceiling, rather than the loose frangible skin hanging from his arm or his stomach, which sways with his trembling movements, or the saggy ball sacks, which rhythmically slap against my backside, or the spittle on his cracked lips, surrounded by a ray of fine multitudinous creases. You'd think in my profession, senectitude wouldn't bother me. But it does.

This is my job, I keep thinking to myself, and it will all be over soon. I haven't the right to be so picky. This is a luxury, to be able to make money so easily and in such little time, to elude the grueling grind of a 40-hour workweek.

But the inner turmoil takes a toll I hadn't anticipated. I'm weary and broken inside. And every new stranger I invite inside to further defile me feels stranger and stranger, and the strain becomes greater and greater every time. Whittling me down.

He's not the cuddling type, thank god, and the whole thing is over quickly enough so I don't even have to cancel my dinner date later. But I am almost late scrubbing my skin raw in the boiling hot shower, trying to cleanse myself of his essence.

Chapter Twenty-One

When I arrive at the restaurant for my next date, I don't linger on the corner for long. I go ahead and go inside, because the sun's gone down already and it's freezing. The restaurant is way too fancy for my liking, but it's not important what I think. If anything, it indicates my date is wealthy.

"Can I help you?" the host, dressed in black trousers and a white button-up, asks me. He looks me up and down, then smiles at me in a patronizing sort of way. He tries to conceal his judgment, but I've been trained by a lifetime of inadequacy to easily spot it. But that doesn't mean it's any less belittling.

"Yes. Umm. I'm supposed to meet someone here," I mutter self-consciously.

"Name? Do you have a reservation?" he asks me.

"Umm." I look down at my phone at the guy's profile. BigBoyXXX is his username, and in our conversation, he never bothered mentioning even his first name. "I don't know. He might be here already." I scan the tables hopefully but see no one seated alone. "I guess I'll just get a table and wait on him. My name's Lilith." His eyebrow arches ever so subtly, and then his eyes rake over me again.

I feel more like a hooker than ever in the knee-high boots and netted stockings I had mistakenly thought of as sexy and chic—in a French kind of way—while getting ready. The dress I'm wearing is far too short for the cold weather. The host guides me to a table in the back, which forces me to walk through the dining area on full display for all the other classy diners. I stick out like a sore thumb amid all the rich customers in their suits and cashmere sweaters and blousy shirts and silky cascades of board-straight hair. It's mostly wealthy couples sharing intimate dinners, or small groups of women sipping cocktails, chatting about how exasperating their nannies are, or what work they've had done recently or whatever.

I notice a particularly beautiful couple near my table. The girl looks to be about thirty, the man in his early forties. She has luscious, dark-brown curly hair and thick, arched eyebrows that are slightly darker, so that they provide a stark contrast to her ice-blue eyes. She's definitely had work done. Her lips are too plump and her porcelain skin impossibly smooth and tight. And the mounds of her cleavage are way too high and perfectly round to not be augmented.

The man's raven-black hair is so slicked-back that not a single strand is awry. He has a few creases on his face, but they only make him look sexier and more mature, not at all like the baby-faced Tinder dates I've endured. And forty seems still-youthful compared to my last client. I shiver as I recall the traumatic, too-recent experience.

Like the woman, his eyebrows are also very prominent and immaculately shaped, and eyes a piercing blue. But they are more vivid and intense, like the deep ultramarine in a Vermeer painting. And he probably spends a lot of money on his appearance. It's true what they say about being rich: it does make you prettier. These two are of an elite class I'll never belong to.

I can't make out what they are whispering to one another, but it seems to be rather intimate, considering the woman's leg is rubbing against his and they're both smiling seductively at one another, as if they might tear each other's clothes off at any moment right there in the restaurant.

The woman catches me staring over the man's shoulder and smiles. I glance away self-consciously, embarrassed that I've been caught.

I'm saved by my phone vibrating on the table. It's a text from the guy I'm supposed to meet. I'd been so distracted by the beautiful couple, I'd forgotten about him.

"Running late," he texts. "About five minutes away. You there?"

"Yes, I'm here. Table in the back. Ask for the name Lilith," I reply curtly. I feel a little perturbed not only by his lateness but by the beautiful couple sitting beside me. He's bound to notice them when he does finally arrive, and I'm specifically worried about the girl. I'm accustomed to being the most beautiful girl in the room. But now I'm not. So it throws me off. But I'm supposed to be exuding confidence and sensuality, so I pretend everything's fine.

A waiter comes to my table and I feel a spike of anxiety. I haven't even glanced at the menu.

"I'm sorry, I'm not ready yet," I whisper, my voice heavy with remorse like I've committed a crime. I really don't belong here.

He emits an exasperated noise and rushes off.

When I do actually look at the menu, I feel a sinking dread. The food is not only unappetizing, but also incredibly expensive, with measly-portioned tapas of pureed organs and caviar-laden toasts starting at $20 and some well over $80. Even a single glass of wine is more than I'm willing to pay. If he doesn't show, I don't want to waste my precious money on this crap.

The minutes tick away with agonizing slowness, and when twenty minutes elapse, I realize he isn't coming, and don't bother with following up again. Then my phone pings. My worst fear is confirmed. He says he has to cancel, but would like to meet me tomorrow. So I block him. And now I'm sitting here in this bougie restaurant for nothing, feeling like I must order something, but I'm going to be humiliated, regardless. There's still the other date later tonight, but my pride has been so injured I'm not sure I have it in me.

I can feel the couple glancing my way over their wine glasses with mild curiosity.

Then I see the waiter returning, and doom resounds in the pit of my stomach.

"Have you decided on anything?" he asks in a clipped, perfunctory fashion as he readies his pen poised upon a tiny notebook.

"Sorry, but I'm not going to order anything," I say in a flustered voice and hand him the menu.

"Excuse me?" he asks defensively.

"I'm really sorry." I feel especially bad, given that he's already wasted his precious time and energy bringing me the water without being paid or tipped a dime.

In the past, when I was at my peak, I would've been pragmatic about the situation, and relatively unfettered. Everything was like that back then. Everything was easy and I was invincible. I used confidence and sexiness. And now—what's happened to me? I didn't know reverting back to the young girl I was in rural Tennessee—trembling, self-conscious, socially-inept, easily brought to tears—was possible.

"I was supposed to meet a man here but…but he stood me up. So." My words turn sticky in my throat as the tears surge to my eyes and strangle my speech. Admitting the truth seems so simple yet so mortifying, when it's actually spoken so plainly, so profanely, out in the open air for everyone to hear.

The speechless waiter pulls a shocked and affronted expression.

I glance over at the beautiful couple and see them watching me. The woman whispers into the man's ear, her arched eyebrows raising in some provocative question. He answers back with a wry smile that is dastardly handsome. I try to compose myself as best I can and start to walk off; that seems to be the natural course of action. I don't want to linger long to find out what the waiter's next response will be.

"Wait," the beautiful woman calls out. "Please. Come sit with us!" she says as I rush past them with tears flying from my eyes, probably making a mess of my mascara. The faucet's been turned on now and there's no going back. I'm mortified as I freeze in the middle of the restaurant, then turn to face them.

"That's okay," I mumble. "I was really only here to meet someone. Some guy. He stood me up." I'm sure they already heard everything. But I'm in a pitiful pit of despair now and must wallow in it.

"Only a worthless asshole would stand you up," the woman says, lifting her glass with a lazy, bone-thin hand. She hands me a tissue from the table, which I graciously accept.

"Thank you," I say self-consciously, dabbing at my eyes and trying to compose myself. It makes me uncomfortable, receiving a compliment from someone more beautiful than I am. I realize, then, that I've surrounded myself with ordinary people. I wonder, for the first time, if it was done with some vain intention.

"Come on, take a seat," she begs with a pouted bottom lip that's definitely been injected. There is something pernicious about the two of them, I can tell. There's that vampiric look in their blue eyes. Their effortless charm and sexy sinister smiles make my skin crawl, but they are also extremely alluring.

"Thank you," I say, surrendering to their gracious plea that feels more like an insistent command. But, to me, it is an order I don't want to refuse. In fact, I feel compelled to obey it. "Sorry, I feel so out of place here," I mumble, also feeling compelled to apologize for my very existence. In the current state I'm in, I'd probably apologize if someone ran me over.

"Why is that?" the man asks, commanding my attention with his piercing blue eyes and brooding brow. It's his first time directing a single word to me. His voice is so deep and compelling, with its husky vibrato, it sends chills up my back, and I feel it reverberating in my chest. But I can't hold his entrancing gaze for long. It makes me too flustered, and after all, he's not available; he's with this gorgeous girl, who could easily be an Instagram model and probably is, actually—I'll have to ask for her handle. Needless to say, he's totally off-limits, and I feel shameful holding that stare for too long.

"Because I'm from bumfuck nowhere. Tennessee to be precise."

"I thought you sounded different! That accent is adorable, darling." She puts her manicured hand on mine for a moment, and it feels like I'm being blessed by the touch of some holy saint.

"My name's Ashley. And this is Lance."

"Hi. I'm Evelyn," I murmur with a shy smile, avoiding Lance's gaze. I can feel the steady, penetrative intensity of his stare in my peripheral vision, and it makes me quake in my chair.

"I think that was my great-grandmother's name!" Ashley shouts excitedly, gripping Lance's arm. He cracks a wry smile at her, and it's suddenly apparent who the brains of this operation is. I wonder why Lance is with her. Maybe she really is just arm candy. A dumb bimbo with fake tits. A mere source of amusement to him. I wonder what their sex is like. I wonder what he likes in bed. If he's demanding or overbearing. I wonder if he can make her come. I wonder if he gives her an allowance. I have a sickening level of intrigue about them, this mysterious, beautiful couple.

"Evelyn." Lance says my name languidly in that sultry, sinister voice, pulling me out of my daze. "Tell me, how did a little Southern Belle wind up all the way in Portland, Oregon?"

And suddenly, I'm self-conscious again, as soon as those eyes are on me, watchful and penetrative. Joseph's gaze was, too, but it was more curious than intrusive, and not cold or formidable. I can't tell if Lance's gaze has a chilling or arousing effect, or both—I only know that it causes goosebumps to prickle op my arms, and my breath to turn shallow.

"Give her your card," Ashley urges Lance, giving his arm a light squeeze.

By his mildly irked reaction, I can tell he's not a man accustomed to being ordered around. He emits a perturbed little exhale then digs in the pocket of his blazer, from which he proffers a blank, white card.

"Huh?" I say confusedly, taking it anyway. There's nothing on it.

"Turn it over," he softly commands. But before I can even obey, he reaches towards me, his fingers caressing mine and sending tiny, electrical surges through my body, shuddering down from my fingers to between my legs at the root of my female sex. I clench my thighs together reflexively. I put up my mental walls and erect my emotional armor around my heart, still tender from its recent wounds. What is this swift unraveling? What is this fire he's lit from the bare touch of his fingers? My wick is suddenly, involuntarily ignited as he wills my hand to move with his, turning the card over with an almost obscene slowness. I want to move my hand away, because this feels illicit, but I can't. And I wonder if Ashley can detect the erotic nature of this seemingly innocent touch.

And then I glance over at Ashley and see that she's wearing this secretive smile, and her eyes are glued to me, knowing and studious. She's completely fine with him touching me like this. In fact, she encourages it, and she bids me with those icy blue eyes to look down at the card now overturned in my palm.

His name is imprinted in a stark, white typeface against a black background. *Lance Vanderbilt.*

Underneath his name is a phone number in much smaller font, and below that, in even tinier and almost inscrutable letters, the word "dominant" is engraved in silver.

"Wait. Vanderbilt…" my voice trails to a faint whisper of disbelief. I have some vague recollection of high school and having to memorize the names of business tycoons and robber barons in American history class.

"He doesn't like talking about his family much." She caresses his arm gently with her hand as she speaks, and he remains as still as a statue.

"I'm a self-made man. Or, to what capacity a man can credit his fortune to himself," he explains smoothly, the turns of his voice as rich and layered as coffee. I catch a whiff of his subtle cologne, faintly musky and sweet like vanilla or tobacco, but mostly smelling of money.

"Right. I reckon you didn't grow up in a roach-infested trailer," I dryly retort as I look at the fine black coat slung over his chair, the material I cannot identify looking simply expensive and luxurious.

"Excuse me?" he asks with a quizzical smile, sounding somewhat affronted by the surly tone of my voice. I've gone too far.

"You're so cute," Ashley quickly interjects, coming between us. "I love people that come from humble origins. But class can be learned too, you know," she tells me. She thinks I'm classy, or could be, with the right tutelage. *Me, classy?*

"Really, it seems fairly congenital to me," I look at Lance pointedly, and he looks back as if he's scrying into a crystal ball, trying to glean some mystic truth about me. I shift my gaze self-consciously.

After several minutes of awkward conversation, during which I've most certainly crossed the line and made a cocky fool of myself in a way that's probably going to make me wince at myself for weeks to come, I stand up suddenly and say, "Thank you for sharing your table with a peasant like me. I really ought to get going and let y'all get back to your meal. See you," I mutter, though I probably never will, though I can't help the excited, fluttery feeling in my chest as I leave the restaurant, making sure to look pointedly at the waiter.

It's raining out, but only sprinkling, and the world is gray but in a soft, luminous sort of way that is almost cozy rather than bleak.

I hear something clicking loudly against the wet sidewalk pavement. I turn around to find Ashley chasing me down in her stiletto heels. "Wait. Evelyn!" she yells, and her perfect fake tits are bouncing so hard she looks almost ridiculous. She has to stop to catch her breath, even though she's not even run a block. But with those cumbersome mounds on her chest, it must be quite the exertion, and for once I don't envy her at all.

"What is it?" I ask, worried I forgot something. I pat my coat pocket, but then she grabs hold of my wrists and pulls me close to her. For a moment, I think she's going to kiss me, right there in the middle of the street in the rain as her head draws nearer to my own, so close I can smell her shampoo. I wouldn't mind, honestly. I get wet just from her closeness, something that rarely happens even with men, and I realize I'm attracted to her in spite of my jealousy. But instead, she whispers conspiratorially into my ear, "Can I ask you something?"

"Of course," I reply, even though my insides are churning anxiously.

"You're like me, aren't you?" she asks. She watches my reaction. I feel discomposed and caught in the act of a crime I do not know and I'm not sure I committed. I'm not sure how she deciphers all that, but she smiles knowingly and states certainly, "I had a feeling. You're an escort."

"Yeah, I am," I say with a sigh of relief at being able to profess the truth for once without fearing any judgment. And she sighs with relief too. It must've taken guts to accuse a new acquaintance of such a thing.

"I knew it." She laughs excitedly, smiling broadly now, and releases a shaky exhalation. Her teeth are blindingly white, but the enamel is transparent, giving them an eerie, bluish glow. "Our kind has to stick together," she winks, and there's something about her conspiratorial friendliness that sets me on edge. Why is she being so friendly? She must want something. I'm too jaded and experienced to believe otherwise.

"Really? But shouldn't we be at odds with one another, like competition?" I ask, but the reality is that she's in an entirely different league than I am, so to perceive her as competition is ridiculous.

"Competition? No!" she winces at the dreadful notion and forbids me from ever thinking such a thing again. It must be easy for her, being so diplomatic and sanguine, since she has no competition to speak of. It follows that she'd dislike the antagonistic nature of competitiveness when she's at no risk of ever losing. Other people simply don't have a choice in fighting. I never thought about it before this moment, because I hadn't been at much risk either.

"We look different, yes, but it doesn't matter what you look like. Yet, it means everything."

I look at her with a puzzled expression. "I don't follow…"

"It doesn't matter how good you look, if you're not a guy's type. And every guy is different. Every guy has a type."

"That's true," I consent. "But I still don't look anything like you."

"It's more than just looks. And you're Lance's type. That's why I made him give you his card."

"How did you know?"

"He whispered it in my ear, right after you walked in."

"Why didn't he just give me his card, then? And isn't he with you?"

The more she tells me, the more confusing it all gets.

"Well, Lance is surprisingly reserved, to start. But looks can be deceiving, don't you think? He can be…eccentric. He has eccentric tastes," she says delicately, and hesitates as she struggles to find the right words. I watch as something akin to distress passes over her face, disturbing those smooth, paralyzed planes ever-so-fleetingly.

"I'm leaving Portland soon," she digresses suddenly. "I'm moving to Boston, where my family lives. Next week, actually. So he needs someone to replace me."

"Oh. So you really are his escort?"

She ignores this gauche question that I immediately regret, but then she says, "Call him. Before he finds someone else. Have you ever had an arrangement?"

"Not like what y'all have," I say without hiding my envy. I've never been lucky enough to get one of those dependable, sugar daddy arrangements. It would be such a relief to no longer have to hustle for my money, constantly putting myself at risk, and just see the same guy once or twice a week. "Is there an allowance, then?"

"Of course. Like you wouldn't believe." I'm nearly tempted to ask how much. My curiosity is suddenly piqued. But I can't get my hopes up. I'm still wary. "He's very rich." Her eyes go wide and serious, in an attempt to convince me of the gravity of it. She must be able to detect the doubt in my eyes, though, because she leans forwards and whispers the number delicately into the shell of my ear. Then my jaw drops, and I reckon there are dollar signs flashing in my starstruck eyes, just like a Looney Tunes character.

"Then why on Earth are you leaving?" I ask, because when something seems too good to be true, it usually is.

"Oh," she averts her gaze, looking suddenly hesitant and pained by my question. She's visibly deflated (except for those absurd breasts and lips, of course). I can see the walls going up around her as she retreats inside herself, no longer the bubbly, plasticized girl from before. "It's complicated. I've got my reasons." I'm sure she can detect my suspicion after that abrupt shift in mood. But I like that she finally seems real. The pretty, plastic version was also too good to be true. Nobody has it all. There's a deep sadness lurking behind all that manufactured happiness. And the cracks in her manicured façade reveal that there's something fishy going on with this Lance too. "You should know by now there's no such thing as a free lunch," she whispers darkly. I think of the silver word at the bottom of the card I still have in my pocket, and all the connotations that word entails. *Dominant*, it had read. I've never been the kinky type, and BDSM has always seemed bizarre and formidable to me. But I can't help but be intrigued by the erotic, the forbidden, and the unknown. "But it's worth it, for a time. If you can handle a little pain," she whispers enigmatically.

"This is all very *Fifty Shades of Grey*," I chuckle, but all humor has been drained out of my voice. Because I don't like pain usually unless it's self-inflicted.

"You have no idea," she says without even the barest hint of a smile discomposing that exquisite mask. This time, I definitely don't laugh. "Just consider it," she says as she turns to head back to the restaurant, but still looks over her shoulder at me as she walks away. "I'm offering you a once-in-a-lifetime opportunity. Even if there are consequences." Then she adds alluringly, "Not many girls would pass this up."

Looks *can* be deceiving, I suppose. She's certainly smarter than she looks. And it only makes me distrust her more.

As I walk home to get ready for my next and last date, I turn the card repeatedly in my coat pocket, in the same way one turns a thought over in their mind. And I am.

Chapter Twenty-Two

I play that conversation with Ashley over and over again in my head. It's all too thrilling and mysterious. I feel excitement as well as doubt swirling queasily in my gut, and fear, a quiet fear dwelling beneath all that potential pain she'd alluded to.

I hate being gripped by indecision, at a standstill, confused and powerless.

But mostly, I just want a reason to binge.

Any inner strife or minor inconvenience or environmental stressor is enough for me to crumble, rationalizing that weak desire.

Next thing I know, that disgusting, animalistic impetus I'm all too familiar with takes over me. It derails the conscious part of me capable of restraint and judgment, causing me to get on the bus to the store, and then the donut shop, and then two different restaurants, and leads me to accumulate about $120 worth of binge food. I text my date scheduled for late that night to cancel. Then I order a Lyft—which costs $17, plus a tip—to take me uptown to my apartment where the feeding frenzy finally begins. I proceed to gorge myself whilst staring transfixed in my bed, at nothing in particular. My mind and those nagging thoughts of inferiority and humiliation and self-conscious dread, together with the dilemma of indecision, are finally, blissfully silenced.

My mind and my body are numb, and the food tastes good. And it feels good to surrender to the urge which has stalked me the past few days since my last one, and since Joseph. It stalked me before then too, when I was good. It didn't fade with time. It didn't get better like they said it would. There are distractions. But distractions never last. I'm always left with myself. And I don't like myself lately. So I wasn't really good to begin with.

And then, after about an hour of stuffing my face nonstop, my stomach gets so sickeningly distended with the copious amounts of food, I feel as if I cannot breathe and my stomach might explode. And the food no longer tastes good. It tastes revolting, or like nothing at all.

It takes some time and effort to get the food to come back up, but then it's easy, and at the same time, it isn't. It hurts and my heart pounds as if it's going to explode out of my chest from the force of vomiting. And my eyes feel like they're going to squeeze out of my skull, but when I check them in the mirror, they are only bloodshot and watery, and my face looks tired and flushed as well. Otherwise, it's the same me. Still alive, but still weak and worthless. "And still pretty," I whisper hatefully at my reflection. Not as pretty as Ashley. But still pretty. And because of that, I'll never have to truly suffer the consequences of my actions. Until one day when I'm not pretty anymore. And then what?

The next morning, I look haggard and my stomach feels queasy. My head is aching from the exertions of the evening. I had ended up binging and purging three times in a row, going out for more food in the middle of it. I figured I might as well, since this is the last time I'll do it for a while. I used to tell myself after these episodes it would be the very last time forever, but I've learned how unrealistic that can be, and when I hold myself accountable to unrealistic expectations, I feel even worse when I do inevitably fail.

After weeks of being good, of eating wholesome meals and even indulging in the occasional treat, or dieting on rabbit food, the allure to binge just becomes too seductive not to give into it eventually. It's the best reward my primitive brain can conjure, even better than money, or fucking, or getting high or drunk. Or maybe I'm just weak and making excuses for myself.

I think my brain's wired that way because I grew up so poor, with little to no food in the house, let alone the calorie-dense treats I saw lining the shelves in the supermarket or on billboards or posted on the windows of glowing fast-food restaurants. I used to fantasize about food all the time then too. Now, I can afford to gorge on as much as I like, and I live in a food-lover's paradise. But I also have to be thin and pretty. There's the rub. That's the only real asset I've got, after all, besides my wit, which doesn't count for much. So bulimia and I go together like two peas in a pod, much to my torment now as someone who can see the myriad problems with it—the negative repercussions on my health, my social life, my body-image, and my finances. Not to mention the reign it has over my freewill. It's like a sort of imprisonment, having bulimia. I'm stuck in the cycle; I'm stalked by it. And I can't escape.

I have good intentions going into the next week, determined to be better and get my shit together.

But my mood is as changeable as my body image. One moment, I feel crusty as hell and down in the dumps like a heavy, morose cloud is perpetually looming over me, and then another moment, I feel like I'm the sexiest bitch that ever strutted down Northwest 23rd Avenue and could easily conquer the world and bring every man to his knees.

But I still feel not really up to the task at all when Wednesday rolls around and I finally text him. Of course, he's been on my mind constantly these past few days. I've been holed up in my apartment, waiting for the right moment, avoiding socializing even with my closest friends.

I never like to hang out shortly after my slip-ups. I'm so overwhelmed by a sense of shame that I feel like the evidence of my episode is palpable on me. I feel like I don't deserve to just pretend everything's all right and wear my cool collected mask so shortly after. The days following are like buffer days. I'm fragile and I'm friable. I have to shed the cocoon of shame. I have to let myself heal. I have to revive myself.

So a few days later, I'm sitting alone in the gloomy dimness of my apartment, and it's pouring outside, the rain beating against my windowpane, and I feel hollow inside—but it's the good sort of hollow—that lovely hollow feeling after undereating for two days straight, eating only the odd piece of fruit or nibble of bread every few hours to sustain me, and copious cups of coffee with sugar-free creamer to stave off that ravenous mental and physical hunger that usually stalks me.

But in the meanwhile, I've kept Lance's card in my jacket pocket and fingered it thoughtfully on the bus, walking down the street, sitting in the coffee shop, reminding myself of its existence, the sturdy and smooth piece of cardboard a small consolation, the plain typeface of his phone number ever-beguiling.

I think that maybe this is the out I need. As the urge to binge creeps into my conscious again like a sly and slinking creature, whispering those enticing thoughts. I turn the card in my hands. This could be my escape from it all. A welcome distraction. A new life. I need the money too. I can't believe I've already spent all of the money I got from the last client, and it was all on food, and most of it I threw up. I might as well have thrown it in the trash. I'm no closer to making rent, and at this rate, I'll have to transfer another couple thousand from savings. I'm so stupid. But there's the card, the mysterious, enticing little card and the promise it holds. But then those tiny, silver letters gleaming in my lamplight scare me again, and I set the card down just as I receive a new text from an old client.

He happens to be the creepiest, most disgusting cretin I've ever slept with, perhaps even more so than the last guy, the decrepit sixty-year-old urchin that seriously made me rethink my life choices.

This particular client is named Dirk. He isn't morbidly obese or particularly hideous, but he kisses in a particular way that is so revolting—yes, even more revolting than the last client—that I can't even pretend to be okay with it during the act. It seems to be a common trait amongst men that pay for sex, being terrible kissers. Dirk is the worst because, not only does he probe the inside of my mouth with the same dental precision as the last guy, but he also full-on licks my face. He slathers my chin, my cheeks, my neck, and even the waxy interior of my ears with his slobbery tongue. And his breath is rank with the taste of tooth decay that's likely turned into an infection, perhaps even an abscess. The odor is so putrid, it reminds me of feces.

But he is stingy. He always tries to barter. That's one reason I hate him. Perhaps I could forgive all his flaws were he more generous.

"Three hundred okay?" he texts me.

"Five hundred I could do," I say. With him, I'm unwilling to go low, even if I'm desperate for money.

"Three-fifty," he replies, and I feel a flare of annoyance, but remember my bank account with mounting angst.

"Four hundred is lowest I'll do," I finally acquiesce. I wince as I hit send. I can't believe I'm doing this.

"That's very high," he texts, and his own annoyance is palpable on the other end, and it makes me recall how insistent he is in bed. I remember him gripping my neck and putting his hand on my face last time, pressing it uncomfortably against the mattress as he came with a strangled, guttural moan. The thought of it makes me shiver with revulsion.

"But okay. Fine. Four hundred. Only because I haven't seen you in a while, Bama," he replies, finally relenting. I wish he could see my eyes rolling into the back of my skull. Oh, he's doing me the favor. I have to repress it all.

I'm about to correct him that I'm actually from Tennessee, but I just say, "Roll tide," and wait for him to arrive.

I shiver again when I first see him, but blame the chilliness outside and usher him in.

At least he's given me an excuse to procrastinate even longer about texting Lance. Ashley had warned me not to wait too long, so I promise myself I'll text him after I'm done with Dirk.

I had forgotten several other things about Dirk. Things that make the experience even more unpleasant. I had forgotten about his body odor, and tendency to perspire very heavily, despite being a man of slight build. His soft belly hangs over his pants and gleams with perspiration, as does his large forehead, and the stench is immediately detectable, like steamy onions. I feel the dampness of his armpits as he embraces me, and then he starts with his tongue, wriggling it all over me like a wet worm. God, it's awful. I squirm and I flinch in his arms, but he hardly notices somehow, he's so insistent on obtaining his own orgasm, it seems, and using me for it like some inanimate object.

I had also forgotten that he never likes to pay in the beginning, and instead waits on me to beg for it. He also probably hopes I'll somehow forget, because he would like to cheat me out of my money and fuck me for free, which is preposterous, considering how grotesque he is. I realize I cannot be left in suspense through the whole dreadful ordeal, worrying if I'll get compensated for all my suffering.

"Did you bring me something?" I ask in a flirty voice, dripping with insecurity as I draw away for a moment. I'm happy to have any small moment to breathe. He looks put-out as he reluctantly takes out his wallet to hand over the money. "Thank you," I say, and unable to help myself, because I distrust him, I begin quickly counting it out.

"What, you don't trust me?" he asks, affronted.

"People make mistakes. Just want to doublecheck," I say in a shaky voice.

"I can count, obviously," his says.

Even though he's only in his forties, his face looks like the molten wax of a candle left out to burn for too long. Pouches of drooping skin pool beneath his eyes and his neck-fat jiggles as he humps me.

I had forgotten about how hard he likes to fuck me. "Yeah, you're a little whore," he grunts, his words rendered with such vitriol and resentment. "Take that cock," he orders in a cruel voice. "I'm gonna fuck you until you're sore." But I'm already getting so sore tears spring involuntarily to my eyes with each dry thrust.

I had forgotten about the ass-slapping, too. He slaps me so hard, I wince and let out a gasp from the searing pain that worsens with each repetition. I wonder if there will be a welt or a bruise. The tears that had sprung to my eyes fall freely now. I guess I need to get used to it, though, if I'm to enter into a sadomasochistic arrangement with this Lance guy. But, stupidly, I assume it will be easier with him because he's attractive, and because I'm not repulsed by him like with Dirk, and because the payoff will be infinitely greater.

When I finally beg Dirk to stop, he doesn't, instead continuing to slap me with what seems even more enthusiasm, thinking the plea is simply to egg him on in some twisted, kinky kind way. But it's not. I don't have daddy issues. That's not my kink. My dad was loving enough when he was alive. A hard man and a hardworking one. I got my fair share of butt-whoopings when I misbehaved, like any kid in the South. The "woke" Millennials from the Pacific Northwest would label it child abuse, but no one there did, and even in hindsight, as an enlightened and fully-debauched literal adult, I don't perceive it as such. I'm not scarred by it. But this—Dirk slapping my ass and saying awful, demeaning things as he rams me hard until cumming with a shuddering groan, panting and sweating like a pig—this will definitely scar me. My father is probably rolling in his grave. Sadness, shame, and self-disgust descend over me in a redolent wave. It's weird how I sometimes think of them during these moments, because I have a sort of out-of-body experience, and am surprisingly less dissociated from the carnal act, and can see it for how debauched and degrading it truly is.

When he leaves, I pretend I'm sad to see him go. Keeping up that agonizing façade for those few additional seconds scars me even more.

I strip my mattress and can still smell his odor wafting through my stuffy apartment. The heat being on doesn't help, creating a warm stuffy stink-bomb. I open the windows and let the cold, bracing night air filter out of the lingering stench. I throw the sheets in the hamper, unable to suffer another second with this stench polluting my skin and take a scalding hot shower. Then I go and load the washer in the laundry room with the tainted sheets. When I'm walking back down the hallway, I bump into one of my least favorite humans: Katy.

"Hey, you!" she exclaims ever-gregariously, a fake smile plastered on her cute little face.

"Oh, you. Hey," I say, hardly friendly, but polite enough to acknowledge her existence. I look at her through narrowed eyes, and I hope she'll get the hint and kindly fuck off.

She doesn't get the hint though.

"I saw a man leaving your room. He looked kinda scary."

"Oh, you did? Hopefully not a burglar. You never know with this city," I say, my voice ripe with sarcasm.

She laughs some five seconds later after staring at me, utterly nonplussed. "Well, I thought for sure you knew him. From the sounds I heard coming from your apartment. Weird noises to make with a burglar," she remarks snidely. I take a quick breath and try to command composure.

"These walls are paper thin, aren't they? Funny, I've never heard noises coming from your room," I remark in a cutting tone. It's because

215

I don't lurk through the halls like some sad loner desperate to make small talk, like her and that other annoying guy whose name I can never remember. Even though I am definitely a sad loner. Even though half the reason I've avoided the hallway is because I'm afraid I'll hear her moaning out Joseph's name, or, even worse—god, the worst thing that makes my heart stutter frenziedly in my chest with a sickening fear—the sound of Joseph's unmistakable moans.

Before she even has a chance to fulfil my curiosity—as morbid as my jealous yearning for Joseph—I quickly add, "He wasn't my boyfriend. I'd have to blow my brains out if that were the case."

"Then why would you—" she stops incredulously, then laughs, feigning modesty. "I mean, you were, right?"

"Yeah, we were fucking. I fuck a lot of people. Just not for free, you see." My voice is as smooth as butter and my countenance composed. If I was flushed, I'd feel the warmth, if I was nervous, I'd feel my pulse in my throat. But I'm as cool as a cucumber. The ice queen is returning from her lair of dormancy, it seems, freshly undone.

And the idea alone that she might be wondering if Joseph ever paid me delights me more than it should. Even the potential that the question might've once—just once—crossed her mind, even if only fleetingly before being promptly abolished by reason, amuses me, titillates me, delights me immensely in the most wicked and exhilarating way. I watch as that hint of curiosity disturbs her soft features. And it makes it worth the entire horrific ordeal with Dirk. I just hope she doesn't say anything to Joseph. Or maybe I do. Because fuck him.

Chapter Twenty-Three

I'm lying in bed some forty minutes later with new sheets on it. I'm freshly showered, and my apartment is immaculate again with no evidence of what's transpired here. Then, in the solitary quietude, the urge to binge creeps into my brain again like a pernicious bug. I'm very hungry, but I'm also sad again for no good reason—after all, I have some money now and everything's fine. I could just eat a meal and be done with it, but I want so many things, yet nothing in particular. There are so many empty and lonely hours stretching out before me, and there's nothing else I want to do. I don't want to be alone with my thoughts. That's the worst thing of all. It would be so nice to just zone out and eat for hours and hours and watch Netflix.

But I shouldn't binge, and I certainly shouldn't spend any of the money I just earned. Not a single dime. I need it all to make rent. I need to replenish my savings. I can't keep going around and around this toxic carousel of self-sabotage. I need to at least forestall this urge until I make more money. Then I see the card lying on the stack of books against the corner wall where I've last left it, the black side gleaming alluringly.

"Fine," I sigh and lift it up into the light. I type out the message on my phone, then delete it, then retype it. Rinse and repeat, ten times at least, until I finally press the "send" button with the following text:

"Hey, it's the charming, scrappy little peasant girl from Tennessee you kindly shared your table with last week. You probably don't remember me, but you gave me your card. I've been thinking of you."

I've just had one of my worst experiences as a prostitute, yet here I am, texting a guy that's into BDSM not an hour later. I trace my finger along the card again.

"Evelyn." He replies right away. I can practically hear that slick, sinister voice of his reverberating sensually in my chest, saying my name. "It seems I can't take my mind off of you."

"Me too," I say, smiling inwardly, but really, my heart's threatening to explode. Because it's true—I have been plagued by the thought of him and how rich he is and how he might be a form of escape from all this, as well as the sickening thrill at the prospect of danger. But then, I've also been consumed by my other problems that aren't so sexy or beguiling. At least my mind hasn't been possessed by thoughts of Joseph 24/7. The bulimia and depression and prostituting and inner turmoil are almost a relief compared to the agony of his existence. But I don't need to think about him now. I've got this Lance guy—my golden ticket.

"You can't?" he asks, and I can practically see the insidious little smile playing at the corner of his mouth. That's all he says. I put my phone on the kitchen counter and leave the room to dry my hair, forgetting about it momentarily, yet willfully, and hopefully adding to his suspense, even though I'm sure he's immune to such pedestrian games. I remember him in the restaurant, all dark and silent and studious with those penetrative eyes.

But when I look at my phone again, I see that he's already texted me back. I feel the first tremors of excitement. He's said, "You didn't seem very scrappy to me. Nice to hear from you."

I feel my insides knot with nervous excitement, and I fire away a quick text, feeling wholly unworthy of this attractive, wealthy man's attention, even if it was only twenty seconds' worth, or the time required type out those two brief texts. Given how rich he supposedly is, I can imagine his time is very valuable. I can't imagine what some people pay for his time.

"Well, that means a lot coming from you," I text back with instant regret. It sounds clichéd and not witty at all. I've always been the enigmatic charming intelligent one that drives the conversation. But it's hard not to feel inferior around someone like him, someone who exudes cool importance. Someone who seems to ooze wealth.

"So, when am I seeing you again?" he asks, as if our reunion is imminent.

I think of Ashley and hesitate. I can't recall when she said she'd be leaving exactly. "I don't want to step on any toes…" I text, then wait with my heart pounding in my throat.

Seconds, then minutes pass, those three dots flashing across the bottom of the screen, implying he's either typing some long message, or fraught by the same indecision I feel, which I highly doubt. He's a man of measured certitude and unwavering poise, after all. But there are those dots. They stop again, and my heart freezes with suspense. I wonder with frustration when he'll end my agony.

Then, my phone starts loudly ringing. My heart nearly jumps right out of my chest. I look at the caller. It's his number. I already have it memorized after staring at his card so many times. I don't even have my own mother's number memorized.

"Hey," I answer in a shaky voice. I rarely talk on the phone. And then here I am, talking to this formidable man.

"That Southern drawl," he chuckles from some other faraway dimension, one probably wreathed in finery. His laugh sounds the same as it did in the restaurant—deep and throaty and with honeyed chocolate undertones. It even has the same reverberant effect that makes my spine tingle and insides unfurl. "I called you because I hate texting, to be honest," he confesses matter-of-factly. "It's too much effort. I find talking to be much more efficient."

"Really? How ironic," I laugh, but he doesn't seem to get my joke. Though it wasn't a very good one. "I mean, that's not very modern of you. There is text-to-speech, you know," I say in a lightly teasing tone.

"I can't be bothered."

"Hey, if it ain't broke…"

"Precisely," he whispers. "Besides, I'm not a Millennial like you."

"Lucky for you, I like older men. I was quite disappointed, actually, that you weren't older."

He doesn't laugh at that joke either. I make a mental note to never try to be funny again.

"So, who were you referring to exactly when you said you didn't want to step on any toes?"

"Oh, Ashley," I say, even though it's obvious. He wants me to do all the legwork in this conversation. I guess he's used to that, in all realms of life. And I'll gladly play along. For now. To an extent. I don't know if she told him everything she'd told me outside the restaurant in the rain that day. "She was so nice to me." I recall fondly.

"And?" he says, sounding utterly unmoved.

"And, you're with her, aren't you?"

"She *was* with me," he corrects, a little sharply, though his voice remains as soft as silk. "But that doesn't matter now. She's left Portland. There's nothing stopping us from meeting right now, at this very moment." Something tells me it wouldn't matter regardless. He's not one to be told what to do.

"All right. I'll bite," I reply, intrigued but also a little afraid. I've learned not to trust anyone over the years. I try to disguise the fear in my voice though, because you never want men to smell your fear, if they are indeed monsters. "Where do I meet you?"

"My place. What's your address? I'll have a car pick you up."

"Umm." I freeze. I usually use a nearby address as a front in case they're the weird stalker type. I usually have that address memorized. But for some reason, right now my mind is drawing blanks and I stutter out my real address before he has the chance to get suspicious of me.

"Great, it'll be there in five minutes."

Five minutes?! I realize then how unprepared I am, but all I can mutter is, "Awesome. Umm. Thanks. So see you soon," in a trembling and wooden voice. I look down at my phone. He's already ended the call.

I stand there for a moment, shellshocked, then frenziedly begin to get dressed once I've snapped out of that dumbstruck stupor. I check my reflection in the bathroom mirror and emit a despairing groan. My hair is still damp from the shower. At least I look good in the outfit I've thrown on, the same dress that could easily pass for a negligee, along with some heeled loafers and an oversized trench coat I thrifted. I figure I might as well go for the "just rolled out of bed" look since my hair cannot be saved. I pat on some foundation and run some mascara over my lashes. I'm certainly no Ashley. But I wasn't looking my best when we met either.

Soon, the car is outside. I get a text from Lance, telling me it's waiting for me.

The ride itself only lasts about three minutes, and I realize I could've easily walked here in fifteen or so minutes. He's in the next neighborhood over—the Pearl District—on the Bowery blocks, in one of the renovated industrial buildings. What used to be mills and factories has been converted into modern condos with loft-style beds and open floor spaces that go for over a million. I've been in one before. I've had clients from all around. But this is without a doubt the sleekest and wealthiest area.

I walk in to find him looking very casual compared to the first time I saw him. But then, he is in his own home, not in a fancy French bistro. Now, he's in sweatpants and a t-shirt, the thin fabric of which reveals his defined pectoral muscles beneath, as well as his bare, muscular arms. I hadn't expected him to be so ripped. He'd only seemed slender and tall in that dark, tailored suit he'd been wearing the first time I met him.

"Wow. This place is amazing," I say, walking around the space as he hangs up my coat. It has an immense open floor plan with lofty ceilings, exposed pipes, and a brick wall, but the rest of it is chic and ultra-modern, including the furnishings. He has a huge bookshelf lining one wall, filled with books that grabs my attention. And there is something very familiar about this condo.

"I think I fucked a guy who lived in this building once," I remark casually as I attempt to feign nonchalance, which is lately not my forte.

"Oh?"

"Yeah. He was a children's doctor," I recall, wrinkling my brow as it all suddenly comes back to me. I had forgotten about him, like I have many of my clients. So many memories have been stored away into the dark recesses of my conscious, perhaps willfully so, and can only be retrieved with a specific trigger, like a scent or scene.

"And was he a paying client? Or just a hookup?" he asks with equal bluntness, but his exacting tone is also razor-sharp, and frightens me.

"Oh. The paying kind," I say sheepishly, no longer quite so cavalier. This is the first time I've told him the truth of my vocation, but then, perhaps, he already knows. He must. It doesn't make the frank confession any easier, though.

"Don't act so self-conscious!" He laughs one of his deep, throaty laughs. "Ashley told me," he explains. "She's surprisingly good at reading people, isn't she?"

"Yes, it *is* a surprise." I wonder what else Ashley told him.

"People can be surprising. You should never judge someone based on their appearance."

"Never judge a book by its cover," I whisper and run my hand along the spines of his book collection. I feel like a pianist gliding her hand gracefully over the black and white keys.

"Or people by their pretenses. We all have to conform to one. But otherwise, Ashley is an airhead. So don't worry, you weren't too far off the mark."

"W-what?" I stammer, whipping around to face him.

"She's like everyone else. She's got street smarts, but she's nothing special. Not like you. You're different. I could tell the moment I saw you. And she did the rest."

"You don't know anything about me. I'm a high school dropout. I didn't go to college."

"Well, I know that you casually quoted Mark Twain and Epictetus during our little meeting. The latter I had to look up. I love stoic philosophy," he remarks, visibly impressed.

"Huh? Oh." I had forgotten about that. But I suppose I did. I was showing off and being cocky, as I'm wont to do. It's how I became so charming, reading and educating myself in spite of being a dropout. "Epictetus. The mentor of Aurelius. Knowledge is power," I remark with a shrug, my confidence partially restored. As if I know anything.

I think of the sad little stacks of books in my own apartment, piled and spread out in disorganized clutter, marred by coffee cup rings. I think of how long it's been since I read an entire book cover to cover. I used to be so productive and constructive with my free time. At least I'm half-heartedly learning French—I can impress him with that later. I feel compelled to impress him and turn tricks, even if intellectual ones, because I feel inferior and poor, not only to him, but to Ashley. Who, however kind, is still my competition, even if she's out of the picture, because he'll be comparing me to her, even if unconsciously. He's a man, so I have to make certain allowances for him, even if he seems to transcend all of those inexorable, gender-specific pitfalls. And I still know so little about him, and these mysterious sadomasochistic leanings. But my curiosity doesn't quite overshadow the fear, so I'll wait for him to bring it up.

223

"Education isn't a prerequisite for knowledge or success," he states.

"I bet you went to Stanford or something," I scoff dismissively.

"Actually, I didn't go to college either," he walks closer towards me, and I feel my heartrate quicken from the narrowing chasm between us. I can practically feel his raw power and virility thrumming through the tense air.

"What?" I ask with genuine surprise. I had expected some Ivy-league education.

"I'm a developer. An entrepreneur."

"And a man," I point out. "A handsome, charming one. With connections, I take it." I don't mention the obvious generational wealth that makes my tone sour with resentment.

"That's true. I'll consent that a man can never be entirely self-made. That's why I like to share my wealth with people like you."

"Sex workers?" I ask, raising my eyebrows provocatively, testing him.

"People I like," he answers with a blithe smirk playing at the corners of his perfect yet cruel mouth. "Beautiful, intelligent women, specifically."

"Ah. Well, I'm honored," I chuckle sarcastically, but my heart is racing. I'm out of my element, for once. I'm usually so calm and collected with clients. But those are per meet and I'm in control. While this is an arrangement where he decides the terms.

"So, what do you want, Evelyn?" he asks, stepping closer—so close, he's now pinned me against the bookshelf. I don't correct him and tell him to call me Eve, like I usually do. I'll let him call me by my full first name, the name which sounds old-fashioned and ill-fitting. Because all of this feels ill-fitting. I don't belong in this expensive condo with its exposed brick and modern furnishings. I don't belong with this handsome man whose perfect hair is slicked back without a strand awry,

224

and whose eyes are impossibly seductive, and whose cologne reeks of wealth. A millionaire who's a solid ten, and Lord knows what he wants with me.

And then there's his question to which I do not know the answer. I don't know who I am, and I don't know what I want. So I'm forced to look inward during that fraught and frozen moment. I hate being introspective.

"I don't know," I begin uncertainly, my gaze jumping from the books beside me to the abstract painting hanging on the wall directly behind me, to the fur rug, then the spotless kitchen encapsulated in stainless steel. "I want to be different. I want to be a part of your world. A world that has always seemed inaccessible to me. I want to be able to walk into a fancy restaurant and not have that sinking feeling of inadequacy that's stalked me since the day I left Tennessee. I want to enter a room without slouching and meet the gaze of people like you with confidence, without feeling inferior. I want to forget—"

I stop abruptly as I almost say Joseph's name, and look down, my courage suddenly failing me. Did I really just say all that? Did I really just admit to the most obvious desire that afflicts every member of working-class America? It's so pathetic, so obvious and predictable. I had always looked down upon the trite Cinderella fantasy, yet here I am. No woman is immune to that Cinderella fantasy, I suppose.

"Yes?" he breathes, his low voice a serpentine susurrus, sending chills down my spine. He grips my chin and brings my face upwards, forcing me to meet his hypnotic gaze. My heart is beating feverishly in my chest, so anxiously that it might explode. And I'm wet. I feel the hot seeping wetness between my legs, and yet there is an animalistic fear entangled with my pulsing desire, which even I hadn't anticipated. I want him to kiss me.

"It's silly. It's so clichéd. But...I want you to transform me."
Maybe I'll be resurrected as a different human entirely, and all my
problems will disappear.

"I can make that happen. But first, you must do something for
me..." he commands darkly. Another shiver snakes down my spine.

Chapter Twenty-Four

Lance takes out a vial from his pocket just as I think he's about to kiss me. Amber-colored liquid fills the tiny bottle.

"What's that?" I ask with a sense of doom rushing into my heart, extinguishing all desire with equal swiftness.

"I'm a man of eccentric taste," he says with some hesitation as he enunciates each word delicately. "For some women, it's too much to handle when fully-conscious. This will help ease you into it at least. You won't feel a thing. Well, maybe just a little. Enough to make it fun for me. And it will dull the pain after."

The promise of all my consciousness being dulled, held within the tiny bottle that glints like an amber jewel in the low lamplight, is almost enticing. But it's also terrifying. I don't even like drinking or smoking excessively.

"The pain?" I peep as quietly as a mouse.

"Don't worry, I won't leave a single scratch. Maybe a bruise or two." He draws my face close to his, so that all the warmth of his evil mystery envelopes me. Then he kisses me. He's a good kisser, a ravenous one. A greedy one. But not sloppy. I feel myself begin to unfurl again, but not quite, because while I am attracted to him physically, there's the ever-present fear holding me back. Something feels inherently wrong about this, and it cries out from the pit of my stomach. And the cry says *run.*

I wonder if Ashley ever drank the liquid. Did she drink it every time? "What's in it?" I ask as he pulls away, pressing the vial into the palm of my hand.

"A mixture of things. I had a chemist friend concoct it," he says enigmatically, failing to elaborate which actual drugs constitute it. "Chemist" could be a euphemism for meth cook, for all I know.

"I'm okay without it. This time around." Then something inside me switches like clockwork. Part of my body resists this unconscious shifting, but then I do it anyway: I go into performance mode. "I'll do whatever you want," I murmur seductively into his ear, wholly acquiescent. Even though I'm still sore from the last guy.

"That's what I like to hear. Next time though, you might change your mind. And the vial's always here."

He leads me to his bedroom, his grip cold and hard. "I'll go easy on you for now. Since this is your first time," he says, as if I'm some kind of virgin. But suddenly, I do feel like one.

When he pulls me into the bedroom and presses me onto the bed, I'm almost excited. But maybe I'm just confusing the fear and anxiety with arousal. And when his huge cock springs from his boxers, I feel resounding dread in the pit of my stomach. I will most certainly bleed if he's as rough as he lets on. I can see how he's hard to handle.

The sex isn't too bad. It's painful, yes, but no more painful than when I'd been with Dirk. Tears spring to my eyes. I bite my lip as he thrusts deeply inside of me. At least he's clean and attractive. But when sex is painful, there's no way for me to enjoy it. There's no chance of my battered pussy and frazzled nerves to register any sort of pleasure from those harsh, insistent thrusts. And I'm quickly beginning to realize I'm not attracted to him—I'm attracted to the idea of the life he's offering me.

He puts his hand around my neck, clutching it with a crushing force. Just as trepidation seizes my racing heart, he orgasms with a shuddering groan, releasing me and collapsing onto mattress.

Afterwards, he's strangely gentle and detached, as he hands me a towel and draws a bath for me. I'm sore and I'm bruised, and there's a stinging pain inside when I get up and go to the bathroom. I watch as faint tendrils of blood float like ink through the cloudy water of the bathtub when I sit down in it. Lance pretends not to notice as he drains the tub for me. After washing and redressing, I'm antsy to leave. I want to be alone in the dark of my own apartment.

When I get to the kitchen, he's making himself some tea, and there's an envelope on the bar.

He motions for me to take it.

"I didn't know how much you wanted, so I went ahead with what Ashley usually received, plus a little more for inflation. I hope it's satisfactory."

The envelope is so thick with bills, I'm scared to count it. I have no idea how much it actually is. I can only go off of what Ashley told me, which was one thousand. Usually, I can eyeball it with a quick glance, thumbing over the bills. But this is so much. And yet I have the pressing need to know. What's the cost for blood? Is any amount ever enough?

I remember what Ashley had whispered to me: *it's worth it, for a time. If you can handle a little pain.*

And it's only gonna get worse from here.

"How much is it?" I ask in a thin whisper.

"Twelve hundred," he announces loudly, his voice echoing through the lofty ceiling. I stand there in silence for a moment, dumbfounded by an amount I can't quite wrap my head around. That's all my bills for the month, earned within the space of less than three hours. The only other money I'd need would be for food and lattes and extra things. With one more meeting, I could have plenty extra leftover to replenish some of my savings.

But I haven't a clue yet just how much money he's willing to invest in me in addition to that inordinate sum.

229

"I'll also be signing you up for a couple credit cards. You'll need them to pay for all the appointments my assistant will set up for you. They'll be hair and makeup and whatever else Ashley did. And you'll need new clothes, for our occasional outings." He adds bluntly, "I like my women to have a certain aesthetic."

"So I really will be transformed, won't I?"

"You wanted to be like Cinderella, didn't you?"

"So you're my fairy godmother?" I laugh wryly. At least I'm not jaded enough to have lost my sense of humor. But he seems intent on stamping even that out, because his smirking demeanor shifts abruptly to one that's dark and stormy, with a solemn frown as he pulls me to him, gripping my waist with those callous hands he used to strangle me, then jerking my chin up to meet his steely gaze.

"No. I'm your master. Understand?"

I give him a tiny, submissive nod. He releases my chin, satisfied, though he's still holding me close to him with one hand.

"Good. Now leave. There's a car waiting outside for you," he instructs with the same brutal coldness. I can feel his cock, rock-hard against me, with a surge of despair intermixed with something akin to lust. He releases me and quickly turns away.

Chapter Twenty-Five

Not even two weeks have elapsed before I get an entire new wardrobe and make about five trips to the salon, where I receive facials, a haircut, a keratin treatment, and some kind of chemical relaxer that has probably damaged my hair, but makes it look silky smooth and straight as a board. I spend about eight hours one day in Sephora, where they instruct me on how to reconstruct my face with contouring, and how to achieve that smoky eye look and Kylie Jenner lips and sculpted eyebrows, sending me off with fifteen different products totaling over $800. All charged to Lance's credit card, of course.

In the end, I look like an entirely different person. I'm so manicured and beautified and covered in makeup I'm unrecognizable, but I know it's still me beneath it all. Every time I see myself, I feel exhilaration after that momentary shock and sense of total detachment which never seems to fade. I find myself stealing glances in shop windows, car mirrors, puddles, and other people's awestruck gazes. Lance has been keeping tabs along the way, and even attended my first salon appointment, but had to leave for a meeting halfway through. He wanted to make sure I was in the right hands, but more so, he likes to keep me on a leash. He's asked me to keep sending him selfies after every appointment.

"I don't know about all this," I had said reluctantly after the first salon appointment. "I don't even look like myself."

"You wanted to be transformed, I thought."

"I did. I guess I just didn't realize how strange it would feel. To look like an entirely different person."

"You don't look like an entirely different person, Evelyn," he'd assured me vacantly. "Wear it like armor. Everyone has a mask."

I haven't posted a single picture on Instagram during my metamorphosis. For all my vanity, I'm still ashamed. This isn't the real me, after all. Posting how beautiful I am now would be too obviously self-conceited, probably prompting people to question me about it. They'd ask me why and how I did it. It's strange, wanting people to look at you, to notice you, and wanting to be invisible at the same time, and not have to suffer the world's probing gaze.

I get a text from Stephanie as I'm grabbing a latte. "I haven't seen you in forever. Did you die?"

Oh yeah. Friends. I haven't been active on social media, and I've been even more neglectful of my friends.

As for Stephanie, I ignored her last text two days ago, asking to hang out. I've been too busy, too absorbed by this new world I've just entered.

"No, not dead. Would that be such a bad thing for any of us, though?" I text back, thinking I'm funny. But she doesn't take kindly to my nihilistic sense of humor.

She calls me right away.

"I was afraid I'd have to call your landlord to check on you. Can you imagine if they found you dead in your apartment?"

I get a gruesome visual of what that would be like, and the various stages of decomposition that would've already afflicted my corpse by the time I was discovered. How long would it take, I wonder, for the smell of my rotting corpse to emanate through the crack of my front door?

"Well, I hardly can imagine being dead or decaying. It's not an experience anyone's been able to recount, really," I say, chuckling at my

232

own sarcasm, pretending I didn't just play that precise gruesome scenario in my head.

"Stop being so goddamn nihilistic and go out to eat with me. I miss you. You haven't texted me in ages."

"I'm game. We'll catch up. But promise not to scream when you see me. A lot has happened recently and I look...a bit different."

"What? Did you finally let yourself gain weight? Did you get a therapist?" she asks in a hopeful voice. "You're too thin," she chides.

I suddenly regret ever telling her about my eating disorder. I think I've actually lost a couple pounds since last seeing her. She won't be happy with me about that either.

"No, not exactly. You'll see. How's two for a late lunch?"

"Fiiine," she whines. She hates suspense.

My outfit is a black trench coat with sheer tights and tan, knee-high boots and a blouse tucked into a mini skirt. My bag is Prada, purchased at Nordstrom with Lance's store credit card. I look like a page out of *Harper's Bazaar*. Now I can buy whatever I want without even looking at the price. I felt a wicked thrill when I bought it. There are children starving in Africa, after all.

I take a Lyft and charge it to Lance's card, which he's kindly linked to my own Lyft account. It drops me off a block away, and as I walk down the sidewalk, a biker gets distracted by me and almost crashes into oncoming traffic. I've definitely peaked. But at what cost?

I walk into the café Stephanie wanted to meet at, which serves vegan macro bowls and aesthetic gluten-free pancakes, and has a sleek white interior filled with cascades of green philodendrons. Their leafy tendrils hang from the ceiling, making the place look like an urban jungle. The sort of people filling the white tables are rich housewives and Instagram influencers and would usually make me feel incredibly self-conscious. But today, everyone turns to look at me. I watch as both

233

curiosity and jealousy discompose their perfect, contoured masks. The certitude of being both the prettiest *and* most put-together person in the room feels like a superpower. There are not many men in the restaurant, but the few there are gawking with lustful awe as I float by on my platform boots. The expenses of clothes and car rides alone adds up to more than what I made seeing three or four clients a week. I can't imagine how much money all of these things are worth, and if I saw it written down, it'd likely make me sick. That's the beauty of using someone's store card with no limit.

Stephanie is already there, nursing a latte in the back. When she sees me, she doesn't scream—just like I made her promise—but her eyes do go as wide as saucers and she gasps so loudly a couple people turn to see what the fuss is about. My layers of foundation thankfully hide how self-conscious I suddenly am, as I feel warmth rush to my face. Because Stephanie knows the real me. She knows what lurks behind this mask.

"Eve?" she blurts, flabbergasted.

"In the flesh. Just slightly improved," I answer, laughing, then embrace her. She's wearing a simple knit cardigan and jeans with boots.

"Who even are you?" she blurts, gawking still. "You look like you belong in a museum."

I sit down beside her as her eyes continue to pass over me in disbelief.

"I got a sugar daddy," I explain, whispering conspiratorially into the delicate shell of her pierced ears. We used to look more alike. We both shopped at the same places—vintage and consignment shops, fast-fashion stores, discount racks. Neither of us used to wear makeup or do our hair or get our nails done. Now, she looks so plain-faced and pure and dowdy beside me. Her nail polish is chipped where mine is manicured, and her curly hair is frizzy and unruly where mine is sleek and smooth. We make quite a strange pair.

"A sugar daddy?" she repeats, much louder than I would like. And of course, at that precise moment, our waitress walks over. I lightly kick Stephanie's leg. The waitress looks vaguely amused. Maybe she hears this more often than one might expect. She'll be getting a good tip for not being judgmental.

"What can I get you two ladies?" she asks with a cloying smile and overzealous tone I find slightly deterring and causes me to second-guess her tip. I've become a little too godlike with my newfound wealth. Before, I'd just give the standard 15 percent, unless the service was deplorable.

We both order. I insist on paying. Stephanie doesn't take much persuading there, and I can tell she's itching to ask how much I'm making now. Especially when I add, "I've entered a very lucrative arrangement."

"So he paid for all this? Your makeover...the clothes...everything?"

"Everything. He set up all the appointments, made the calls, knew exactly what I needed and from whom. Because I didn't know what the hell I was doing. And he gives me an allowance that's way more than I've ever made taking on several clients a week. I used to dream of getting a rich sugar daddy, like a truly rich one that would give me a proper allowance. I can't believe it took this long, honestly. But I can't believe the luck of it either. I didn't even meet him on the site. I met him at a restaurant after being stood up by another client. Can you believe that?" I chuckle in disbelief, but my ego is actually swelling. It's a lot easier to brag about sugaring, as they call it, than prostitution or escorting or even stripping. If you think about it, some of the most powerful women in the world are glorified sugar babies. "So no more hoeing around for me. Now I'm someone's full-time mistress. And believe me, looking like this is a full-time job." I flick my hair back theatrically, then wince at myself. I sound like I'm reading from a script, yet I don't care at the same time.

"I bet. I couldn't do it," she says, but only to make herself feel better. I can detect the envy hiding behind that righteous, self-assured tone and smug smile.

"You're more or less a kept woman too, you know. I just get paid more," is my surly quip to her insincere spar. "You're Stephen's mistress," I tease. If I'd said it more earnestly, she would've been offended.

"How much is it?" she says, probably to change the subject. But her eyes glitter with genuine curiosity. Everyone's obsessed with money. It's inescapable in this capitalist hellscape. I think to myself how proud Joseph would be at that thought, and I cringe at myself again. I haven't thought about him in a while.

"A lot," I state bluntly, with no indication I'll embellish any further.

"But what's the amount you get, like, per week?" she asks, practically itching with curiosity. It's something she can't simply glean from her tea leaves or star charts, I suppose.

"Don't be tacky," I chide her.

"Fine. Well, Stephen has never tried to tell me what to do. I bet you have to do things for him you don't want to. Don't you?"

That comment silences me, and her expression softens as she patiently watches. I can't stand that familiar, friendly gaze. I think about the vial of liquid I now readily down to drown out my senses. I had been so staunchly against it in the beginning, but now it's like my regular nightcap. I've gone to his condo four times since the first night. I haven't noticed any bad side-effects yet, only a little grogginess and a mild headache the day after. And, of course, the lingering soreness. Nothing a quad-shot and green juice can't kick. But then a shiver runs down my

236

spine at the thought of his feather-soft, unraveling touch. Of course, I'll never tell her or anyone about that—the anticipatory wetness I feel when he ensnares me in his callous embrace. I don't tell her about his twisted inclinations, his whips or his ropes or his ruthless desire for domination, either.

"I mean, yeah. He's in a wealthy circle. He wants me to fit in with them—with his friends and colleagues at all these fancy parties and work events he wants me to attend with him. He wants me to shine. I've entered a whole new world."

"Like in *Little Mermaid*."

"'A Whole New World' is from *Aladdin*."

She looks dubious.

"I miss the old you," she whines like a petulant child. She can't suffer being corrected or reprimanded, however small the reproof. Genuinely, though, I do think she misses me. But I don't miss her. I don't miss anyone, not even Joseph. Maybe that's because Lance's potion has made an unfeeling husk out of me.

"I'm right here. I'm still me," I assure her, but my words are hollow.

"No, you've changed," she whispers sadly, though her tune changes when the food's brought out and I insist on paying. At least I can buy her love.

When you perceive yourself as the most attractive person in the room, when your whole life begins to revolve around your appearance, and vanity consumes you, of course you become someone else. I no longer have time to wallow in depression, obsess about food, or cry over men that don't care about me, but I also don't have time to read, or practice French as frequently, or visit Charlotte in the nursing home, let alone hang out with friends. Being so absorbed by this new life provides a much-welcome distraction, but it's also distracted me from the things that once mattered most.

Speaking of which, I have an appointment to get waxed, which turns out to be one of the most excruciating experiences of my life. More painful, even, than the rough sex with Lance that left me bruised and bleeding some nights. When the lady at the waxing salon sees the bruises mottling my leg in faint purplish hues, and the ligature marks striped across my wrists and ankles, she gives me a sympathetic look, like I'm some helpless victim of domestic violence or sexual assault. I'm tempted to tell her how ironic and hypocritical such a look is, coming from an esthetician who inflicts pain upon poor women for money so that they can adhere to today's beauty standards. Isn't that a form of torture as well? Stockholm Syndrome at its finest? I used to roll my eyes when I passed places like this. I used to subscribe to a superficial feminist persuasion, but that's all been thrown out the window now.

When I contemplate saying something, my eyes flicker to the sign posted on the wall by the front counter, which reads: "We reserve the right to refuse service to anyone."

As I'm leaving the waxing salon, I get a call from my mom. It's been a hot minute since we last spoke. Before Lance. Before Joseph. Before I began to gradually unravel. I have to organize my lies and categorize my thoughts, so that I don't let something slip or give her cause to worry. The mask is more difficult to maintain than ever.

"Hey, mama, how are you?" I say, answering the phone and wincing as I walk home. My pussy is still burning from the waxing. I decided not to order a car because the salon's only ten-or-so blocks from my apartment, but now I'm sorely regretting it.

"How am I? I'm fine. How are you?" she asks more pointedly, her maternal voice both injured and concerned. "I haven't heard from you."

"Well, I haven't heard from you either," I reply defensively, serving her the same dish, even though I'm wracked with immediate guilt. She always insists that I call her, for some reason, and rarely buckles and does the deed herself. I've never understood why. Perhaps because she has some internalized resentment towards me for moving away. I was the one that left; it's therefore up to me to keep in touch, or something like that. But as the child, I don't see it that way. She's my mom. It's her job to be worried. I could use someone being more worried about me. And yet, her worrying gives me anxiety.

"How is everything going? Anything new? Are you healthy?" she asks, the concern in her voice deepening with each question. I digest them with uncertainty. When I'm forced to see things through my mother's eyes, it doesn't matter how logically I've rationalized my actions, they always seem sinful and seedy and sordid. Because—if she could see me drinking that vile potion and being sodomized by Lance and subjected to his perversions and being paid for it with tainted money and being plucked and polished for the sake of a man—she'd be traumatized. But at least I haven't purged for two weeks.

"I'm great!" I answer in a hollow voice that I'm not even convinced by. My mother's perceptive, so I doubt she's convinced either. She can always see through my lies. I know she can. But she rarely confronts me about it. So I sit there, punished by her long and painful silences.

"Hmm," she eventually responds. "Are you still working at that restaurant?" I left waitressing years ago, but still use it as a cover. Luckily, my mother's never visited me. "I've been thinking of coming up to Portland," she says, reading my mind. "Since I've never been up to visit you."

"No, you don't have to do that! It's so expensive. And you'd hate it. People smoke weed in the streets. There's homeless people and dispensaries and strip clubs everywhere."

"I don't see why you'd want to live somewhere like that," she says for what seems like the eightieth time. A self-righteous Christian would never understand what a utopia it is here for us "liberal" heathens.

"Well, I do. But it's okay. I'm great, really," I try to assure her, and myself.

"You never post on Facebook anymore."

I'm glad I chose not to post photos of my recent transformation now. If anything, it would only alarm my family and raise their suspicions. And they're all nosy as hell. The only way to avoid their prying questions and gossip is to give them nothing to work with. So my Facebook, as well as my Instagram, has become a dead zone. I don't need that extra outlet for attention and validation now. The truth is all too palpable when I look in the mirror, when Lance pays me thousands of dollars per week, when people stop and stare and whisper with reverential awe as I pass them on the street.

"I've been busy with work."

"And you're too busy to visit for Christmas, I reckon?"

I remember that Christmas is only about a week away. I can't believe it. The months are just slipping by. There are storefront displays with Christmas decorations, and the huge tree in Pioneer Courthouse Square has been put up, and the trees lining the streets are strewn with lights, but it doesn't seem real, and it only makes me sad to see. There isn't a word in the English language for that sad, sinking feeling triggered purely by nostalgia.

"No. It's too crazy at work right now. I can't get off. I asked, but my manager said no way," I lie. "I'll come visit soon, though. Late January, how's that? And I'll stay a couple weeks."

"Okay," she says sadly.

"I'll send some money over too—" I start, but she cuts me off.

"No. Absolutely not," she interjects in a stubborn tone. "Out of the question." Whenever I've tried to send her money in the past, she acts like it's an affront, or something shameful, to get money from your own daughter. If only she knew how shameful I truly was. "I should be the one sending you money," she says sadly. "But you know it's been hard here. Ever since your father..." her voice trails then fades to silence,

240

and in that silence, there are so many things left unsaid. The word, the event, the reality of his permanent absence, lingers like the smell of something putrid in the air. My dad has been dead a long time now, but it still feels like an open wound. A heart attack took him one day at the factory. Out of the blue. None of us were with him. I never even saw his corpse after that. Weird. To refer to your father as a corpse. But now he's not even a corpse anymore, I reckon. I'll be like that one day too. We all will. I hate mortality more than anything.

The funeral had a closed casket. Not because he had a grisly death. None of us could stand to see him dead like that, though, all rigid and powdered.

Nothing was the same. I moved to Portland shortly thereafter. I didn't want to die in a factory like my father did. I didn't want to be surrounded by grief.

But I think it made my mama resent me, for abandoning her and my own grief. It's easy not to think about it, when there's nothing here in Portland to remind me of him. But now I'm on the phone, and it's as fresh and intense as ever.

"Please let me. Tips have been insane lately. Lots of rich folks coming in. I made three hundred last night alone," I lie again. But it's not so far-fetched. Waitresses make a ton here, not like back home, where they make two dollars an hour, plus whatever measly tips they can get.

"Fine. And you'll visit in January?"

"Yes," I say, though I'm silently dreading it already, and I wonder at what Lance will think of me leaving for so long, if he'll allow it, or if I'll have to end it, and if so, what the repercussions will be.

I get off the phone and see that I have some new texts from Lance, and more appointment reminders.

I miss a bunch of my French classes because of all the appointments Lance has scheduled for me. He doesn't bother asking if I have prior engagements. He feels entitled to every second of my day, it seems, calling me up and ordering me to come over whenever the mood strikes him. I guess that's just yet another sacrifice.

But because of all the money I have coming in lately, I decide to hire a personal French tutor who can work around my schedule. After meeting only a few times with her, I'm not quite fluent, but I feel confident enough to go to France eventually, especially now that I have the financial means. My cup is overflowing. Why, then, does it feel so empty? I feel like a hollow husk. I feel sapped and spent. And no amount of money can buy me more time to hang out with my friends, or visit Charlotte at the nursing home, or go back home to see my mother, let alone fly to Paris. No amount of money can buy my happiness. I look in the mirror again at the beautiful stranger.

Chapter Twenty-Six

Now, it's gotten to the point that every time Lance texts me, my heart fills with dread.

"Tonight. Eight o'clock. There'll be a car outside waiting on you," he texts one evening.

And then I'm there in his dark apartment, knocking back that magic tonic with heady anticipation. Everything becomes murky yet lurid, numb yet visceral, as it all starts up again. I come to a few hours later with fresh bruises.

"You have an appointment tomorrow at eleven for your lips," Lance tells me in the kitchen as I regain consciousness over a cup of chamomile tea.

"My lips," I repeat in confusion after some delay. My brain feels so slow after being drugged.

"Sure. Don't you want them to be bigger? Ashley had hers injected," he says matter-of-factly. "Yours are a bit thin, after all."

"Oh," I say, swallowing hard, too weak from the previous exertions and the effects of his potion to argue.

"There'll be a car about thirty minutes before then to pick you up at your apartment. I had my assistant send the driver your number so he can call you."

"Your assistant has my number?" I ask, feeling suddenly violated. Maybe it's just the fact that I'm still sore from being freshly fucked. I ought to feel more violated by that, though. But I've long normalized being used for sex, of being subjected to various forms of sexual sadism, but never such a crude form of paraphilic rape. I've become acquainted with terms like "biastophilia" and "sexual sadism" after entering this twisted arrangement with Lance, in an attempt to understand him, and myself.

Because I'm fucked up too. More fucked up than I thought.

Here's the thing about me: I don't come when he fucks me. I'm hardly conscious as it is. But I do get wet. And part of me is filled with a sickening thrill.

And yet, for some reason, the idea of his assistant, some stranger, knowing my personal phone number, elicits a more visceral reaction.

"Of course he does. Is that a problem?" he asks. A test. One of his thick, dark eyebrows lifts provocatively.

"Well, I've never met him," I answer tentatively, my whole body tensing as he approaches me. It tenses, but it also begins to unravel, an unconscious reflex I still don't comprehend.

"That's probably for the best. He happens to be very charming. Ashley even called him cute once. I'm a jealous man," he tells me. I realize then that I haven't been able to witness this infamous jealousy of his first-hand. Not yet, at least. I'm going to my first social event with him in a few days, a Christmas fundraiser his company is sponsoring, so perhaps I'll see it there. "Speaking of jealousy," he says, and his voice trails as he walks off purposefully, piquing my intrigue. He returns with a thin manilla folder. "Our test results came back."

I look at him confusedly. I try to search my memory, but the exertion of that alone is too mentally taxing. My brain is so slow and foggy lately. It could be from the lack of sustenance on my strict coffee and fruit diet lately. But I also fear it's from his mysterious elixir.

"From the clinic," he reminds me. Then it all comes rushing back—the cold, metallic bite of the syringe as it drew my blood, the swab at the back of my throat and the clinic's grimy, tiled floors. The nurse's stale inquiry about how many partners I'd had in the past three months, which I was unable to answer decisively. "We both came back squeaky clean."

"Oh, right. That's great," I say, though my voice is tremulous as he takes out another sheet of paper. He had mentioned this as well. I'd forgotten. "Now, the exclusivity contract." I sign it obediently after a quick read-through. After all, he's paying me an excessive amount as it is. The contract doubles my allowance for agreeing to be exclusive and not wear a condom—how can I turn that down?

He signs it as well, then puts all the papers back into his thin folder. He leaves and I enter a trance, staring into my mug, the last dredges sunk to the bottom, where I try to glean my future. A month ago, I would've never guessed I'd be here. "I like to keep my favorite pets on a tight leash," he whispers behind me. I jump a little. I hadn't noticed him return.

He's standing behind me know, and I'm still sitting there gripping my mug of tea. But the mood has shifted, and my body is tensed again, every fiber rigid with apprehension. He grips me by the hair and wrenches my head back so that he can run his bared teeth along the sensitive skin of my neck, and I can feel his incisors digging along the bony ridges, tickling me, unraveling me. "So I'm not the only one?" I ask. I've never really considered that he might have multiple mistresses. An expensive habit of his, to be sure. But we did just sign an exclusivity agreement. But then he could be lying to me. I wouldn't doubt it.

"You are now. Didn't I say you were the favorite?" he hums, low and guttural, then bids me not to speak. I obey with a quivering sigh. He turns away from me and leaves the room. The abruptness is jarring. He often does this. Mistreats me, manhandles me, teases me, then leaves for an unknown duration, expecting me to stay like a loyal dog. And I do. I don't leave until he tells me to. He gives me the money. He orders the lift. He commands me to get dressed and announces the car is outside, his voice leeched of all warmth or affection. But then it always is. A machine. A cold, tall, and muscular machine with perverse and esoteric inclinations.

But he isn't bidding me to leave just yet. Not tonight. When he returns, he has a rope dangling from his hand. And his cock is rock hard, forming a taut tent in the crotch of his gray sweatpants.

"Again? We already did it tonight," I gently plead, though I know such protestations are futile. I can leave when I want. It's not him that's keeping me here. It's the money. I have to always bend to his will, or he won't want to see me anymore. He could get someone else. The hardest part of the arrangement is that it's me who's torturing myself, agreeing to be tortured, permitting him to do as he wishes. So that I'll get that fat envelope at the end. "I'm still sore," I complain as he puts his hands on my shoulders.

"Are you trying to go out of your way to defy me? You know that'll only make me harder," he hisses, his low voice serpentine in my ear.

"Harder here?" I ask, feigning innocence and donning a childlike voice. Then I reach behind and grip his bulge, feeling the throbbing length, a sense of power swelling in my chest. "Or harder on me? I don't know if I can take another round," I say as I barely shift and feel a sting of pain.

"You can always use the potion again," he kindly offers. So chivalrous of him. I consider it. I haven't taken that much in one night before. I probably shouldn't.

"No. I'll take some Ibuprofen."

"Just go ahead and take it," he says, sliding a fresh vial across the table. He always has a ready supply. I wonder where his stash is. The idea of overdosing on it seems mildly appealing. Certainly not a bad way to go. I'd feel nothing. "I'll pay you double for all your pain and hardship," he promises in a wry tone, lifting the vial up to my lips. He likes that it makes me forget. It means he can do whatever wretched things he wants to me.

By the time the potion has snaked down my throat and into my belly, and my brain begins to buzz, I've grown wet and swollen. Shamefully, I yearn to be corrupted again, even though I'm still sore, and the idea of more pain makes me wince reflexively as well. At least I have the potion. At least I have that sweet nothingness.

I don't like the pain. I'm not a masochist. Not really—despite all my poor, self-destructing coping mechanisms. It's some other aspect of it I like that I can't quite put my finger on, that I dare not dissect for fear of what troubling truth about myself I might unearth.

It's something about the masculine domination. The strength and vigor and roughness. If only I could have the roughness without the pain, the domination without the degradation, the subjugation without that total terrifying feeling of powerlessness, that harrowing vulnerability. It's like I want to feel like I'm being raped without actually being raped.

Sometimes, I even fantasize that it's Joseph raping me, not Lance. I fantasize that he's the one holding me down, so consumed by his desire for me that he's driven to madness and brutality.

But Joseph would never be hostile towards me. And when Lance takes out his restraints and instruments of torture—the ball gags and flogger, or the leather whip and studded rod—that fantasy is shot dead. The instruments are not my cup of tea. They only represent pain and posturing to me.

My stomach pools with dread, and my body tenses with impending doom whenever I see him open that huge closet where he houses all those sadomasochistic sex toys, and I dry up like a river in a drought. Everything starts to grow very hazy right around then.

I barely know how I get home later that night. And the next day, I awake with the same resounding dread filling my chest as I do when he opens his closet, or proffers one of those amber-colored vials, or caresses me with his callous hands. The excitement of the money has waned. But the greed for more has only intensified. An envelope sits beside my bed filled with crisp Benjamins. The faces stare at me with lurid smirks that deepen my dread. But today, something else entirely is filling me with dread. I look at my phone at the calendar notification lighting up the screen. I have an appointment to get my lips injected.

I never in a million years would've elected to do it before. Yet I find myself going along with it as if I'm some sort of puppet or machine, with zero reluctance. The whole thing feels surreal. It's as if I'm in a trance. And then it's done, and my lips are ridiculously swollen, as if I've been stung by bees or had an allergic reaction. I stay locked away in my apartment for two days straight before emerging to go to the gym and eat.

Lance had intentionally scheduled it a few days before his gala— our first big event together. A charity fundraiser his firm is sponsoring. He wants the swelling to go down before then.

I've been preparing in other ways too—I've been to the gym two hours a day this past week in preparation and eating as little as possible. Mostly baby carrots, apples, and coffee. So naturally, all I can think about are donuts and pizza and hamburgers and anything processed, carb-laden, or with saturated fat. But I won't binge. I can binge when I'm old, just like I can sleep when I'm dead, except I need my sleep— nine hours, lately, in fact. My beauty sleep, I call it, but really, it's just depression sleep.

Chapter Twenty-Seven

Then it's the big day. Then the day turns to night, and I watch my life slipping away. I go to the bathroom to get ready. I emerge like a beautiful butterfly from its cocoon some two hours later.

Lance escorts me into the expansive foyer where the gala is taking place. It's in an old hotel downtown that I can tell has been hosting fancy parties and balls for well over a century. He's in a fitted tux and I'm in the slinky black evening gown he picked out himself and had tailored to fit me like a glove. I feel invincible despite the fact that I'm being kept on a tight leash, and I fear I'll make a fool of myself. Because I fear his wrath if I do.

A man and woman are standing by the open bar, chatting while daintily holding up martinis with perfectly spherical olives poised on the delicate rims, which glint in the low chandelier light. They look perfect, not a hair out of place or blemish marring their smooth faces. The woman has Botox, I realize upon closer inspection. The man might have it too. I wonder if Lance does. I shudder as I realize he'll probably be scheduling a session for me soon. And I've already gotten lip injections, so why not? Go ahead and fill my face with paralyzing toxins as well, while you're at it. Inject me with silicone and hyaluronic acid and all things unnatural.

Lance introduces us, telling them I'm his date and nothing more. They look mildly intrigued.

He leaves me with them when someone calls his name from across the room. "An important investor," he whispers into my ear. "I'll only be a moment," he promises, then abandons me.

I'm alone with the sharks now. They eye me hungrily. Fortunately, I'm a great conversationalist. I just have to keep up decorum and not revert to my crass ways. For what I'm getting paid tonight, I'll happily play the clown or sacrificial lamb.

"So, tell us how you met Lance. He's quite the catch," the woman says.

"Well, I was sitting alone in a restaurant…"

Some twenty minutes later, the man and woman have ventured off in search of the toilet, and another man has come up.

"What do you do for fun?"

"Fun?" I ask, chuckling with derision. "I hardly know what that is."

"Don't act so jaded. You're young and you're beautiful. No one could ask for more."

I realize there are several other things one could ask for, but I see his point, and I see how selfish and spoiled I am. But that's no surprise, either.

"You speak French?"

"I'm taking lessons. I guess that's what I do for fun."

"I lived in Paris when I was younger. The best two years of my life," he says, waxing nostalgic.

Suddenly, we're speaking in French to one another, practicing rudimentary conversation. I'm attempting to respond in turn, though it is quite the challenge.

"Evelyn," I suddenly hear Lance's low growl of a voice behind me. The hairs on the back of my neck stand on end. I can feel him—his presence—as his soft breath grazes my prickling skin. "Since when do you speak French?"

I whirl around to face him. He doesn't look pleased.

"I thought I told you I took lessons," I say innocently, but I know I haven't. We don't talk about our day-to-day much. We don't have the same stimulating conversation we had in the restaurant, or over the phone. Even though he said he was so drawn to me because of my wit, because I was different. The idea sounds so foolish now. How could I have been so naive? And here I thought I had discarded my naivete long ago, in the piney wilderness of Tennessee. But then, if I had, I would've known he only chose me because he saw me looking so desolate and distraught, alone in that restaurant near tears and ripe for the kill. Playing the sacrificial lamb again. I'm just figuring that out now. It's no surprise I like playing the damsel in distress as well.

"Is this one yours?" the man asks Lance, referring to me, and he's smiling, unaware of how exacting that question is.

"Yes, she is. Will you excuse us for a moment?" he asks in a clipped but polite tone, though I can hear the anger, an icy river, raging beneath that placid veneer. He takes hold of my arm and jerks me away.

"Of course," the man chuckles, none the wiser.

He leads me through the sea of people in that crowded room until we're at the entryway, his grip tightening, his short nails biting into my tender skin. He leads me down an empty hallway, the sight of which strikes fear into my heart. I had thought it would be different than when we're alone in his condo. But the hallway is dark and deserted, and there's no one here to keep his impulses in check either. He pulls me into a darkened enclave in the wall.

"What was that back there?" he asks sharply. A couple stray strands come loose from his slicked-back hair as he snaps his head towards me, so that his face is inches from my own. He grasps my chin. I can feel his hot minty breath against me. "That wasn't just taking classes. You were showing off. You were flirting with him."

"First of all, I'm pretty sure that guy was gay." I laugh in his face, not sure why I'm being so insolent. The man did have a gay vibe, but

251

one can never be sure in Portland. And now is not the time to test Lance. "And I've been trying to learn for a while. I've wanted to go to France since I was a little girl. You just never asked. You never ask me anything. That's why."

"So you're arguing with me now?" His dark sapphire eyes look more wolfish than ever. "I called for you and you never came. You were so engrossed in your little French conversation," he states spitefully. "That's very disobedient. I wanted you on your best behavior here."

He doesn't actually care about the French. It was just that I was having some fun at the party, and with another man, and that I wasn't at his beck and call for once. I've stoked his jealousy and he's glad I have. He loves for me to be disobedient, because he loves punishing me.

"What are you going to do about it?" I ask, donning a sexy voice and disguising my fear. Playing along like I always do.

I can feel his heart beating wildly against his chest, against mine. I look away, glancing at the empty hallway as the sound of heels click and clatter, echoing loudly, but I don't cry out. This is, after all, an arrangement, not some nonconsensual form of sexual slavery. I can leave any time I want. And yet I'm pinned to the wall, frozen by fear and something else—the threat of being discovered. It excites me. Being admonished excites me, I realize with a throbbing ache deep in the trenches of my twisted soul. I feel him hard against me. Perhaps this is the only good alternative to true love—and that agony I felt with Joseph. If I can't have him, this is all I can have: pain and perversion.

"You just want to keep me all to yourself, don't you?"

"Of course, and I pay good money for it," he growls insidiously.

I feel a sting of resentment, even though it's true.

But even after all these years of solicitation, prostitution and degradation, it's still sometimes a little soul-crushing.

"Then why not some other girl, someone more obedient? You could have anyone."

"Maybe I like a girl who will defy me from time to time. Otherwise, I'd have no reason to punish her. And that's the best part," he whispers wickedly into the shell of my ear, his hot breath antagonizing me. "And those girls can't quote Epictetus or speak French."

Even though I know that isn't true now, and that he doesn't actually give a damn about my wit or my knowledge, he does genuinely prefer me. His eyes didn't linger long on the other women in the room when we first entered, even though some were equally beautiful and far classier. And he does give me a grotesque amount of money just to get a taste of possessing me. Part of me does want him to possess me, because that would allow me to finally relinquish my own self-possession. His cock is so hard it practically springs out when he unzips his slacks.

"Now turn around," he commands, hiking up my dress, careful not to rip it, and turning me to face the wall. He does not show the same care as he forcibly bends me over then rams his cock inside me, but I'm dripping wet by then, so it does not hurt as much as he'd like. It feels good, actually, surprisingly. It's the first time it's felt this good. Which means he can't punish me as well as he'd like—he wants me to resist and wriggle in his clutches, he wants me to wince and cry out in pain—so I can't show signs of enjoying it.

But he has to show some restraint as well. He has to be slower and quieter than usual, and be on his guard, here at this work event with his colleagues, business partners and investors, in such close proximity. A mere wall separates us from the hallway. If someone were to walk down this hall, they'd catch us. But that's what makes it so hot, so thrilling, the stakes so high.

I've never had public sex. I didn't think it was something I'd ever be into either. I'm not voyeuristic and I've never indulged in kinky fantasies. But the hum of the people on the other side of the wall, reminding us of their presence, adds to the suspense. And he's made me realize I like being chased, dominated, and possessed. And the vigor with which he fucks me, savoring each thrust with a pant or a beastly, guttural groan, only makes me feel more desired, arousing me in spite of my disdain for him. And it's also because of the resentment I harbor for him that I cannot show him my pleasure, even as the longing to moan out with ecstasy builds in my chest, and my loins ache to tense and shudder against him, to achieve my own orgasm, but I must restrain that growing, insufferable urge. And it only makes it better.

He stops for a moment, and his cock suddenly slips out of me, still hard, the swollen tip trailing along my tender opening with agonizing slowness. A whimper escapes my trembling lips.

"You're soaking wet, you little whore. You're actually enjoying this, aren't you? Did you have too many glasses of champagne, or are you just a slut?" He asks in a hot, reproachful breath, then jerks me around and pins me to the wall as I try to wrench myself free.

"I am. I'm yours. Only yours. Fuck me. Please," I whisper with some resistance with my cheek pressed against the wall.

"Oh, now you're begging?" he snarls, not seeming particularly pleased by it. But with him, it's impossible to know what he truly wants, because his perverse predilections are no easier to comprehend than my own.

He hoists me up, using the wall to brace my weight, but also using his strong biceps to support me. I wrap my legs around his midsection and then lower myself onto his cock. His slacks have fallen to his ankles, a pool of black folds around his feet, and his long, lean legs are beginning to tremble. If someone caught us now, there'd be no saving us. What would be the consequences if they did? Would we be publicly humiliated, or reprimanded, or even arrested for lewd conduct? The possibilities are as titillating as they are anxiety-inducing.

I let out a moan as his cock thrusts within me in the most delicious way, better than the first bite of chocolate cake after dieting for days. Which says a lot, coming from me. My moan is loud—too loud—and he's growing short of breath, but he reaches up and clamps a hand over my mouth to silence me. "Don't make a sound or we'll be caught, then I'll really have to punish you," he tells me darkly, but I call his bluff. He can't support me for long with one hand, since the other is clamped over my mouth, so he has to move it away eventually. His hand returns to my ass to hold me up, his fingers digging into the soft flesh. Not that there's much. I've lost weight, even though I shouldn't have. And yet, I'm glad I did, because it's made me lighter, and Lance likes being able to manhandle me with ease. So that he can flaunt his brute strength. "You're as light as a feather," he whispers with awe between his breathy pants, and moves me up and down so I'm sliding over his cock in a rhythmic motion. "I could snap you between my fingers," he says, all breathless and husky.

I'm so turned on by that masculine strength of his, by his subjugation, and particularly by the people nearby, by the party waiting and the exciting risk at being found, despite my simultaneous hatred for him. It all makes my heart hammer frenziedly in my chest, coinciding with that mounting pressure as I approach my orgasm. People often mistake fear for arousal. There've been studies on it. But then when fear is intertwined with arousal—what do you call that?

And then Lance begins to shudder and quake and move me so quickly up and down onto his turgid cock, I can't take it anymore. Maybe it's because I haven't come in so long. Maybe it's because it feels better without a condom. Maybe it's because I didn't take the potion beforehand, so I can feel everything. Maybe it's because he's not being too rough with me, and so it actually feels good for once. Or maybe it's just a combination of all those things, along with my new level of recklessness.

Then I come undone, damn him. He does as well, a fragment of a second after I do, with a hot spurt and tense jerk. He pushes deep inside me. I quiver and clench around his throbbing cock. And we both release an anguished sigh of relief.

He catches his breath, then slowly releases me, easing me down and slipping out of me. I can feel some of his warm cum seeping out and I clamp my thighs together. My legs are limp and quivering, so it requires some effort. Occupational hazard.

We were so close in that fraught moment that my heart almost ached for him with something akin to affection. But his cool façade returns as soon as we regain our breath. The frantic excitement of the moment dissipates. His mouth settles into the same hard, cruel line. He pulls his pants up and adjusts his shirt, then his voice cuts like a knife as he brusquely orders, "Go get yourself cleaned up. You're a mess." He looks me over as though I disgust him, and my hatred for him returns just as abruptly. He turns and rushes off, I take a bit longer to move from that darkened spot, a brief sanctuary from the party and from myself. I'm not quite ready to be reunited with my reflection.

I feel like a fool as I go on my walk of shame down the hall and to the restrooms. I wonder if he's angry at me for enjoying myself. I'm certainly mad at myself, because I despise him and everything he represents, yet I allowed myself to forget all of that. And I didn't even drink his elixir of drugs this time.

In the restroom, I encounter a woman from the party who's condescending eyes rake over me critically, lingering on my disheveled hair and fallen shoulder strap, and that feeling of inferiority that's stalked me since I was born suddenly returns, despite all the makeup and designer clothes. Along with that sinking feeling is a rush of overripe resentment. She shoulders past me with her head held high. I wonder if she's been laid in the past year.

I look in the mirror and gasp in horror. The damage is worse than I thought. My mascara has smudged beneath my eyes in inky blots. With the fillers, my swollen lips look grotesque and comical. My lipstick is smeared across my face. I had wanted to look like Angelina Jolie, not a clown.

I hadn't noticed any lipstick smeared on Lance's face, but it had been dark in that shadowy alcove. I'm sure he's cursing me now in the garish light of the men's restroom, looking, hopefully, as clownish as I do.

But he looks as flawless as ever when I return to the party. I was able to clean up for the most part as well.

"And then I told him if you're not willing to take risks, you shouldn't have gotten out of bed this morning," I hear Lance's deep voice saying in the midst of a circle of other rich bastards. They all wear the same exact black tuxes, and they all burst into laughter at his stupid joke. No one has the faintest clue what he's just done, or how twisted his perversions are.

Women hang on the men's arms, as dainty and pristine as I am, their contoured faces aglow. Fake tanner and bronzer hide their malnourished and pallid façades. Injections and implants making them balloon out only where they should, so that they look both gaunt and simultaneously voluptuous, defying nature while miraculously adhering to impossible societal expectations.

I take it Lance wants me to be his arm candy as well, so I reluctantly go up to him.

"Ah, there you are," he says when he sees me in his peripheral. My body tenses, but I force a breezy smile. I take his outstretched hand, and once he's reeled me in, he wraps his arm around my waist, clutching the small of it possessively. It's as if nothing happened. Like we've just been mingling at this stupid party the entire time. "Peter here was just bragging to everyone about your mastery of the French language."

"Mastery? I'd hardly call it that," I scoff with a shy smile.

"*Il est difficile de vaincre ses passions, et impossible de les satisfaire,*" he says eruditely, telling me with perfect enunciation that it is difficult to master one's passions and impossible to satisfy them.

It's definitely a quote, and not at all relevant to what I said, but at least it sounded cool. Everyone in the circle laughs delightedly, in awe of his impeccable accent, and how effortlessly the flowery words flow from his lips. Even though they have no clue what he said. I barely do. And the source of that quote eludes me. I might know plenty of English quotes, but I don't know a single French one.

Lance looks down at me expectantly, and I realize everyone else is awaiting my reply as well. They expect me to explain to them what's just said. And they expect me to speak French back. It's a test. A test for their amusement. I'm the entertainment here. I'm already dressed up like a doll. I'm not really one of them. I can only function as the amusing diversion or the pretty ornament. After all, Lance paid good money for it, I think—with embittered resignation—as I try to summon my wittiest riposte.

But my mind is blank, because being witty and speaking French at the same time after drinking an unknown number of glasses of bubbly wine is impossible, so instead I begin slowly with, "He's just told us that it is difficult to master one's passions and impossible to satisfy them. But I have no passions, so I need no satisfaction," then, as I regain some of my confidence, I quickly add in French, "And yet I am a woman, so I am still eternally dissatisfied."

The man translates that last part for everyone, and they all break out into boisterous laughter. Even Lance chuckles to himself, though I'm sure it's just for show.

One of the women, a thirty-something-year-old, is eying me suspiciously. I meet her gaze with an easy, open-mouthed smile, yet I secretly feel uneasy. She dislikes me because she wishes Lance would go for someone more his age, like her. She resents me for my youth and beauty and my knowledge. She's jealous.

Or maybe she's giving me that ugly look because she sees right through this manicured pretense of mine and is reminding me that class cannot be bought or bequeathed or acquired, and that I'm still trailer trash.

I'm so distracted by trying to maintain that fragile pretense, that I hardly notice the male server passing around hors d'oeuvres on his silver platter. "Have some, Evelyn, you look like you could use one," one of the men in tuxes mutter to me. I wonder how he remembered my name so quickly. Everything that's happened tonight is a hazy blur.

"What are they?" I ask as I take one, but my voice is so quiet it's probably inaudible. I am ravenous and even a little faint. The evening has been particularly taxing. The effort of conjuring up something witty in French took what little energy I had left. My head is throbbing. Was it all the champagne or did Lance slip something into my drink?

Lance raises his glass and says something, but I hardly hear it. I'm chewing my food and look up and almost choke at what I see. Not because of the food—though it is very strange and off-tasting, and I still can't tell what it is—but because of the server holding out the platter towards me, staring intently.

It's *him*.

Chapter Twenty-Eight

It's Joseph, serving me hors d'oeuvres on a silver platter.

Soft face, gentle gaze, hard lines, piercing eyes. Wearing a busboy uniform, complete with a white button-up and black bow tie.

He hasn't shaved. He still has the same stubbly beard with the soft, cherubic hairs. His high cheekbones are still prominent. He's gotten frailer like I have. But he's still beautiful, rugged and pure, where I've just become plastic and preposterous. And everything that's transpired between us is silently spoken in that flickering glance. Our eyes lock for a fragment of a second. My heart stutters and—I think—almost stops. I'm suddenly disarmed.

His stare, I realize, is incredulous and critical in a curious sort of way. It's as if he's judging me for looking so different and being here with these people. He thinks I'm a sellout, I realize, and he's wondering how it happened. And he's not wrong. I am a sellout. That's precisely what I am. But he'll have no answer from me. I stare back with a raised, perfectly arched eyebrow, challenging him, because now I'm in the superior position, aren't I? I don't feel that way, though. I feel as if my mask has been suddenly ripped off and my britches pulled down. It's like I'm on the stage again, on display naked and ashamed. All the ridiculous posturing, and only he can incite this level of shame. I involuntarily replay all the moments he fucked me and left my heart split wide open, laid bare. I feel more foolish than ever.

Something tinkles in the background. Joseph tears his gaze away from me, then walks off. He has a job to do, after all, and I've changed. It's as if the knife has been pulled out from the wound, left to bleed. He doesn't care about me anyway, I remind myself. He used me. He's no better than the rest. The wound scars over temporarily again.

"What's the matter? Don't you like foie gras?" the man who'd spoken French before asks me in a concerned tone. It all happened so quickly, no one realizes the cause of my despondent expression.

"Foie gras?" I pipe up, my voice quivering as I digest what he's said. The food isn't quite as easily digested. I can already feel it turning in my stomach like something rotten. "That was foie gras earlier?" I ask for clarification, my voice quivering because I can't believe it.

"Yes, it's quite expensive. A delicacy, some might say." His jovial face shifts as he takes in my horrified expression, which I can't hide for the nausea quaking in my gut. I'm standing here as it all crashes down on me in a wave of self-loathing at what I've become, and the brutal reminder that I don't belong with these people, and I never will, and I don't want to, even though part of me will always resent the fact and resent them in my confused and envious way. "What's wrong?" the man asks with concern.

"She looks like you told her she just ate an infant's heart," another man in a tux laughs.

I'm tempted to retort that the truth isn't far from that, and to remind them of how cruel the process is, which has been banned in many countries, because I'm sure they've never taken the time in their self-obsessed lives to find that out. They never put that on the description on the menus in their fine French restaurants and tapas bars.

"Don't you know what foie gras is?" one of the girls titters in a patronizing tone behind her upraised champagne glass before she takes a sip. She's trying to make fun of me for being low-class.

I'm tempted to tell her that yes, I do know, and I likely know more than she does about that and everything else.

"Yes, I know what it is. I was just unaware that I was eating it. And I'm surprised they'd serve it here at a charity event. Foie gras involves the force-feeding of geese and ducks, which are reared for approximately one hundred days before being slaughtered for their fatty livers, which grow to be six to ten times the ordinary size from the force-feeding alone."

I stop there, though I am tempted to go on. But I can't because Lance's grip has tightened around my waist, his fingertips are biting into my skin, almost puncturing it, bidding me to cease speaking, so I do. I release a shaky exhale, half because talking about the inhumane practice has gotten me worked up, raising my blood pressure and increasing my heart rate, and half because Lance is hurting me, daring me to continue, attempting to subdue me with that painful and punishing touch of his, and behind it the threat of a harsher punishment in the not-so-distant future. Perhaps tonight.

And there is the omnipresence of Joseph. I can't see him now, but his figure looms somewhere nearby, and knowing that and having seen him has me particularly on edge. Even after the transformation, and all the changes I've undergone, despite the immaculacy of my mask and the poise an abundance of money can afford, I am still utterly disarmed by him.

The woman I've just directed my rant to regarding foie gras is gaping at me speechlessly. I realize the blunder I've made, chastising one of Lance's colleagues, or clients, perhaps. And Joseph is nowhere in sight. He certainly won't be saving me tonight. Why do I keep getting myself into trouble and harm's way, expecting there to be no consequences or for someone to rescue me? Why am I so horrid?

"I apologize for my date," Lance says, his fingers still biting into my flesh where my dress is cut out in the back to reveal an expanse of bare skin. "She's not accustomed to hanging out with oblivious people like us. If only we had time to worry about the welfare of waterfowl," Lance remarks facetiously, then his tone darkens as he sarcastically adds, "We're too busy keeping the economy afloat." His fingers bite deeper into the flesh of my waist as he says this. I almost whimper in pain.

Everyone bursts into nervous laughter, and I try to excuse myself. Lance grabs hold of my arm and wrenches me back. "I think you've had too much to drink, darling. I didn't know alcohol turned you into a crazy vegan." I think to myself that wouldn't be such a bad thing. I should go vegan, but I'm too selfish, and suddenly I feel like more of a spineless hypocrite than all the people surrounding me, pretending I actually care, lecturing them. "We should call it a night."

"It's only eleven!" a girl protests, disappointed at his departure. Because she obviously wants to fuck him. She can have him, for all I care. He might've made me cum the once, but that was just because of how messed up I am, not his direct doing. And Joseph was somewhere very nearby, waiting hand and foot on these affluent assholes. God, I really am horrid. The idea should make me happy and triumphant, but I just feel dirty and shameful. I'd rather it have been him, even now, and I hate that. I loathe myself and what I've become. I've always hated myself, deep down. So I suppose not much has changed, despite my shift in circumstances and inflated ego that had falsely convinced me otherwise.

We wait in the lobby for the car to arrive. Outside it's incredibly chilly, and snowflakes begin to fall. The first of the season.

I go out, abandoning Lance to feel the snow on my face. The idea is strangely appealing. I can hear Lance's voice behind me fading as he shouts that I'll catch a cold. The door shuts. But I don't care. Why should I?

I want to run away from it all, I think, as the ice-cold flakes fall on my face, which is upturned towards the black night sky.

A plane ride to Paris sounds nice right about now. Why haven't I booked one yet?

A car slows at the curb. The driver rolls down his window, about to speak to me, when Lance breezes past and whispers in my ear, "This one's not for you. You'll get the next car. I've ordered it for you. I'll see you at the apartment." His voice is clipped and restrained, and I can hear the anger brewing beneath it as he slides into the car and refuses to look at me.

He's punishing me, making me ride in a separate car. He doesn't want to be in the same vehicle, perhaps because he fears his own dark impulses. I've only caught a glimpse of the untold monsters lurking beneath that cool veneer of his. The aggression he's shown so far could be a mere taste of his real desires, and perhaps he likes me taking the potion because he can do worse than I realize, because I always forget what happens and my brain feels all foggy.

My brain is beginning to feel foggy again now. Perhaps it's the effect of the cold, which penetrates my very soul. But I am aroused suddenly from my sad meditative stupor when the other car rolls up, wheels slowing over the icy streets with a soft crunching sound. And then there's Joseph.

I hear his voice first as he calls my name from behind me.

"Evelyn," his voice intones, husky and strangled by some emotion I can't decipher—why should he feel emotion? He is just as much a cold and unfeeling machine as Lance is. So I have my guard up as I turn to face him.

"What do you want, Joseph?" I ask, feeling weary and weak in his presence, with all the burden of consequence weighing down upon my shoulders. But my voice sounds sharp and steely, which is a relief to me. I was afraid it would tremble and crumble as quick as my resolve. I hold my head up high, feigning resilience.

He's standing there in his white button up and starched trousers, his sad, sweet face looking as beautiful as ever. A beautiful boy. So young and innocent compared to Lance. But he's even more lethal, and he seems to know that. His brooding brow is furrowed in that weary, melancholic way, shadowing his sad eyes. The same expression he wore when I was dancing up on the stage. Those eyes once disarmed me, but now, with the snow settling on my naked shoulders and falling all around me, they only trigger a bitter sort of resentment.

I'm better than him now. I'm out of his league, and the chasm between us is as palpable as the snow falling and the expensive evening gown I'm garbed in, glittering under the streetlights. It's a stark contrast to the stripper clothes he last saw me in. I say it again: "What do you want?"

He opens his mouth to answer when the driver calls out from behind us.

"Hey, lady, are you Eve?"

Every fiber of my being resists as I turn away from Joseph to walk up to the car and answer the impertinent driver. I have to make that turn look effortless. The driver is a young man, drumming his fingers on the steering wheel impatiently.

"Hi. Yes, I'm Eve. Lance sent you, right?"

The driver nods, expecting me to get in, but I hesitate. I glance back at Joseph, still standing there, my heart swells with both relief and adoration. I had genuinely been afraid I'd turn around and not see him there, and that he'd grown impatient and left. God, I hate myself.

"Can you wait just a minute, please?" I ask the driver. I'm not ready to part with him, though I contemplate the idea and how satisfying it would be to watch him watch me go with that sad wounded expression. But I can't bear it. Not yet. Why haven't I learned?

"I mean..." his voice trails uncertainly. If he leaves without me, I don't know what I'll tell Lance.

"Lance always tips really well, I promise. Please," I beg, batting my eyelashes.

That seems to appease him. "Okay. Five minutes. That's it," he says, glancing at the digital clock that reads 11:38 p.m.

265

I go back to Joseph, wobbling on my heels. The effort of even walking is such a strain lately, and my head is swimming by the time I reach him.

If he were to take me into his arms right now and kiss me and profess his love for me, or even simply insist upon driving me home, I'd let him in a heartbeat. I would leave Lance without a moment's hesitation, and our arrangement and the three thousand dollars. All of it. Because Joseph is the one who's truly got me shackled. And he always will. I despise him for it. And for his aloofness, because he does not declare his love for me and never will. I know all of this as I continue to stand there, hanging on his every word.

But he simply looks back at me expectantly, as if his mere presence suffices.

"Look at you," he finally murmurs softly. "You got all fancy. You barely look human." I meet his gaze and see that he's looking at me with genuine awe, but also irony and disappointment, perhaps even resentment. Either way, I will not show the ruinous effect he still has on me. I keep my face passive and taut.

"I don't know what you want from me, Joseph," I say wearily, reiterating my last question again, because he's refused to answer it, and I'm growing impatient.

"I don't know either," he says, lifting up his arms and exhaling. His puff of breath is visible in the frigid nightly air.

I look at him for a long moment. He really is expecting me to be the one to buckle. That way, he's not culpable of the consequences—that annoying, inevitable wringing of my heart and those problematic female feelings. That way, he's not the one being totally vulnerable. That way, he has the upper hand. But I already know this about him. So why, still, haven't I learned?

I'm the one with more money and someone waiting on me, after all, even if it's with a rope and a gag. They desire me all the same. How ridiculous that sounds, though, in my head amid all the fraught irrational grappling. Joseph doesn't know about the kinky sex stuff. He just sees me in an expensive evening gown looking better than ever, with a handsome man who's much richer than he is. Yet he has the nerve to expect me to be the one to buckle. I see it in his eyes. And for what? One more fleeting night from which I receive nothing, not even a shred of real affection or an ounce of hope, let alone monetary compensation?

He stands there, waiting for me to start it all again. But I'm tired and I'm fed up, and my pride is too wounded and simultaneously inflated for all of that.

"I wish I had my coat to give you again, to keep you warm," he says as I shiver and glance back at the driver. I rub my arms, covered in goosebumps. I think of when he carried me, saved me, fed me and drove me home, then made what felt like love to me. But it wasn't love. I have to remind myself that, because—otherwise—I'll delude myself again. The elixir's effect seems to linger in my bloodstream, fogging my senses and grasp on logic. "Then you'd have to give it back," he adds pointedly, smiling that same sweet, sad smile that makes me crumble every time, no matter what I tell myself.

"I wouldn't. I wouldn't call you," I state, remaining strong, severe, and as frigid as the nightly air.

"Oh," he says, sounding both wounded and dumbfounded, and not expecting such coldness. His stupid beautiful face looks as though it's been punched. But he still does nothing. The driver honks his horn. I jump a little at the irritable noise. It's my signal to give it a rest.

"I have to go, Joseph," I say, my frustration suddenly coming to a head. I want to slap him and scream and cry and curse his existence, but I don't. I maintain my cool veneer and turn away from him, floating across the sidewalk carpeted by snow to the dark shelter of the car. He does nothing for me. I'm better off without him. He's just a server, a busboy, a handyman, going nowhere, just letting life pass him by.

267

I don't look through the window at him as we drive off. I'm the ice queen again now.

On the ride over, I know Lance won't be exercising the same restraint as before. He didn't have his ropes or other instruments of bondage in that alcove. With the people in such close proximity, he couldn't sodomize me either. It won't be pleasurable or titillating, only tedious and painful and wholly degrading, and like every time before, I will long for it to end with agony. I decide I will take the potion again this time. The fog from the last time has almost lifted completely. Before, my wavering logic was probably more due to my fragile female heart than any mind-altering substance, though I hate to admit it. Maybe I'm just rationalizing my actions like I always do.

I never change. Always the same. Always these circles, endlessly running around and around, like a mouse in a maze, meeting obstacles and choosing different routes, but still with the same result: never escaping my problems or myself.

Chapter Twenty-Nine

I consider telling the driver to drop me off before we get there, closer to my apartment, and then I could walk back and never see Lance again. But I fear his wrath if I defy him even more. But this is the twenty-first fucking century and I can do what I want. I'm not his captive, even though it feels like that. It's only my fear shackling me, and, even more, the greed that's infected me like a disease. Greed and selfishness and hunger for more money and more finery, which I've grown accustomed to so very rapidly. Surely I can adapt. I'm a Capricorn, as Stephanie would say; I'm resilient. But then there's the money I haven't been given yet, the dues which were promised me: three thousand for attending the party with him. And I had thought to myself, getting ready this evening, that, with the money from tonight, I can end things and go to Paris. This is the last time, I assure myself. If I make it out alive. I always have the vague yet nagging worry that I won't. I've become accustomed to that feeling, always waiting for strangers on street corners at night, forever flirting with danger and the unknown. I remain cocksure and reckless to a fault.

When I get there, he's waiting in a chair in front of the door, the rope in one hand and the rod in the other. He's tapping it on his leg. That vial with the awful amber-colored fluid is sitting on the counter, waiting for me as well.

"What took you so long?" he asks when I enter, and stands up, still holding the rope but letting the rod clatter to the floor. He looks taller than ever.

"The driver was late," I explain, swallowing hard. My throat is bone-dry. The potion actually sounds refreshing now. But maybe only because I fear the impending punishment. It's already evident he knows.

He is a predatorial wolf, preying upon me, the helpless lamb, with his pointed teeth and lupine smile.

"No, it wasn't," he says, catching me in my lie and beginning to stride towards me, a devious smirk playing at his lips. "I can see on the app where it is at all times, darling," he reminds me, his facetious tone sickly sweet. He pulls a stiff smile, his white teeth glinting insidiously as he informs me, "It arrived at the pickup location seven minutes before you actually left."

"Yeah, well, I had to pee," I say with mounting desperation, as if another lie will save me. He's so close to me now; he's ensnared me; I'm backed up against the wall.

"Well, while you were 'peeing' I called the driver. I can do that too, you know." My heart plummets into what feels like the pit of my stomach. "He told me you were busy talking to a man. A serving boy?"

I can barely summon the courage to speak. All that comes out is a faint and listless whisper, "Oh, well, I—I was, yes."

"Why would you lie to me, unless you were doing something wrong, hmm?" He pins me to the wall and puts his hand around my neck, clasping the frail length of it with his long fingers, slender but strong. So strong he begins to strangle me, and I genuinely fear for my life. And that is a terrifying feeling. I wish I was the type to fight back— but I'm not. Instead, my limbs are stricken by paralyzing fear. "Who was he?" he demands, barely loosening his hold so that I can speak. I have to think fast. But my brain is all foggy again.

"I can talk to other men, can't I? The contract doesn't forbid me from speaking. But it doesn't matter. We didn't do anything. He was just an old friend," I try to assure him. Such assurances are futile now, after he's already caught me in a lie.

"Then why didn't you tell me that?" he demands, his hand tightening again.

"Because I'm afraid of you," I state solemnly, the thin whisper of my strangled voice dripping with spite. "Did Ashley fear you too? Did she hate you?" I'm tempted to ask, but I don't. Looking back, she had seemed so encouraging and optimistic. I can recall no hint of despair or desperation in her voice. Maybe she was just a brilliant actress.

He sighs, seeming satisfied by this admission, and lets go of me. After all, he wants me to fear him. But he also wants me to desire him, and all desire has been extinguished from my eyes. I can no longer even pretend; I despise him too much.

"You better take the potion. You won't like what I'm about to do to you, babe."

"Why are you like this?" I find myself asking as he walks to the counter and picks up the vial. He had anticipated everything unfolding precisely this way. He was looking forward to terrifying me. His cock was throbbing in expectation, I bet. I can see he's hard now, still, despite my obvious hatred for him.

The thought sends chills down my spine as he grabs me and presses me close to his rock-hard bulge.

"Because I'm a possessive man. And I want to possess you, and keep you for my own," he snarls into my hair. "And I know that you want to be punished. You crave it. Because you know you're bad. Rotten to the core. Just like I am." Then he hands me the vial. And I drink it. But this is the last time, I silently promise myself as the bitter-tasting liquid slides down my throat.

He picks me up and hoists me over his shoulder, carrying me like a cadaver to his room. I'm not wet. His callous touch doesn't have the same affect after my reunion with Joseph. I have no sensation whatsoever. Only a sweet numbness that takes over my weakening limbs as the potion filters through my bloodstream. The room is growing fuzzy as my vision blurs. I black out as he ties my arms and feet together then blindfolds my eyes.

Chapter Thirty

I awake to the sound of an alarm going off. I'm still tied up, though the ropes have been loosened. The foul stench of vomit pervades my nostrils as soon as I look down to find it dried and sticky between my breasts. I wonder if it's the alcohol from last night or the potion that caused it. I'm lucky I didn't asphyxiate. Lance is nowhere in sight. My breath catches and heart seizes in horror when I look down at my legs, which are striped by welts and bruises rippled across my pale skin. Some are friction burns, others full-on contusions that are painful to the touch. I almost cry, because it looks so bad, and I know it will take ages to heal completely. I fear some of the injuries will never heal and bear some permanency. The alarm is still sounding, it's shrill beeping incessant. I get up and limp sorely over to the digital clock by the bedroom door and turn it off. Who even has actual alarm clocks anymore?

The bruises are only superficial, I remind myself as I go to the bathroom. I can't bear to look at myself in the mirror. I get in the shower and let the hot water cleanse me of the vomit and everything else, and soap my face until the old, caked-on layers of makeup have washed off as well.

The inky mascara is smeared down my face when I get out, making me look like a drowned zombie. But otherwise, I'm clean. Then, as I peer through bleary sleep-drunk eyes at my reflection in the foggy bathroom mirror, I notice bite marks marring the pale flesh of my neck. There are also rope marks striping my wrists and ankles. Lovely.

Lance is still MIA when I leave the bathroom. The living room and kitchen are empty. Silence. And I feel a flood of relief. I'm guessing he planned all this out, as he plans everything, so meticulously. He had set the alarm clock to wake me up. He had loosened the ties so that I could easily escape, he had left everything for me on the kitchen counter. My money is there in a manila envelope, sealed, as well as a note from Lance which tells me he plans on returning a couple hours after I wake up, and expects me to be gone by then. He apologizes for being rougher than usual.

I chuckle incredulously at the note and his vacant apology, then read the last bit with a gasp:

"I've tripled the agreed upon amount as compensation. I hope that is sufficient for your troubles. I look forward to seeing you again soon." That means there's nine thousand in here, I think, as I hold the large envelope in my hands. For the first time, it doesn't feel worth it—this excessive sum which no longer feels adequate for the injuries and mistreatment I've endured. My hatred for him is not even marginally tempered by the extra money. But my concern over the bodily injuries he inflicted has admittedly been somewhat mollified by the compensation.

I go back to the bathroom, dry my hair, redress, call a Lyft, then get the hell out of there. At my apartment, I lock the deadbolt, and as soon as I'm safely shuttered away from the world and from him, I count the money.

I have almost fifteen thousand in my savings account now. This will put me at close to twenty-five thousand. I could live for a year off that if I budget wisely. I feel light with the relief of that comforting fact. I could stop this now. I could talk to Lance and I tell him that I can't go on any longer, and I'm sure he'd understand, especially now, if I show him the bruises which have darkened to a lurid purple on my legs. But what if I earned just another couple thousand, or three or four? Then I'd have enough to go to Paris and stay for a month and travel around Europe at my leisure and forget about my problems and Joseph once and for all. And that's all I've ever wanted, isn't it? But then I could keep earning more and more money and pushing the limit in perpetuity—and when would it ever be enough?

I never learn. Eternally dissatisfied. And rotten to the core.

I lie supine in bed, staring up at the ceiling with chestnut cream slicked on my elevated legs. My head is still swimming from the vile potion's lingering effects, and dehydration, for once not caused by purging *intentionally*, but a gnarly hangover instead. And I think on things.

I think back to the nursery rhyme my father used to sing to me when I was acting out as a child. A poem by Henry Wadsworth Longfellow. It goes like this:

There was a little girl,

> *Who had a little curl,*

Right in the middle of her forehead.

> *When she was good,*

> *She was very good indeed,*

But when she was bad she was horrid.

I feel the most horrid I've ever felt. But I suppose there's still time yet. I still haven't stolen or cheated. I haven't physically hurt anyone, not even emotionally, at least not intentionally. Except, perhaps, Joseph, walking away from him the other night. But that was out of self-defense. My own heart was bleeding too. But now it's frozen, I assure myself.

I see scissors on the bathroom counter. I stare at them for a while as my vision warps and blurs. I reach for them, like an automaton, then stumble back to bed.

Lance doesn't call me for a few days. I'm relieved, even though I'm undecided as to whether or not I'll continue seeing him. But his silence is a welcome reprieve. Now, for once, I can breathe and recover. I've been erecting this mask for so long. I've had to be this perfect plastic thing. I had wanted to see what it was like—to be rich and perfect—but it's way more work than I anticipated. I don't know how women carry on with it indefinitely.

So for now, at least, I can let loose and stop caking my face with makeup and shaving myself daily and going to salons and other beautifying, demoralizing appointments every fucking day of the week. I've been starving myself on acai bowls and kale smoothies and black coffee and skinny teas, and now I have a chance to gorge myself in the private sanctuary of my apartment. I put on loose-fitting joggers to cover my bruises and eat a very late breakfast at the brunch spot across the street, ordering pancakes doused in maple syrup and gravy-smothered biscuits. And then I order Postmates for dinner and get cakes and cookies and an entire baguette at the grocery store nearby, and basically binge two days in a row. I eat all the foods I've deprived myself in order to have a flat stomach for Lance when he fucks me bloody. How ridiculous. How ridiculous I also feel eating all these ridiculous unnatural processed foods and wondering what humanity has come to that this is the epitome of comfort to me. That this is how I most want to waste the endless hours of the day. And that other humans are hellbent on drowning their problems with alcohol or pills or drugs or maybe food as well to escape themselves.

I'm as weak and horrid as ever. But one thing's changed— somehow, I don't feel motivated enough to purge my food. I don't care anymore. I've got a lot of money and zero fucks. But then I have the ever-present worry lying dormant in the back of my brain, sometimes resurfacing when I see my phone light up, that Lance will text or call and demand I be there in an hour. I'd be faced by a dilemma.

I feel bloated and awful after my two-day binge-fest, and when I look in the mirror, my belly is no longer flat with hip bones exposed and abs rippling the taut skin. Instead, it's distended, featureless, gassy, and indisputably unsexy.

But when my phone lights up and buzzes, it's not Lance. It's Gertrude.

"Hey. Can we meet today at Prasad?" This is unexpected, considering how we left things. And even more unexpected is her suggesting we meet at one of the vegan restaurants Stephanie and I always go to, because she hates anything remotely healthy or hipster. I think the coffee shop was even featured on an episode of *Portlandia* and mocked for its flatulence-inducing fare. Gertrude has chronic dyspepsia and IBS, and I'm already bloated and still full, so there's no way I can go anytime soon.

Then she sends a follow-up text. "Also, I'm sorry about the last time we met. I'll treat you?" she says, sounding mildly desperate. But maybe that's just the way I'm reading things.

I'm reluctant to say yes, given my bloated stomach and the new pimples that have sprouted up on my face. I need at least three days before I'm presentable to society again. "Okay. Tomorrow," I agree anyway, despite being consumed by anxiety. I even care what Gertrude thinks of my appearance.

The next day, I put on some concealer to hide the fading breakout and dark circles under my eyes. I'm wearing some leggings with an oversized turtleneck and giant puffy jacket, not only to keep myself warm in the freezing winter weather, but to also conceal my bruised and swollen body. Then I put on a pair of sneakers and tie back my greasy hair that, in its current state, no amount of dry shampoo can salvage.

Walking the twenty minutes to the restaurant is agonizing. My head is throbbing, and my body is sore, not just from the bruises but from the water retention—a symptom of binging—as well. But why does my head hurt so much? I get dizzy for a moment. My vision begins to blur as I cross a street.

A car honks loudly, then skids to a stop inches from me in the middle of the road. My heart nearly stops in my chest. "Hey! Watch out, stupid bitch!" the guy in the car yells at me as I skirt around his stopped vehicle. The honking of his horn still pounds in my ears. I have to sit down because the dizziness and headache make me suddenly nauseous, and I think I might vomit. I look so fat and clumsy and ugly, and I feel like shit, and the whole world is cruel.

I recover somewhat, though I feel oddly frail as I continue walking.

When I get to the restaurant, I loathe the people's eyes that immediately go to me, like metal to a magnet. I wish that I were invisible so that I wouldn't have to suffer their hateful stares. I dread Gertrude seeing me and the state I'm in—I just hope I don't look as bad as I feel.

I'm surprised to find Stephanie there, sitting at a table with Gertrude.

I'm about to ask why Stephanie's here and why Gertrude didn't bother mentioning she would be, considering Gertrude and Stephanie had a falling out and don't get along, when Gertrude looks up at me and blurts, "Jesus, you look awful. You're rail-thin."

"Do I?" I ask. I glance at my reflection in the mirror on the wall and see that my face does look gaunt. The hollows of my eyes are deeper than I remember. And the shade of my skin has a sickly pallor. But I looked so fat a second ago. It must be these mirrors.

"You look anorexic," Stephanie gasps, confirming that which I cannot believe.

I should be overjoyed. Or relieved, at least, considering my severe body dysmorphia this morning.

"Or strung out," Gertrude remarks, eyeing me suspiciously. I feel a swell of anger in my chest.

"I'm fine."

"You cut your hair."

I reach up to touch the single lock of hair that's come loose. It's been cut short and is dangling over my forehead. I forgot I did that. I'm not even sure I remember doing it.

There was a little girl,

Who had a little curl,

Right in the middle of her forehead.

But my hair is limp and straight, not curly, so not the effect I imagine I had hoped for at the time.

"I'm fine," I repeat hoarsely.

"Then why are you walking funny? Are you on something?" Gertrude asks with her eyes narrowed.

"Oh, just this stuff Lance gets me to take sometimes," I tell them, sitting down. "It's harmless, I think. It makes my head a little foggy. But it does miracles for repressing emotional trauma, lemme tell you," I say in a flippant tone, trying to be funny in an ironic sort of way. But they don't look amused. I shift awkwardly in my seat. Tough crowd.

"Wait—what stuff?" Stephanie asks in a frightened voice, her eyes wide with concern.

"It's a liquid. He keeps it in a vial. I take it at night before we—you know. He likes it rough and it's just not my cup of tea, so it makes it easier. And he pays me so much money."

"What's in it? Do you know what it is?" Stephanie asks, her voice heavy with concern. She does have a flair for melodrama, but then so do I.

"A cocktail of barbiturates and trazadone, probably," Gertrude says. She does a lot of random research for her writing, so she's an encyclopedia of information. Plus, she loves to flaunt her knowledge. "LSD, maybe? Molly? Roofies?"

"Maybe it's something off-market, that he concocted especially for his mistresses," I whisper facetiously, just to annoy them. They don't seem to appreciate my making light of it. "It's only occasional," I try to reassure them, as their concern begins to transform into annoyance. "It's not like I do it daily. Maybe once a week, or twice, or three times, tops. And this whole arrangement is temporary."

"No, Eve. It's over," Stephanie says emphatically, as if she's my mother or the police. "You're not seeing him again."

Now I'm the one who's getting angry. I had tried to take their criticism with an open mind at first. But now they're just being bossy and obnoxious.

But, hey, it's also kinda nice having someone concerned about me for once.

The latte I ordered earlier at the counter comes out with their food. I didn't order anything else because the last thing I need is extra calories. And I'm especially glad now that I didn't, because I don't plan on staying long.

"Okay, fine. Y'all're right," I concede, unable to bear those insufferable stares. "I shouldn't be taking that stuff when I don't even know what's in it. I mean, that's common sense, which I seem to lack a lot lately. I won't take it again, I promise."

I'm about to add that I'm still going to keep seeing Lance though, when Stephanie interjects, "It's not like you to take it in the first place. This man obviously drove you to do it with whatever twisted shit he makes you do."

"He doesn't make me. I choose to. And I can choose to stop whenever I want to."

"What about what you need to do, Eve? What about what *we* want you to do?"

"You really need to stop this, Eve," Gertrude adds. So now they're ganging up on me. Strange, considering they used to hate one another.

"It's easy for you two to say," I retort in a defensive voice, then stand up dramatically, downing the last dredges of my latte. I set it down back on its saucer, where it clatters loudly. "Stephanie, you're such a hypocrite. Stephen is more or less your sugar daddy. You depend on him. You depend on your rich parents. I don't have a safety net or privilege like you. You've never really had to worry about providing for yourself. Plus, it's really rich you judging my occasional drug use when you smoke weed and god knows what else daily. And Gertrude," I say, taking a breath and looking at her so that I don't have to witness Stephanie's wounded tears, "You've got your writing. You'll always have that. I don't have anything like that. I never have. So don't try and walk in these shoes. We all know the only thing I've got is my charm and my looks—"

"That's not true. You're smart, Eve," Gertrude insists. A compliment I hadn't expected to receive, but it doesn't change things.

"Yeah," I say with a bitter laugh, scoffing in her face. "What does that amount to? Where has it gotten me? Where has it gotten anyone? It doesn't mean anything unless you've got a fancy piece of paper you pay for."

I can feel the frustration mounting in my chest, and soon there'll be tears, too, unless I leave now. I hear Stephanie sniffling and can't bear to look at her.

"I have to go. I can't take this right now," I say in an exasperated huff of air as I stand up. But I also can't take parting with them like this. They are my only friends. And if I leave now, they might abandon me, and I'll be completely alone. "Please don't hate me, but god, this is ridiculous." And then I yell as I storm off, "I'm a grown ass woman!"

So why don't I feel like one?

I get home and fall into the cozy sanctuary of my bed. It's been very seductive lately—the plush embrace of its soft mattress, the luscious warmth of my cloudlike comforter which shelters and protects me from the outside world. Lying down in it and sleeping—a sleep which makes the whole world and all my problems disappear, even if only temporarily—I am able to finally surrender to the soreness and the lethargy that's been weighing me down all day. So I take a mini depression nap, because every movement seems to be a strenuous one lately. I could hibernate for five years, even though I know it's not healthy or normal, and in the back of my brain, I fear it'll just get worse and worse and I'll sleep my entire life away, and my muscles will atrophy and I'll end up homeless because I don't have the energy to do anything, let alone work, and so I'll eventually run out of money, if I don't die by then from whatever's plaguing me. And eventually, I will die—I'll just slip away into nothing and be a dusty imprint on the sidewalk.

All these worries persist and fester in the back of my brain. But then the undeniable desire to sleep and forget it all and slip into that sweet, delicious nothingness of slumber supersedes it, alleviating all my worries. For a time.

Chapter Thirty-One

I awake to a text from Lance. His usual text, asking me to meet him tonight, though it reeks of false remorse. He's at least aware that he went too far last time. I hope he found me that morning with as much horror as I experienced when I awoke, and it forced him to realize that maybe his twisted fantasies weren't so controlled or safe or innocuous after all. But I doubt it, and I have no desire to find out. There's too much risk now, and I don't trust him. I never did. But now things have changed, and I suddenly care about my well-being, though God knows why. Now that I've entered this inescapable, depressive mire, you'd think I'd care less about survival, that I'd be more flippant with my life. But I've never been suicidal. I'm too narcissistic for all of that. My vanity disallows me from total self-annihilation.

Lance wants me to meet him at 8:00 p.m. and it's already nearly four, meaning I have a few hours to decide what I should do. Of course, my friends—if I can still call them that—would tell me to run as fast as I can away from the perverted asshole. They'd urge me to block him and cancel any cards or accounts he gave me access to, and perhaps even report him to the police. And to move out of my apartment. To move in with them.

But I've already heard their side. And there's still the tight hold he's got on me. I feel it pulling…and as I consider agreeing to his wish, because I want the money, because I've got nothing else to live for, the anxieties surrounding my bloating and bruising resurface as well, amid all those toxic thoughts swirling abysmally in my head. What if he's angry with me, or worse, disgusted by me? I might hate him and fear him, but I still want him to see me as desirable, and I know how fucked up that is. That him deeming me ugly and rejecting me is the worst possible thing that could happen. But even worse is if I text Joseph. The urge has been a barely audible whisper in the back of my brain, tempting me since the night I saw him. And now it has reemerged again, that nascent, pervasive seed rooting itself in the trenches of my conscious, refusing to die. Until it's consumed me and it's screaming.

But I have to be as strong as that night I walked away from him and didn't look back.

And I've been strong since then. I've been repressing that urge and silencing those quixotic whispers. However, there's been the binging, the total lack of energy, the overwhelming desire for sleep, the both painful and disorienting side effects of Lance's elixir I very likely imbibed too much of. I've been consumed by all these other things up until now. And now, it seems to sweep over me with the same all-consuming power of hunger. I want him to save me like he did that night at the strip club, to rescue me from my dismal mess of a life, and to shine all his magical radiance on it.

Would he do that for me? He would. He would in a heartbeat. And during that brief moment, it would feel like a revelation and an epiphany, and he would bless my existence like an angel of light. But then he'd just flutter right out of my life, a devil disguised by that cherubic countenance and impish charm. And I'd be drowning in a deeper species of misery than before. Then what? But I have no one else, so I despair, and I cling to the only thing which I know to bring me happiness, even it is fleeting and false and leaves a sour taste in the mouth. A blessing is actually a curse. But the nectar is too sweet and too irresistible to deny. I've already had the taste taint my lips.

I get my phone out and hesitate when I see again the text from Lance. It waits there, silently demanding a reply, and my resolution wavers. Both paths are so destructive, yet I cannot stand still and do neither. I cannot simply do the sensible thing—I must choose one form of undoing. Otherwise, I really might jump off a cliff, as I teeter on this precipice of madness.

This is no question for Stephanie or Gertrude. They'd vehemently disapprove of both.

But then there is still someone else I can talk to, I realize. Someone who might better understand my struggle, because she's led a hard life too, unlike my friends, who were born into privilege with talents and resources. She was a vagabond and a woman scorned, and a relic of the days when looks were the best thing a woman had: Charlotte. She didn't judge me when I told her about the stripping, or even when I hinted at the escorting.

I haven't visited Charlotte in a while. I think it's been three whole weeks. I feel guilt pooling in my gut. I've been so obsessed with earning money, so entangled in Lance's twisted fantasies, so enraptured by his pretty, vacuous world, I've neglected those most important to me—including my friends. I'm so selfish, the first time I've thought of her is out of my own need for advice and consolation.

I struggle to rally the motivation to get out of bed.

The more I think about the amount of time that's elapsed since I last saw Charlotte, the more worried I get. She is in a nursing home after all, and when I'd last seen her, she'd just gotten a cold. What if she's...dead? I think of my father with the same sickening dread. But she's not my father. And nothing will save the time I lost or took for granted with him. Still, I get dressed again and rush off, not caring how I look. She hasn't seen me since before my transformation, though I'm sure she'll notice the lip fillers right away, I think with nagging anxiety—but god, why am I so fixated on how people perceive me? She could be dead, for all I know, and that's the most pressing concern I should have, not my looks. When I first saw her, all frail and tiny in her bed, looking like a wrinkled doll, I was actually envious. It's deplorable, I think as I finally resolve to leave my apartment.

"I wish I was invisible," I whisper under my breath, just as a man walks by and his eyes scan the length of me, assessing me, analyzing me, stripping me bare and forming his opinions, as people always inevitably do. I cannot escape it, being human and being social, whether I dress in stripper clothes or an evening gown or in sweats and an oversized puffy, like right now. Everyone will always have some opinion about me. I wonder how nice it must be to be no one at all, formless and free.

When I get to the nursing home, Charlotte's door is locked. I try the knob with my heart pounding. The fear rises in my throat like acrid bile. "Charlotte?" I call out in a tentative, feeble voice. A nurse is walking down the hall and sees me.

"Excuse me, ma'am, can I help you?" she looks me over and her eyes light up in recognition. "Oh, you volunteered here, didn't you?"

"Only for a little while. I still come by occasionally to visit Charlotte though. Why's her door locked? Is she okay?"

"Charlotte Theriot?" she says in sudden recollection, her voice ringing sadly, and I know that tone. It makes my chest ache and my breath hitch and stomach plummet with doom. I know that she's dead, and that I'm too late.

I nod, but I can't find my voice. She looks at me with this sappy sympathetic expression that is well-intended but makes me sick. There's something too practiced and mechanical about it. "I'm sorry. She caught cold and it took her in the night a few days ago. She was just old. And lonely. It was her time."

"Her time?" I repeat with horror, my voice shaking. I had decided on the walk over that I was going to tell Charlotte everything today. Not only about my arrangement with Lance, but about Joseph too. And I was going to speak to her in French. I'm nearly fluent now. She would've been so proud. I was going to ask her what I should do—ask her for advice. I was going to hug her, even though we've never hugged before and to be honest, she didn't seem like the hugging type. But I

285

was going to, and for some reason I thought it would enrich her life as much as my own. The idea now seems preposterous and conceited. She was barely clinging on to life as it was. I wasn't enriching anything. And she's dead now.

I feel stupid too, because I was no one to Charlotte. I'd only just met her a couple months ago. I'm not her daughter or her cousin or her friend, even. I'm just a stranger and a prostitute who visited her occasionally to make myself feel better. If she knew what I truly was, she might've not even wanted me to visit. She might've been disgusted by me. But I was the only one she had. And now she's gone. No one to remember her or honor her legacy. Every experience and memory and interaction has slipped away with her life, and it was as if she never existed at all. I wonder what they did with the body and shiver violently.

"Here, come with me," the nurse says in a grave tone that compels me to follow her down the white clinical halls, which seem more inhospitable than ever and resound with the echoes of our footsteps. We go to the old closet I was left in my first day here. Inside, there's a small cardboard box with trinkets and photographs sitting on a dust-covered table.

"We already cleaned her room out. This is everything she owned. She didn't have any relatives listed to claim it. We usually just put all this stuff in the dumpster. But I guess it's yours, if you want it."

I think of her daughter as I take the box with trembling hands. It's so light. There's barely anything in here. A whole life that can fit into this tiny box, lighter than a couple hardback books, and that's it.

"What about Collette?"

"Collette?" the woman repeats the name confusedly.

"Her daughter," I explain. Surely the staff knows about Charlotte's only surviving relative.

"Sorry. As far as I know, she didn't have any family." She shrugs and leads me out of the dimly-lit closet to the lobby. She apologizes and escorts me to the sidewalk.

It's not until she's gone that I slump down against the brick wall of the building, still holding that tiny box, and begin crying as I stare at it with the vision of Charlotte. Such a pitiful thing, to die all alone. That'll probably be me. I'm hit by the harrowing realization that being totally independent has its consequences, not only is it lonely, but it's terrifying. Sure, unlike Charlotte, I have my family back home in Tennessee, but here in Portland, I live such a solitary and independent life, that if I died, they wouldn't even know. They're too far away to check in on me, and my mother rarely calls. It doesn't help how much I've isolated myself.

If I died alone in my apartment, none of my friends would know, because I have no friends, at least not anymore. The only two close friends I had are rightfully fed up with me. My corpse would begin to decompose in my locked apartment. My rotted remains wouldn't be discovered until the stench got sufficiently foul enough. It's the scariest thing I can think of.

I try to stand up, the box feeling like a great burden in spite of how light it is, and my head feels dizzy, and the world is spinning again, and my heart is pounding like it's gonna explode any second as my vision blurs and I collapse back down onto the ground and try to catch my breath. It's like when I was in the strip club. But that time, Joseph was there to save me. Always so self-destructive. Always playing the damsel in distress. And here I thought I was resilient.

I guess I could die here. At least someone would find me pretty quickly and I wouldn't have decomposed by then. There's no one in the street to see me or help me. I'm all alone. I did this to myself. It's the potion I willingly took, or the poor eating habits and the binging and purging in the past, or something else rotten deep inside of me.

My heart is still pounding like a frenzied drum, but not nearly as hard.

I feel my phone vibrate with life. Only one. A text, an email, a notification. *Something*. Someone cares about me, I tell myself reassuringly. Even if it's just some spam email or some stranger liking my old Instagram photos.

My hand fumbles in a futile, searching motion for my phone. Then I smell the acrid stench of smoke wafting into my nostrils.

A nurse appears, a cigarette in her hand, a weary expression on her haggard face as she takes a long drag then exhales languorously, her head tilting back. I watch her intently, trying to focus, so that I don't slip away. She sees me, drops her cigarette and stamps it out, then rushes over to me with a look of concern.

"Hey, you okay, honey?" She leans down so that she can study me more closely. She checks my pulse with two of her cold, tar-stained fingers.

I see her face shift between concern and indecision, until she says, "You need me to call an ambulance? Do you need to go to the hospital? Did you take something?"

"I—no," I wince as a bright shard of sunlight cuts through some tree branches, blinding me. It's setting. Golden hour. I reach for my phone again ineffectually. It falls from my inner coat pocket and into my lap.

She seems relieved when she sees the iPhone, the screen protector unscathed. I wonder if she thought I was houseless, and I internally fret over my appearance. Even in my indisposed state, I'm vain enough to worry about how rough I must look.

"You need to call someone?" she asks, taking the phone tentatively from my lap. "Someone who can come and pick you up?"

I summon my strength and nod to her, hoping she can read that tiny movement. "One-Two-Two-One" I tell her emphatically, though those four short syllables require so much energy to utter. My father's birth month and day. I realize it is today. Or was it yesterday? I can never keep track of the days.

She enters in the passcode, unlocking my phone. "Joseph? Is Joseph a good person to call to come get you?"

I breathe in sharply at the name. His name must've appeared on my phone because he's the one who texted me. I don't know how he did it. I can't remember if I ever gave him my number. "Yes."

I almost black out while she's on the phone with him. I strain my ears to make out her frantic conversation, but my head is throbbing. The world is pulsing. Next thing I know, his pickup truck has rolled up and he's shouting my name.

Chapter Thirty-Two

"Hey! Evelyn! What's wrong? What happened?" He jumps out of his truck and runs around from the driver's side to me. My hero. My hipster knight, clad in flannel and Carhartt rather than shining armor. The sound of the door slamming is jarring, and the Earth teeters and shakes on its foundations, but it's still music to my ears. Just like that husky, honeyed voice of his.

"She was just lying against this wall, looking like she'd passed out. I checked her pulse and her blood pressure's really low. She might need to go to a hospital."

"She probably just hasn't eaten," he tells her under his breath as if he knows me so well. And he does. "I can't keep saving you, you know," he says to me earnestly, taking my face in his hands. "I'm no knight in shining armor."

"You ought to be," I say, meaning many different things, but too weary to elaborate, or to spar with him. My guard's down now. But he knows what I meant, and I see that comprehension in his beautiful grass-green eyes, eternally soft and searching.

"So this is why you didn't reply to my text earlier?"

"My friend just died. She lived in this nursing home," I explain succinctly.

"Christ. I'm really sorry, Eve."

Don't say my name. I wince at the sound of it, voiced so empathically from those lovely lips. My heart wrenches at the sight of his stricken face. Will those lines delicately creasing it ever lose their power?

"Let me help you up," he says. He lifts me up easily with both arms, just like he did that night at the strip club. My faintness has left me starry-eyed and quixotic again.

"You probably haven't eaten in a while, have you?"

"I ate yesterday," I mumble dismissively, as if that's an acceptable answer.

"Yesterday? It's half past four," he informs me.

"And?" He doesn't know how much I'd been eating before that. If he did, he'd be horrified, and I, mortified.

"You've lost some weight, haven't you?"

"I guess," I say, because I have, relative to when he last saved me at the strip club. But I was much thinner at the party. Hadn't he noticed how tiny my waist was in that svelte black evening gown? Hadn't he seen how beautiful and perfect I was? "Why did you text me earlier today?" I still haven't had a chance to read it, in the midst of fainting and being lifted into his truck.

"I was in your neighborhood," he says simply and shrugs. I hate it when he shrugs. Even now, drained of all energy, I have the capacity for hatred. And my heart wrings with agony at how beautiful he is as I watch him. I'm slumped against his passenger seat. "I actually had a job close to your apartment. I'm doing Task Rabbit now."

"What's that?"

"An app like Uber, but instead of ordering a ride, you order a handyman."

"It's like you're asking to be invited into a porno," I mutter.

"It happens, what can I say?" he remarks, and I almost believe him, with that same sting of hideous jealousy I was so sure had been stamped out of me, until he adds, "But then I'd be charging a hell of a lot more."

I want to ask if it actually has happened. Because my curiosity's been reignited, enough to wake me from my stupor. And it's that sickening jealous species of curiosity. But now he seems wholly detached from me, and I from him, and even when he picked me up and put me in his car, his touch was unfamiliar, his grasp was uncaring, and his hands strangely cold. Why then did he text me? Just to drag things out and prolong my misery?

It's hard to be the ice queen and damsel in distress at once.

We pull into a drive-thru, of all places, and I get a fry and milkshake. "Not exactly the most nutritious," he remarks with the barest hint of a teasing smile, which makes me realize he hasn't smiled this entire time, which, in my experience, is highly unusual for him. A grim expression returns to his tired face. I feel so far away from him.

"You really have the nerve to say that? In a drive-thru?"

"Yeah, well, I'm broke. Sorry. Otherwise, I would've taken you somewhere with kale salad and fancy smoothie bowls."

"I could've paid," I say apologetically. I feel guilty, considering I have thousands of dollars, zero debt, and he's likely barely scraping by. Suddenly, this carton of limp, greasy fries he's kindly handed over to me seems far more meaningful than all the money and expensive food and designer clothes Lance's filthy money could buy.

"Do you even have money on you?" he asks dubiously.

I contemplate that frank question then confess, feeling rather stupid, "No, I don't, I guess." Money is only worth anything when you have it on you.

I'd only brought my phone and lip balm and keys to the nursing home. I hadn't planned on being there long. Now, in addition to those few meager possessions, I have Charlotte's box. Joseph put it in the backseat. Whenever he turns or goes over a slight bump, his truck bounces, and the box makes a clattering noise. There are lots of silver bits and glass frames inside, and the sound makes my chest clench with anxiety every time. Even though she's dead. Even though it was going to be discarded anyway. Even though it's of little monetary value. It's all that I have left, and I must protect it, and cherish it. And I've never been the sentimental type.

"I ought to have money on me. I'm sorry. I'll get you next time," I promise vacantly, doubting there'll be a next time.

"It's fine. It's my pleasure," he says in a clipped voice, not sounding fine at all. He obviously wants me to drop it, but I don't.

"But I should be the one paying. I owe you one."

"I figured you were pretty well-off, seeing you at that hoity-toity party with all those rich people." His tone is ripe with resentment, even as he tries to shield it behind his usually cavalier disposition. Money is a sore spot for him, like it is for me. I remember him mentioning how much he despised money and capitalism on our first so-called date. "And that man," he adds tentatively, voice prickly with something akin to jealousy, but then maybe I'm misconstruing things, as I'm apt to do. "But I guess every one's got shit going on behind the scenes," he says, and I tense self-consciously at his sideways glance, which, like his statement, is heavy with meaning.

"That man isn't anyone to me," I state like some automaton as I sit up straight, utterly rigid with my eyes glued to the road, yet nothing in particular. "He paid me to sleep with him—to do awful things you can't imagine—if you must know. And a lot of other men have too," I profess plainly. My throat is suddenly dry and tight, but I keep talking in that frank but muted whisper with my eyes staring blankly at the road. "I'm a prostitute, you see. A sex worker, escort, whatever you want to call it. That's all I am. I'd never loved anyone before you. I never even liked sex. It was just work for me. Then you came along. I was afraid to tell you. I was ashamed—afraid it'd ruin my chances with you, because I was holding out hope that you'd want to stay around—but you don't even love me. And of course, I can't truly hate you for that. People do what they want, and they have that right. But I should've accepted the reality of the situation long ago." I realize then that I've divulged way more than I meant to. I was just going to tell him about the sex work, but of course I had to go and be and idiot and profess my feelings for him yet again. And he's heard it all before. I say nothing more. I look at him, expecting a response.

He squeezes the steering wheel hard with his clenched fingers, and a throbbing vein ripples across his temple as he clenches his jaw and furrows his brow. Is he angry at me? Is he disgusted? I can't bear his brooding inscrutable silence.

"Well, say something."

"I mean, I had my suspicions, Eve. About you being...well, you know. Maybe that's part of the reason I felt so conflicted about you." He can't even say it out loud.

For some reason, that last part feels like a slap in the face.

After a period of silence strung tight to the point of breaking, I say, "Anyway, I've stopped all that. I've stopped seeing Lance, even. I couldn't take it anymore...his fucked-up predilections. Besides, I've made enough money to last me for a while. Now I just have to figure out what to do with myself."

"The world is your oyster, love," he says in a droll voice that twists with irony. My own heart twists at his cool façade. Beneath that aloof veneer, I can tell how bothered he is by my own frankness. By the truth of what I am. But what am I to him?

"Are you mad at me?" I ask.

"Why would I be mad at you? I don't own you, Eve. I'm nothing to you. So why should I have any room to be jealous?"

The words cut deeper than I expect them to. What happened to the ice queen back at the party the other night, with those delicate snowflakes falling all around her?

"I never asked if you were jealous. But I get it," I mutter, my own cutting voice mercenary now. I might be bleeding, but I can still fight back. I've learned that, at least. "I'm better than you and I have more money." The words seem childish, but they still achieve their goal. He smirks as if he's merely bemused, but his expression is incredibly sad.

"Right you are," he agrees with a dismissive laugh. All a show. All a sham. Stop acting so nonchalant.

I say nothing. I just stew.

"You know it's for the best," he states into the stale air.

"Why? Because I'm a sex worker, or because I'm just plain undesirable?"

"Stop. That's not why. You know that," he says, but adds, "I mean, if we were in a relationship, I'm sure your occupation would pose problems," he treads delicately. "But I've got my own problems."

I knew that already. Supposedly, he has commitment issues. Supposedly, he needs therapy. Supposedly, I'm the exception in his otherwise celibate lifestyle.

"Then why the hell did you text me, Joseph? Why won't you just let me be?"

"Because you won't let me!" he shouts frustratedly. I jump with fear at that unexpected show of emotion. Anger has transformed his placid features and disturbed the already tenuous air. His face softens and he continues, his voice still in plaintive frustration, "You're always so damn helpless, just begging to be rescued, and it's like you're appealing to this part of myself I despise. A part of myself I've always tried to get away from."

"What part is that?"

"You know. The sex part. The part that makes men weak and act like slaves and pigs at the same time. The part I've always tried to ignore or escape."

"You could never be like—"

"But you've got this hold on me," he interrupts, still fraught by frustration. It's palpable on his stricken face. Those brooding brows. "You're like a witch."

I scoff in annoyance. He keeps saying that. "Well, you're able to ignore it most of the time, it seems." Whatever hold I supposedly have on him.

"I repress it. I try not to think about it. I try to forget about you. And most of the time, it works. It doesn't help when you magically reappear in my life, looking like a thousand bucks."

If he's referring to the night at the party, then I had been worth far more than that. Three thousand, to be exact. What wound up being nine thousand. And that isn't counting the money spent on lash extensions or the gown or my hair or manicured nails or lip injections. But I don't correct him. Because now, I feel worse than a crumpled and tattered one-dollar bill. His speech about me has only made me feel worse. He only sees me when he does and texts me when he does and saves me when he does in spite of his better judgment. Not because he wants to. Quite the contrary.

If he had a choice in the matter, he would have never met me. He would've erased me from his reality. If it were me, I'd still waver if the choice was offered. If I could go back in time, or to a clinic like in *Eternal Sunshine of the Spotless Mind*, I'd likely choose to still relive this agony and cling onto my fantastical hopes. Each prayer accepted, each wish resigned.

My phone starts going off then. It's Lance, calling me in a frenzy. I'm not sure what to do. I'm afraid of what he'll do if I continue to ignore him. Then I go to his contact and I block him, and I delete all of his login info on my phone, and make a mental note to change mine as soon as possible. I feel as if a chain's broken loose, and I'm finally free. But those chains that once disempowered me had little to do with

Lance, or his instruments of oppression. Instead, it was all me. Because I was the one allowing it. And all I had to do was say no. It was always that simple. With everything in my life. I just thought I lacked the fortitude to do so. So what's shifted, I wonder? How was the wool lifted from my eyes? Was there some threshold of suffering and stupidity?

And then the idea returns to me—an idea which has been marinating for a very long, long time, but I've never been wholly convinced of it until now. I'll go to Paris. Lance can't find me or bother me there. And I can't bother myself with thoughts of Joseph. A vague shadow of his memory might remain like a faded imprint, but surely the novelty of international travel will quickly eclipse it. And now that I've told him the truth of everything, I can go with some sense of closure.

I could bring a bunch of my cash there and exchange it for euros. I could stay in Paris for a month or two, then travel around the rest of Europe. I could find Charlotte's daughter, Collette, if she does in fact exist. I could finally stop worrying about how people perceive me, because it'll be a clean slate and I don't know a single soul there. I can run from my problems like I did when I first came to Portland. But this time, it will be different.

"I think I'll go to Paris," I suddenly proclaim with marked finality. "Charlotte, my friend that died, was from there," I remark with a little less confidence as the grief resurfaces.

"You speak French now," he says. I recall him overhearing me speak it at the party.

"I have for a while," I tell him, even though it's not quite true. It makes me feel better about myself in a slightly subtler way though, compared to when I openly declared that I was better than him. That was just obnoxious, and I'm already cringing at the embarrassing memory that will probably stalk me for the next few days.

"You should do that, Eve. Well. I ought to go," he says reluctantly, pretending the parting is as painful for him as it is for me, just to indulge me, because he pities me. But what does he really feel? I still don't understand. But it's just that I can't comprehend him, or any man, really. I had thought I understood men, because of the nature of my work. But I was deluded to think that, I realize.

"All right," I whisper thinly, leaving, standing idly there on the sidewalk with the box of Charlotte's things. *So that's it then?*

Yeah it is, he seems to say with his sweet green eyes taunting me. And he's smiling, that son of a bitch. He cranks his truck and drives off into the night.

Chapter Thirty-Three

One month later, I wake up late for my flight. I had intended to save money and take the MAX, but now it doesn't matter what I want, I'm running late and Lyft's my only option for getting there on time. When I order the ride on the app, I don't hesitate. I'm not wracked by guilt. Even though it costs $30 before tip. Years ago, my finger would've wavered over the confirmation button, hesitating for an inordinate amount of time. But I can quickly remind myself of all the thousands of dollars in my bank account, and I can order it without a shred of guilt. It's a good feeling. This is how rich people must always feel about everything, no matter what the cost. They don't look at receipts. They don't mentally calculate their monthly expenses obsessively several times a day. They don't worry that a car ride or a meal or a single purchase will break their budget. Living must be so easy for them. And yes, I can confirm, it's easy. Too good to be true. I don't worry about the cost, but I worry that it won't last. That it will be stolen from me or depleted too quickly. Or that it isn't real at all, and I really am in a dream. Because I'm cursed by chronic imposter syndrome, my childhood poverty sewn into my DNA.

"Thank you, yes," I say to the driver when he pulls up and calls my name.

"Domestic or international?" he asks.

"Paris," I quickly reply, though that's not exactly the answer he asked for. He probably only wanted to know where to drop me off. But it had been reflexive, and now the words don't feel real. Perhaps because I booked a flight for 7:00 a.m., and it's the ass-crack-of-dawn and I'm scarcely awake, and everything still feels like a dream.

And then I wonder: who am I, this woman, this completely human person with her own thoughts and emotions and experiences? She is so lucky to be alive and to have utter control of her own life and her own choices.

That's me. The horrid girl waiting in the streets, in the rain, beneath a man whom she despises, whom she fears, whom she relies upon. But not anymore. I decided that two weeks ago. I threw out my binge food and my scale. I made up with my friends. I've been eating lots of legumes and vegetables and drinking eight glasses of water a day, and I've called my mom too. And I've told myself that's enough to get by. One has to negotiate with themselves what constitutes "enough." And today, I woke up feeling invincible.

I'm that girl. And I'm so, so lucky. I'm having my *Eat, Pray, Love* moment, I think with a sense of bitter irony. I hate that it was precipitated by such selfish, cataclysmic means.

The universe can be brutal and cruel in its random turnings, but *c'est la vie*. And today is different. Today, I woke up feeling effervescent, my cup overflowing, with the whole world waiting to be explored—streets unseen, cities unchartered, people unknown and food untasted. If only I could grasp that feeling every morning upon waking, instead of that abysmal groggy heaviness where the brain is too slow to fathom the wonderment of its own existence. It's on autopilot, too sleep-drunk to perceive this crazy, beautiful, fucked-up world, even as it does through its foggy lens. All it longs for is to slip back into that sickly-sweet nothingness of slumber. If only I could harness the novelty of today to willfully change that stubborn pathway.

I get into the dark warm shelter of his car, which still has that new-car-smell. I say with marked finality again, still effervescent and my cup is over-flowing, and my heart is fit to explode from sheer happiness, "I'm going to Paris. Ain't that something?"

We drive off into the pale-pink dawn, just as the sun is beginning to peek out. I long for coffee like a robust fuck. I think of Joseph with nostalgic longing, then shut my eyes and breathe deeply. I'll buy a triple-shot latte at the airport once I'm through security. I still refuse to cut that one vice. I need some kind of addiction to get me through the day.

I text Stephanie and Gertrude to tell them that I love them. I contemplate snapping a photo of the sunrise. Then, a split-second after, I contemplate throwing my phone out the window into the river instead. Because it's just another addiction I don't need. What's more, it's the most compact purveyor and enabler of pretty much every kind of addiction. And Joseph's number is in it, and I don't have the heart to block him. I can't even remember when or how I got his number, but now it's sacred to me despite claiming that I want to forget about him.

Then, my phone's ringing something frantic as the car goes over the Fremont Bridge, racing high above the Willamette River. And my heart's racing too. I look down and it's *him*.

About the Author

Morgan was born and raised in rural Alabama and now lives in Portland, Oregon, where she works as a software engineer. In her spare time, she enjoys writing and participating in activism.

www.ingramcontent.com/pod-product-compliance
Lightning Source LLC
Chambersburg PA
CBHW061138120626
46546CB00005B/1841